PILOT UPGRADE

Also by Richard L. Collins

PILOT UPGRADE

How to Stay Current in Safety

Richard L. Collins
and
Patrick E. Bradley

An Eleanor Friede Book

Macmillan Publishing Company
New York

Collier Macmillan Publishers
London

Macmillan Publishing Company
866 Third Avenue, New York, NY 10022
Collier Macmillan Canada, Inc.

Library of Congress Cataloging-in-Publication Data
Collins, Richard L., 1933–
    Pilot upgrade : how to stay current in safety / Richard L. Collins
and Patrick E. Bradley.
        p. cm.
    "An Eleanor Friede book."
    Includes index.
    ISBN 0-02-527231-4
    1. Aeronautics—Safety measures. 2. Private flying. I. Bradley,
Patrick E. II. Title.
TL553.5.C55   1989
629.132'52'0289—dc20   89-12536 CIP

Macmillan books are available at special discounts for bulk
purchases for sales promotions, premiums, fund-raising, or
educational use. For details, contact:
    Special Sales Director
    Macmillan Publishing Company
    866 Third Avenue
    New York, NY 10022

10 9 8 7 6 5 4 3 2 1

Printed in the United States of America

Contents

Preface

One of the most important components of safety in general aviation flying is education. Sometimes we miss the boat on this by failing to educate pilots on the true risks of flying. They are not always what we think they are, and it takes a continuous study of the scene to keep an accurate picture of the risks.

The reason it is vital for us to understand risks is because their management enables us to fly airplanes safely. There is no way to get all the risks out of any activity, especially a dynamic one like flying. We know they are there. What can we do to minimize them?

There is another important element in safe flying. There are some risks out there that we may choose to take in return for more utility. It is in these areas that the importance of understanding risk peaks. Night flying: If the engine fails in a single, we have quite a challenge to face in the next few minutes. How great is the risk and how do pilots do at handling the risk? The accident rate at night is terrible; does the poor rate come from those pilots risking it in a single? Engine failure is not the major risk, or even a significant part of it, at night, and we all need to know that. Low IFR approaches: You read about a lot of those in the paper. Many pilots would bet that most happen on nonprecision approaches. That is just a hunch, though, because most of the accidents happen on full ILS approaches.

Aerobatics? Very risky? Not if the pilot manages the risks with a proper airplane, proper training, proper equipment, and a conservative attitude.

Whenever you set out to explore these things, it is inevitable that a lot of pilots won't agree with some of the ideas expressed. That's fine. The important thing is that we all learn to think through the risks, and if we decide to take one of them that is a tad above the norm, to take it with full knowledge and explain it to any passengers so they can catch the next bus if they don't like the risk.

Bradley and Collins have flown together a lot and probably come at the subject from two different directions. This should give you a more complete and balanced look at how pilots might view risks. One of us learned to fly twenty-seven years after the other, so there is no question that some of this view of the aviation world is affected by what went on in the fifties. On the other hand, the elder of us has closer contact with the business of risk management simply as a result of having taken more risks.

Finally, please don't let an exploration of risks take anything away from flying. There is no doubt that the demands of controlling an airplane can be great, but they pale in comparison to the rewards. Consider risk management part of the most enjoyable and rewarding challenge left around today.

PATRICK E. BRADLEY
RICHARD L. COLLINS

PILOT UPGRADE

CHAPTER 1

Preflight Planning

FIRST PART Patrick E. Bradley

A very experienced pilot once opined to me that half of all general aviation injuries and fatalities could be avoided with thorough preflight planning. As a student pilot, I remember being dumbfounded by this little tidbit. Though I had soloed by that time, I still thought that pilots got into trouble as a result of things that they did in the airplane, not on the ground. And as for preflight planning, that consisted of scheduling an airplane for the same time that I could borrow my parents' car. Up to that time, other people made all of the decisions regarding where I could fly and what weather conditions I could handle. It wasn't until further along in my instruction that I began to understand the extent to which thorough planning can make or break a flight. And as for the experienced pilot's estimate regarding preflight planning and aircraft accidents, I tend to think he was conservative regarding the number of injuries or deaths that could be avoided.

Preflight planning, as I understand it today, consists of everything that a pilot must do before walking out onto the tarmac, and maybe a little more. It involves planning and familiarizing oneself with the route of flight, checking airport

approaches for instrument flights, estimating fuel requirements, sizing up the weather, and calculating weight and balance. It involves evaluating a wide range of factors and
ultimately making a number of judgment calls that lead to the
decision on whether the flight will at least begin. Because many
aspects of preflight planning often seem routine, and because
the decision-making process can often be mind-warpingly difficult, I often find the temptation to cut corners nearly over-
powering. Who wants to spend time wearing down pencil lead
or squinting at performance charts when he could be flying?
No one, of course. But it didn't take me many flights to learn
that, without the proper preflight preparation, even the sim-
plest, most familiar jaunt can be transformed into a potentially
dangerous series of humbling and bumbling calamities. With
that thought in mind, I wear out pencils and squint at performance charts, confident that the time spent prior to the
actual flight will stand me in good stead.

THE NIGHT BEFORE

I usually try to complete as much of the planning for a
particular flight as possible well prior to the event, often the
evening before. Even if I don't leave first thing in the morning,
it always seems as though there's too little time right before
departure to sit down and think through your game plan. I've
found that rushed preflight planning simply degenerates into
a fill-in-the-spaces exercise that may fulfill the minimum requirements but doesn't go nearly far enough in enabling me
to fully prepare. I do best when I can take enough time to
walk through the basic steps of flight planning.

My first step is to select the route that I will follow VFR

or file with flight service. It is on this route that I will base other calculations. Of course, when you are planning an instrument flight, the most basic route selection can be rendered entirely academic when you receive your clearance before takeoff—the most direct and thoughtfully selected route may not always be the one preferred by ATC. Usually, though, especially when the route is not a familiar one, the exercise of studying the location of unfamiliar navaids, airports, and intersections can be useful during the flight or even beforehand, when you've got to copy a five-minute clearance along airways and use navaids completely different from those you requested in the flight plan ("Did he say GOOFY or GOOPY intersection?"). I try to make a point of studying the relationship of the VORs surrounding the main checkpoints along my route. That way, if ATC decides to clear me from New York to Wichita via Oklahoma City, I'll know whether I'm getting a raw deal. It's also helpful to know your geography when trying to circumvent weather with the help of ATC. I recall once having a center controller tell me that I could get around thundershowers by diverting toward Westminster. I had to search wildly through my en route chart to find the mysterious navaid so that I could tell whether I should turn left or right.

APPROACH STUDY

In addition to selecting and studying my route of flight, I study the approaches at my destination airport if I'm not intimately familiar with them. It's impossible to know with any certainty which approach you will end up flying, but I find that it is helpful to check the approaches for any potential tricks or for significant terrain. This step is particularly important because I know, from past experience, that I tend to miss potentially critical items during the actual preparation for the approach. An airplane cockpit is an inhospitable environment in which to study the fine print on a Jepp plate, and I've made some ridiculous and obvious blunders simply through oversight.

On a practice flight more recent than I would like to admit, I noticed halfway through the procedure turn on an ADF approach that, instead of flying the published approach, I had flown the entry to the published holding pattern at the ADF. The published approach turn called for a one-minute outbound leg from the navaid followed by the procedure turn. Fortunately, my gaffe occurred in a practice setting with me under a hood and a check pilot scratching her head wondering what in the world I was up to. In the flurry of preparation for the approach, I simply fixated on the holding pattern to the exclusion of the actual procedure. Not surprisingly, I had not looked over the approach prior to my ridiculous first attempt. The same thing could easily have occurred under actual conditions though, and it gives one pause. I am frequently amazed at the complexity of some nonprecision approaches in particular and the ease with which I can overlook or misinterpret the most obvious elements simply through sensory overload.

Another benefit of studying approach plates before starting the flight is the opportunity to note the significant obstacles and where they lie with respect to the inboard segment of the approach. Before a recent flight to Lebanon, New Hampshire, I took a look at the approaches that were available and checked to see whether there were any idiosyncrasies that I ought to know about before getting started. Well, as it turns out, Lebanon Airport is something of a fortress. It's nestled in a wooded valley and is surrounded by hills which, while not the Rockies, are high enough and close enough to the airport to justify an ILS decision height just under 1,000 feet above the ground. I looked a little further and noticed that the minimums for the localizer approach are 1,036 feet above the ground. The airport could be reporting VFR conditions and the field would be below minimums. This is the type of thing that's nice to know before setting off on an instrument flight.

FUEL FACTORS

Another critical factor in the preflight-planning stage is a check of fuel requirements for the trip. For all flights, I plan on landing with enough fuel in the tanks to allow me to fly for at least an hour at economy cruise. It is of course possible that no alternate airport is available within a quarter hour's flying time, and that the FARs would require more fuel for the flight. If this is the case, I will carry more fuel. But there are no circumstances, even during a VFR flight, where it is worth carrying less than one hour's worth of safety fuel. I often read of situations where pilots create their own emergencies where none previously existed simply because of an ill-advised attempt to avoid a pit stop. It happens often enough, it seems, to consider the danger a real one, and there is no amount of pilot skill that will make an aircraft engine run on air. The only answer is to adhere unwaveringly to the minimum requirement. This, I think, is the toughest formula to learn in the area of fuel management.

I have found the temptation to stretch aircraft endurance particularly difficult to resist in certain circumstances. The scenario goes something like this. You've planned a flight that you can just make in a no-wind situation at your cruise power settings. Naturally, you've got wind during the flight, and even more naturally, the wind direction is the reciprocal of your heading. You reduce to economy power, thereby reducing your fuel flow, and for a while, at least, it looks as if you will make it to the airport with lots extra. Unfortunately, the wind velocity steadily increases as you near your destination. The closer you come to dry tanks, the more you think up reasons why you should have more fuel than you actually do have, and how nice it would be not to have to make an additional fuel stop. Before you know it, you rip through your reserves and are looking at an unscheduled, off-airport fuel stop.

GREAT EXPECTATIONS

The problem is one of expectations, I think. If I begin a flight with the expectation that I will complete it with only one fuel stop at a particular airport, then chances are I'm going to work awfully hard to meet my goal. I have found that the temptation is much less consuming when I plan my fuel as a sliding scale depending on the wind conditions that I expect to encounter en route. Prior to beginning a flight where there is a chance that fuel will be a factor, try to develop a fuel plan that takes into account a number of different wind scenarios and the absolute requirement that you will not, except in an unforseen emergency, eat into the one-hour reserve. This way, you can plan important appointments around the worst-case situation, and you won't be in the horrendous situation of having to choose between missing your appointment and making the fuel stop. This way it is also easier to avoid getting yourself to the point where you will be tempted to eat into your fuel reserves.

WEATHER VARIABLES

Weather is perhaps the least predictable variable in any flight, and many pilots don't even bother considering weather conditions until just prior to the flight. Although I agree with this, I still often make a point of checking the television weather to get at least some idea of what to expect. Often this is just a matter of noting where the pressure systems are located and what sorts of fronts they are generating. The real time to check the weather, however, is as close to flight time as possible but early enough to revise the planning variables, like fuel requirements, that may be affected by the weather. This would also be the time to check whether you need to file an alternate and which airport is the most desirable alternate.

Before actually speaking to flight service, I usually try to get as much weather information as I can from other sources. Most often, this involves calling for transcribed weather information prepared by the flight-service station. After I listen to the weather along the route closest to my own, I determine how detailed my briefing will be. For many years, I would just call flight service and tell the briefer, "I'd like a weather briefing for the route." At times this could be a waste of his time and mine. At other times the briefing would leave out some piece of information that I considered important. Now I work from a checklist of weather questions that I keep on a sheet of paper. How good or bad the weather is will determine the questions that I ask the briefer.

When the weather looks questionable, I try to get an idea of the area that the significant weather covers and the direction in which it is moving. The briefer certainly will give you a good idea, and it is also helpful to check the observations at a selection of airports surrounding your route. After I get as much weather information as I can, I remind myself that the final verdict on the weather won't come until I reach it.

CHANGING WITH AGE

The value of even the best briefing from the most knowledgeable briefer is limited by the available information and the amount of time that has passed since the information was gathered. Thus, I am always wary of statements like, "Oh, that front should be through by the time you reach the area." One trap that I have fallen prey to on more than one occasion is the urge to treat the weather briefing, good or bad, as gospel. Although briefers are specialists, experts, I avoid letting them make decisions for me, and I try to put as much faith as possible in my own powers of observation. The weather briefing, then, becomes another piece of information that helps me to make decisions en route.

Perhaps the most crucial step in preflight preparation begins before opening the first chart and continues throughout the flight until landing at the destination. It involves the ongoing question of whether man and machine are up to the flight. The considerations regarding the airplane are fairly straightforward. Are you confident that the airplane that you fly has been maintained adequately, and is all of the equipment working? With regard to maintenance, owners have a decided advantage. They know their airplane's history, and they are intimately familiar with the care that has been taken in maintenance. For renters like myself, the question is more difficult. In the end, I think the crucial factor is the FBO that maintains the airplane. Are they scrupulous regarding inspections and repairs? Do they cut corners? These are critical questions for pilots who intend to use an airplane in a variety of conditions.

I decided some time ago that I would not even attempt an IFR flight in a rental airplane that I have not flown before at least once, and preferably more often. My reasons are twofold. First, I find it essential for my own peace of mind that I be familiar with the type. Nearly all FBOs require a checkout in each airplane type before conferring rental rights, so this usually isn't a serious problem. My second reason for the policy is to make sure that I am familiar with the particular airplane. All airplanes have their own foibles and characteristic idiosyncrasies. Does the airplane normally creak and groan in turbulence? Do the alternate headphone and mike jacks work? What's the actual fuel flow at cruise? And why is the alternator light flashing on and off? These are best detected before undertaking an IFR flight, when what is actually a minor character trait may distract you from the business of flying the airplane. One airplane that I have rented has a notoriously unpredictable electrical system—sometimes it works perfectly and at other times it just quits. I decided that, until the airplane's gremlins are worked out, I will not schedule it except for local practice flights. It wasn't a difficult decision.

SELF-EVALUATION

Determining whether the pilot is prepared for a flight is a much more difficult evaluation. Questions that I ask myself range from "How am I feeling right now, today?" to "How will I be feeling when it's time to return?" Can I realistically expect to fly to an all-day meeting early in the morning, conduct business, and fly back that evening to be back at work the next day? Sometimes it's a tough call, and sometimes the decision on whether to go ahead with the flight will depend on how much flexibility I have in deciding to stay an extra night if, at the end of the day, I don't have confidence that I can still fly safely.

I once conducted an experiment in which I played the part of the guinea pig—a tired one. I stayed awake for two days or so, and flew a number of flights at varying degrees of tiredness. Interestingly, I was able to manage quite well most of the time. I was particularly careful to stick to check lists and to rely on my memory and judgment as little as possible. I made a concerted effort, throughout each of the fatigue flights, to perform perfectly. Even so, from time to time I would lapse, making a potentially significant blunder. The well-rested pilot monitoring me throughout the experiment was able to pick up a number of minor goofs that I didn't even notice. I guess what I drew from the experiment was that, though I was able to put in an acceptable performance even when quite fatigued, consistency of performance was always in question. The major concern was one that we did not have an opportunity to evaluate: How would I have managed in a real emergency situation? I hope I never have to find out.

Another factor that I consider seriously before any potentially challenging flight is the state of my currency. How long has it been since I flew actual IFR? How long has it been since I took a refresher lesson or two under the hood? If I have any question regarding my proficiency, the only really safe choice is to practice first and take on the clouds later. The obligations and the stakes that accompany the flexibility of instrument flying are too high to accept second best.

SECOND PART Richard L. Collins

The NTSB has a separate box to check on its accident-reporting forms if preflight planning is deemed to have been a factor in an accident. And, as the computer shows, this is rated as an accident cause in from 4 to 5 percent of the accidents. But if you read between the lines of the accident reports, there is a strong suggestion that something done or not done away from the airport before the flight was a strong factor in a lot more accidents.

Preflight planning should be considered in three phases. First are the actions that you take before a particular flight, such as checking weather. Second are things done on a continuous basis. These include maintaining and equipping the airplane, staying current, and studying the areas of risk and learning from the mistakes of others. The third is how you respond to the promise of unusual combinations of ingredients on a flight: bad weather and bad business or personal problems might dictate a cancellation, for example. Let's examine all three areas and how they relate to risks.

PARTICULAR PLANNING

We've long preached the necessity of checking the weather before every flight, and the accident records are full of examples of what happens when this isn't done. A private pilot didn't check the weather for a VFR flight in a light twin. There was a squall line along the way and, when it was reached, the pilot elected to tackle it VFR, at low altitude. As the airplane was being maneuvered through the weather, it wound up inside the same cloud as a mountain and the outcome was predictable. That event added five to the number of fatalities for the year and vividly illustrated a risk that need not be taken.

There's also a strong requirement to pay attention to the information in a weather briefing. There's simply no way to wish away an impossible situation, as the pilot of a retractable tried to do in mountainous terrain. The pilot was instrument rated but intended to fly this flight VFR. Two weather briefings were obtained, and both times the pilot was told that VFR flight was not recommended. He elected to go anyway, and later witnesses reported seeing the airplane circling in a valley or canyon area. Then it disappeared into clouds and crashed into the side of a mountain. There was fog and heavy rain in the area.

WOLF CRY

The FSS specialists are often criticized for crying wolf too often in the "VFR not recommended" program. And there is no question that they do this to some extent. But as pilots it is our responsibility to do effective preflight planning, and in the case of big mountains and big storms this might well mean a different route or a different day. The information is there; we have but to use it.

There is good news on the weather-information front, too. There is more information available to pilots now than ever before, and the quality of forecasts has improved in recent years because of new equipment and procedures being used by the National Weather Service. This is fuelled not only by aviation interests. The public is more interested in weather than ever before, as witness the success of the Weather Channel on cable TV. All they talk about all day is weather. And it is a good overview for pilots, with prog charts that give a good idea about what is to come next. And the ultimate in weather information comes through the personal computer. Many different weather-briefing services are available and most also offer flight planning. You can store the parameters of your airplane and, within the accuracy of the winds-aloft forecasts, these will tell you how long it's going to take you to get where you are going.

ROUTE PLANNING

When we plan a flight, the most direct route is usually chosen. But there are often times and places where direct isn't best. Weather or terrain might suggest that a less direct route involves less risk, and a few extra miles is a good investment if it contributes to a safer trip.

A pilot was departing from a mountain strip with a full load on a warm day and quickly turned on course after takeoff. Go direct. There was a ridge line ahead, so the airplane was headed toward higher terrain. The density altitude was high, and as the flight progressed it entered an area of downdrafts. The pilot apparently recognized the problem and attempted to reverse course. Too late, though, and the aircraft struck trees and crashed.

That type of event is best handled in preflight planning.

A careful study of the terrain and the likely wind flows should lead to a plan that has a high likelihood of working and that offers alternatives if the flight doesn't go as planned.

Weather can also dictate a change in plan. I was headed for Wichita, Kansas, one spring day and when checking weather for the usual route, over Columbus, Ohio, and Indianapolis, Indiana, I found a bit of information that was interesting. There was a front out there and the peak wind at Columbus with frontal passage was quite strong—something like 60 knots. The low-pressure area north of the route was strong, with a likelihood that the cold front would overtake the warm front with a resulting occlusion. These can be mean, and the decision was to go southwest and then west, to stay farther away from the low. This added a lot of miles to the trip, but we had a relatively uneventful one. Maybe it would have been okay the other way, but why chance it?

RUNWAYS AND GAS

Another preflight-planning duty relates to the airplane, the load to be carried, and the runway available. The pilot's operating handbooks give takeoff performance; the wise pilot takes the required ground roll and multiplies it by 2.2 for a minimum runway length. That means you can accelerate to lift-off speed in slightly less than half the available runway. If the airplane isn't at the correct speed at the correct point, there is still room for an abort and stop. A pilot attempting a takeoff from a grass strip less than 1,500 feet in length apparently did not do this. The aircraft got off the ground but clearing the trees ahead appeared questionable as a witness said the pilot pulled the nose up too much. The airplane hit the trees.

Determining the required amount of fuel is another numerical calculation that should be made in preflight planning, though it is always subject to change en route. A pilot on a cross-country took off to return to home base with the tanks of his trainer about half-full. When the destination was reached, the surface winds were very strong, which could probably have been anticipated if the weather had been checked thoroughly. The pilot elected to divert to an alternate airport but didn't have the fuel to get there. About ten miles short of the airport, the airplane was landed in the treetops. Perhaps that sounds more like an in-flight decision problem, but if the pilot had planned to go with full fuel, the flight would likely have had a happier ending.

There is no direct risk while a pilot is planning a flight. It is often done at home, or in a quiet airport office. But the quality of the decisions made during preflight planning can have a direct effect on the risks that will be encountered later. If all available information is gathered and used, and every question about weather, aircraft performance, pilot ability, fuel, options, and alternates has a positive answer, then the flight is well planned. If there are questions, or if the plan is to do something that is doubtful or that has proven to be risky, then the pilot has made a basic error, as one did on his planned wedding day. Early in the morning, the private pilot and his best man took off and flew to the vicinity of the pilot's parents' home. There, witnesses said, the aircraft appeared to be doing maneuvers much like those an aerial applicator uses at the end of a swath run. On the final run, a witness reported that the airplane pulled up into a 60- to 70-degree nose-up attitude, rolled sharply left, and disappeared behind trees. Impact was almost vertical, and two more were added to the list. Certainly what the pilot did was planned—an example of the worst form of preflight planning.

CONTINUOUS PLANNING

The preflight activities we do on a continuous basis relate to our proficiency, understanding of risks, and maintenance of the airplane if it is owned or leased for exclusive or shared use.

Proficiency is something that is maintained in a lot of ways. Participation in organized training, such as is offered by FlightSafety International, is one way. To back this up, a study-review program can keep the pilot in the loop on a continuous basis. It is this continuous planning and thought that can lead to less risk in flying. It is here that the mental barriers against buzzing or flying VFR in marginal weather are built. The hours spent reading about the mistakes of others and determining how to avoid such trouble pay big dividends. And it is in doing this that we learn a lot about our outlook on flying. If we look at each wreck with the thought that the guy was stupid, it does no good. Better, ask what factors could lead to a duplication of the feat.

FOGGY PROBLEMS

On one weekend four airplanes were lost in accidents in fog. A light twin shooting an ILS in minimum conditions crashed short of the runway. A turboprop that had diverted from the original destination to an alternate, with minimums but with freezing rain, crashed short on the approach. A business jet shooting an approach to minimums crashed short. And a homebuilt being flown in dense fog, allegedly VFR, crashed.

Four airplanes in one fog system is a lot. And this hyped my curiosity about where in the process we prevent accidents like this. While the accident reports will likely say the pilots of the three IFR airplanes descended below the published minimum altitude without the runway or its lights in sight and the homebuilt pilot continued VFR into adverse weather, that is only part of the cause—the last thing the pilot did. It is possible, and wise, to lay the foundation for the prevention of such accidents in the preflight-planning process.

If, for example, the weather at the destination is forecast to be anywhere near the minimum conditions prescribed for the approach, a preflight review of the proven risks should hoist the warning signs. More general aviation IFR accidents occur in the descent-and-approach phase of flight, and low IFR conditions usually prevail when there is an accident. This is not true because a low approach is of necessity more dangerous than other things. It is true because pilots fail to acknowledge that this is a proven problem area and plan to do the things that minimize the risks. The cure is simple: Don't leave the published minimum unless the runway or the runway lights are in sight. Don't, as they say, "duck under."

It's possible to sit in your easy chair in front of the fireplace and visualize the procedure over and over. Minimums, no runway in sight, go around. It is also possible to visualize what doesn't work. Lights or objects visible straight down but nothing visible ahead is the condition that prompts pilots to fudge. Go a little lower; there is bound to be a ceiling and there is some safety margin in every approach. The fact is there is not always a ceiling and the safety margin in an approach is minimal. The safety margin comes in never going below the published altitude. In Part 91 (not-for-hire) flying we have, at this writing, the right to shoot an approach when the weather is below minimums. For-hire operators can't do this. The airlines almost never lose an airplane on a "duck under." We lose a lot. There is a message there.

VFR

Continuing VFR in bad weather is to VFR flying what descending blindly below minimums is to IFR flying and is a leading cause of accidents in VFR flying. And it is just as easily visualized. The visibility ahead starts deteriorating. Soon the ground is visible only in a smaller circle and there is scud below. It might be raining. Then suddenly there is nothing visible ahead. The usual scenario then is a descent into the ground, in control, trying to regain ground contact, or a loss of control in a too-late, hasty attempt to retreat.

In IFR flying, the minimum safe altitudes are printed right on the en route and approach charts. For VFR, the pilot needs to calculate minimums during the preflight planning. If the weather is marginal, a minimum altitude needs to be calculated that will give 1,000 feet of clearance over the highest obstacles along and alongside the route of flight. Then, if three or more miles visibility can't be maintained at that safe altitude, it's time to head in the direction of the best weather and land at the nearest airport. If that is planned in advance, it is more likely to happen.

BUSY AREAS

We have to consider risk to others in preflight and this takes two forms. If IFR, all the altitudes and separation are taken care of by clearances and controllers. If VFR, a route that doesn't result in low flying over populated areas helps with public relations as well as with possible landing sites in case of trouble. And if the flight is in an area of concentrated high-performance traffic, a good plan minimizes the chance of conflict with a jet. When going to a busy terminal, airlines generally cross from 30 to 40 miles out at 10,000 feet. The approach in use is on the automatic terminal information service. They generally fly at or above 2,000 feet above the ground until 5 miles out on final to the active runway, and they might be at 2,000 for as many as 5 miles before starting that final descent. Those are generalities. It's not the same everywhere, and that is why it is important for every pilot to visit an air route traffic control center and terminal radar control facility in the area and let a working controller explain the traffic flows.

THE AIRPLANE

A final item of continuous preflight planning relates to the airplane. And while you might think that you have control of this only if you own the airplane, that isn't totally true. If it is a club or jointly owned airplane you can have input on maintenance policies. If you rent, perhaps one FBO charges less money than the other FBO. Is that lower rental rate a reflection of the fact that one FBO does everything to the minimum standard, while the other FBO goes beyond the minimum and thus charges more for rentals?

Minimum standards are a big thing when it comes to maintenance, too. The FAA-prescribed minimums, like many other regulations, go back to J-3 Cub days. They have not been substantially upgraded to acknowledge that airplanes have become quite sophisticated. For example, even if you fly a pressurized single a lot of hours a year, and it is as complex as a turboprop or jet, there is no maintenance requirement other than an annual inspection. And if you shop around, you can generally find a shop or mechanic that will do the minimum inspection required in a cursory manner for a lot less money.

The maintenance planning for the airplane should recognize the use of the airplane, and should be based on an understanding of the peculiarities of the airplane. For example, a turbocharged engine works a lot harder than a normally aspirated engine and should be carefully checked at least every one hundred hours even though that is not required unless the airplane is operated for hire.

Some of the things leading to accidents are quite obvious. A pilot flying a Cessna 210 crashed after the engine failed soon after takeoff. The airplane had not had an annual inspection and the pilot didn't even have a medical. Poor planning, and a failure to recognize that neglecting airplanes for a long period of time can lead to some risky flying. In another accident an exhaust clamp that was reported to be installed improperly came loose. Hot gasses subsequently melted and shorted wires leading to both mags, and the engine quit. Not something a pilot would be likely to find on a preflight, but something that might well be avoided if the engine is checked regularly and given top-notch maintenance. After a Comanche crashed, inspection revealed that all the oil had exited, and evidence indicated that the oil line wasn't changed when the engine was overhauled. The line was twenty-two years old. That's why prudent owners plan on the expense of replacing all lines at overhaul time.

Almost 30 percent of fixed-wing accidents come after a loss of power or a failure or malfunction of something on the airplane. In over half the power-failure cases the pilot either used all the fuel or mismanaged the fuel system, which is an easy risk to handle. All it takes is conservative planning. Many of the other failures were of things that were neglected. So plan to spend the bucks to own and/or fly an airplane that gets a lot of tender loving care. Also recognize that everything on an airplane has a finite life, and that some things fail often enough to warrant replacement on a schedule, rather than after a failure. For example on my airplane, I change the alternator, vacuum pump, and the magnetos every 500 hours.

SAFE GADGETS

Safety-related equipment comes in this category because there is no way to add it once you are airborne. Standby power for the flight instruments should really be required for extensive actual IFR flight. Packing flashlights in the flight bag is prudent planning. Making sure the airplane has the avionics—and the backups—for the missions to be flown reduces risk. The equipment that you can add to reduce risks depends a lot on the airplane, but do plan on having an answer for "What if?" regarding the failure of anything on the airplane. That's another thing you can work on while seated comfortably at home.

UP TO DATE

In the context of preflight planning, staying current means keeping up with the latest. For example, when filing Jeppesen revisions for frequently traveled routes and oft-used airports, always look to see what has changed. When they move a VOR, as was done at Harrisburg, Pennsylvania, a few years back, everything changes. Distances, airway definitions, and intersections are all moved around. The rules change on a rather regular basis. Flying is an activity where you do have to pay attention, because so many things are based on everyone marching to the same drummer.

This is true of understanding risks, too. If we develop and maintain an understanding of the things that are causing trouble, we'll be better equipped to ward off the bad stuff. One thing the FAA has historically fallen short on, but that we can do ourselves, is to keep very close tabs on the maintenance history of a new airplane or engine as it goes into service. When my P210 was new, the airplane had a lot of problems. But Cessna did a pretty fair job of staying on top of the problems and getting word out to all owners. Some of their fixes went past what was necessary, but in each case they made sure. For example, after a number of engine failures due to detonation, the operating instructions became super-conservative. In reality the detonation was caused by improper operation and inaccurate gauging, but Cessna exchanged all the turbochargers for units that generated less heat.

THE COMBINATIONS

There are a lot of combinations of events that can and should be dealt with in preflight planning. In most cases the skill is in learning the combinations that should stop the planning for some flights and lead to going another day or another way. Making the decision to go is always easy. Making the no-go decision can be a lot harder.

One of the factors in deciding not to go might be inoperative equipment. A business jet was lost one stormy day because it took on a squall line with a radar that the crew reported as not being up to par. In another case, a pilot undertook an IFR flight with an inoperative vacuum pump. Maybe there would have been no additional risk on a calm or clear day in these two cases, but on the flights in question it was apparently the ultimate risk.

Another factor that has to be considered in relation to conditions is any pressure to go. There is always some pressure on any trip but it is at home, when making preparations, that you can deal with this best. And the way it is best dealt with is through an alternative. If Podunk is below minimums, the plan will be to land somewhere else and drive in, not to take a look and try to get into Podunk. Leaving home with the feeling that you absolutely, positively have to complete the trip as planned sows the seeds for disaster.

And then there is the pilot's state of mind. Life is full of stressful times, and on occasion we have to acknowledge that stress has to be allowed to dictate events or change plans.

This happened to me in 1988, when my mother passed away. She was in Little Rock, Arkansas. I was living in New Jersey and working in New York at the time. The call came about 1:00 P.M., and I took an early train and was home by 3:30. Friends dropped by and a lot of time was spent on the telephone. My plan was to fly to Little Rock in my airplane early the next morning.

Before I went to bed, though, I had a second thought: Do I want to fly tomorrow? The answer was not sufficiently positive to convince me that I did, so, just in case, I called American and made reservations. Then, a few minutes later, I called the limo service for an early pick-up. The preflight planning done up to that point suggested I not fly, and the decision turned out to be correct. I woke at two the next morning and could not go back to sleep. After tossing and turning for a while, I got up and watched *Top Gun* one more time. Later, riding in one of those nice and shiny American Boeings, I wondered how I would be feeling if it was my Cessna and I was in command. The fact that I wondered was enough to verify that the decision to go with American was good.

THE REWARD

The nice thing about good planning is that you head out for the airport with good feelings about the flight. Knowledge about conditions has been gained, the airplane awaiting is in top shape, the risks peculiar to this day and this flight have been analyzed and planned away as much as possible, and there are no unusual factors working against the flight. Many pilots like to spend a lot of time just thinking about flying. This thinking can and should be a continuous stream of preflight planning.

CHAPTER 2

Before Takeoff

FIRST PART   Patrick E. Bradley

General aviation tends to attract people who place a premium on time. For the business traveler, time is a most valuable commodity, and saving hours or even minutes can justify the additional expenses of aircraft payments, maintenance bills, insurance premiums, and the myriad other tabs, tips, and payouts that accompany general aviation. Ironically, though, flying an airplane requires a methodical, careful, and considered approach to even the most routine tasks. Especially the routine tasks. Especially preflighting the airplane, perhaps the most routine of tasks.

In the last chapter, I mentioned that I try to complete as much preflight preparation as possible before showing up at the airport. If I have time and nothing else competing for my attention, it is far more likely that I will dot all of the *i*'s and cross all of the *t*'s. Preflight preparation of the airplane is different, though. You need the airplane, and you need to be at the airplane. And as you are struggling through that mundane checklist or walking around, the airways beckon, distant cities await, and the clock prods. Sometimes doing a complete preflight inspection and preparation can require almost superhuman discipline. And sometimes, what with all of that beckoning of airways and calling of distant cities, summoning superhuman discipline just isn't in the cards. That's a problem with preflight inspections: at times they just don't get done.

MEMORY TRICKS

Since the urge to ignore is so strong during the preflight check, I have a few tricks that usually help me to do the best job that I can. First, I make sure that I have enough time to handle the preflight check list and enough time to deal with the minor delays. That goes without saying. Second, the most frequent delays that I run into during the preflight are associated with fueling and oiling the airplane. Since they can be taken care of while I am running through the check list, I visually check fuel and oil before doing anything else. If the fuel or oil is low, I call in the order immediately and avoid having to drum my fingers when the line people tell me they'll be right with me—as soon as they get done with the G-IV that just pulled in. Another practice that I've found to be helpful is to tell any passengers to wait inside the FBO while I am conducting the exterior check. Especially during cold weather, nothing truncates preflight checks like impatient passengers stomping their feet and rubbing their hands together. Why impose the additional burden when you can just tell everyone to stay inside and have a cup of coffee while you check out the airplane.

Another way to make sure that a preflight inspection does get done is to use a check list. When I mention this to people, they usually scoff. No one uses an exterior check list after his third lesson. It just isn't done. This is how I felt until about two years ago. At the time I was flying out of an FBO in Ithaca, New York, and in connection with a program to revamp their flight school, they had brought on a new chief flight instructor who became the maker and keeper of the rules. One of the more controversial rules imposed upon aircraft renters was the requirement that all exterior preflight checks be conducted with a check list in hand. "This is outrageous," we all complained. "No one uses check lists for the walkaround. It's too distracting," or "It takes too long," and on and on. In fact, I questioned the necessity of the rule, too, simply because I had never used such a check list nor had I ever seen one used. Needless to say, the chief flight instructor prevailed, and I did use the check list. Also needless to say, I started picking up check list items that I never knew existed. There are bolts and guides and microswitches on the Piper Arrow that I had never seen. I was unaware of them because I had assumed that the check list was pretty much the same for the other Piper airplanes I had flown. No two types of airplane are the same, I suppose, and no one ever is too experienced to learn a few more fundamentals.

OVERSEEING OVERSIGHTS

Besides making sure that you're aware of all the items to check during preflight, another benefit of using a check list is oversight avoidance. Everyone knows that you should check fuel and fuel caps before launching on a flight. That doesn't mean that it will get done, though. I once rode as a passenger on a Baron for a relatively short flight from Teterboro Airport in New Jersey to Martha's Vineyard, an island off Cape Cod in Massachusetts. The pilot flying the airplane was experienced and meticulous in all respects. Memories can be fickle, though. About halfway into the flight, abeam Bridgeport, Connecticut, the pilot tapped my shoulder and pointed out the left window. The fuel cap was covering the filler hole, but it apparently had not been tightened properly. Fuel was pouring out of the tank at an even more furious rate than the engines were burning it, and that's a pretty fair rate in a Baron. Although we probably could have made it to our destination on the fuel from the other tank, we decided to make a quick stop at Bridgeport.

Another mistake that I have made during my preflight inspections involves my failure to deal with, or my tendency to downplay, a problem that I have discovered. I think that these mistakes are largely psychological. They center around my desire to avoid finding anything that could hinder a planned flight. Let's say you're doing a thorough exterior inspection—checking all the rivets and cotter pins. If the inspection is too good, and you find something wrong with the airplane, your payoff will likely be a delayed or canceled flight. I fly from a fairly busy FBO, and just scaring up a quart of oil can end up taking a half hour if everything runs smoothly. Remember, the airways are beckoning. Distant cities await. Who wants to waste half an hour, especially when the oil isn't all that low, and it's still above the minimum?

DIMMER AND DIMMER

Even worse, there have been times when I have failed to understand the full import of a discrepancy that I did turn up. I remember one preflight inspection in particular. After starting the engine of the airplane, I switched on the avionics master and noticed that the radio LED readouts were readable but unusually dim. I put my finger over the sensor on the front panel of the radio and didn't see any change in the intensity of the readout. I assumed (correctly, it turns out) that the sensor which controlled the intensity of the readouts was on the fritz. It was a dark day, with about 1,000-foot ceilings and no sunlight and I had an IFR clearance to a nearby airport.

Radio problems were the last things I wanted to deal with. Should I cancel the flight, or should I struggle with the radios as best I could? There was no question that the radios operated fine and that they were readable. But would the condition get worse, or would it get better? Would the radios stay dim but readable, or would they go black? After vacillating back and forth, I finally decided that I would wait to complete the preflight before making any decisions. As the situation stood, it was a borderline judgment call. Maybe I would get lucky and the readouts would die entirely or snap back to life. Either would have made my decision an easy one. My decision was not to be quite so simple, though.

After taxiing to the active runway and completing the runup, there was still no improvement in the faded radio readouts. They hadn't gotten any worse, though, and that was a good sign. I finally decided that I would do the best I could with the radios. If they didn't get any worse, then I would be able to complete the flight without difficulty. The problem was that they did get worse, though—much worse.

I completed the preflight check list, got my clearance and launched without difficulty. The tops of the clouds were fairly low, and within minutes I was cruising in the bright sunlight, thinking, as I usually do in such situations, what a wonderful tool instrument flight is. Before long, New York Approach called with a new frequency for me, and that's when I noticed that the radio readouts had gone entirely black—or at least that's what I thought. At first, I wasn't sure whether the situation I had noticed on the ground had gotten worse or whether my sight was fading. Cupping my hands over the LED faces, I saw that the readouts were probably glowing at the same intensity they were on the ground. The problem was the bright sunlight that had flooded the cockpit when I broke out above the ceiling. The contrast was now nil, and I had placed myself in the unenviable position of having to execute an instrument approach without being able to see the frequencies that I was using.

With lots of hand cupping and vectors issued by New York Approach, I was able to return to the departure airport without much difficulty. In fact, when I got back into the clouds I was able to read the radio frequencies again. So this time, at least, I was able to muddle through a flight that my preflight inspection warned me should never have begun in the first place. Now I try to think through potential problems a little bit more fully before I launch. For instance, I ought to have considered what would happen to the contrast of the readouts when I did get into the strong sunlight. Even more important, I should have considered the options that I would have had in a worst-case scenario. In this case, both of the airplane's navcoms had been affected. It was a reasonable bet that if the readout died on one of them, it would die on all of them. And I was also aware that I didn't have a handheld backup. Finally, I couldn't even mark the present frequency and "count clicks" forward or backward. I knew from experience that to go ahead one on this radio could take anywhere from one to ten clicks. Looking back, I see that there were no good alternatives in the event of a worst-case scenario. It was probably unwise for me to have taken off that day.

FINAL CHECKS

Although we tend to associate preflight with evaluation of the airplane and its systems, there are lots of items that are not included on the airplane's check lists that are really part and parcel of the preflight preparation of the airplane. One consideration that often takes a back seat is loading the airplane. I usually have a reasonably good idea of my weight and balance situation before beginning the final aircraft preparations, but actually fitting all of the gear into the airplane is another question. It's worth giving some thought both to where people and baggage are going to be placed and whether the baggage has been secured well enough.

A point that I tend to lose sight of is that it is fairly easy to be within the airplane's gross weight, but to load it in such a way as to be either aft or forward of the c.g. limits. It's not always enough, then, to know the weight of the people and baggage that you are carrying. Particularly where you're operating close to the airplane's gross weight, placement of people and bags can make a real difference in the handling of the airplane. In nearly all of the airplanes that I fly, the baggage section is open to the passenger section. In the event of turbulence (or a landing that tips the g-meter to its limits), it's certainly worth making sure that the portable iron has been secured and that briefcases and approach books are within reach.

ORDER IN THE COCKPIT

Also, while you're finding a place in the cabin for your library of approach plate books and charts, it's critical to make sure that all of the initial charts have been pulled and are ready to be used. I can recall more than a few occasions where, for one reason or another, I felt the airplane and the ATC system totally leaving me behind because I had failed to get myself organized prior to departure. Getting organized involves setting all of the frequencies and bearings necessary for the initial leg of the flight. To some extent, this requires a little mind reading, particularly where your departure clearance involves a SID. You're never quite sure whether, and if so, when, ATC will switch from the SID mode to vector mode. Of course, the only wise course is to prepare to fly the SID from beginning to end.

But assume that there is a possibility that you won't have to fly the complete SID. I've learned from experience that it's also worth giving some thought to shortcuts you may be asked to take. For example, the SID that I normally fly to depart Teterboro Airport IFR takes you on a circuitous route to an intersection north of the airport. Knowing this, I set my avionics during preflight with the VORs preset with the outbound radial and the intersecting radial. All of the frequencies were set. I would not be taken by surprise. Whenever I think I won't be surprised, though, I invariably am. For this particular flight, you see, I was flying an airplane equipped with an RNAV, and I duly noted this on my flight plan. Unfortunately, I had only been checked out on the RNAV once, and it was entirely different from the type of unit I usually use. Quite frankly, I hadn't even considered setting up the intersection although, looking back, it seems natural that ATC would use my capabilities to both our advantages.

Naturally, when I got to my initial departure altitude, my communications with ATC went something like this:

ATC: Cessna 422PB, New York Departure, maintain 1,700
feet and fly RNAV direct to BREZY intersection.

ME: 2PB roger. RNAV direct BREZY. (Back in the cockpit:
much rustling of paper punctuated by hearty expletives.)
(Two minutes later:)

ATC: 422PB, New York, you were cleared RNAV direct to
BREZY. Where are you flying now?

ME: Er, well, ah 2PB, I'm flying direct to BREZY.

ATC: 2PB, why don't you pick up a heading of 220? Your
present heading isn't going to get you there.

ME: Roger, 2PB, 220 degrees. (Spoken with much humil-
iation.)

With all of the bearing and distance and frequency setting, I had neglected to flip a switch on the RNAV that
would have taken us from VOR mode to RNAV mode, so
during the interval between being given the clearance direct
to my intersection by ATC, I had actually been flying direct
to a VOR. The most irritating aspect of this foul-up was that
it was a problem that could have been completely avoided
by proper preparation. If I had been really on top of the
preflight preparation, I would have preset the RNAV co-
ordinates for the intersection. Then, when it came time to
fly direct, I would only have needed to set in the preselect,
flip the RNAV switch and trundle merrily on my way. Now
I know.

Even if the departure doesn't include an SID, it's worth
having all of the frequencies and information necessary for the
first leg of the flight dialed in and within easy access. Departures can be busy, so it's worth getting as much of the work
done beforehand as possible. Before taxiing onto the runway

for takeoff, I try to have my initial heading set on the DG bug. I also note the initial altitude either on a piece of paper or on whatever instrument or indicator I happen to be using on that airplane to note altitudes. My thinking is that if I can take a memory item and note it in front of me rather than in my head, I have that much more attention to devote to items that I can't note and recall easily.

Whether or not this is an area of high risk, I am not entirely certain. I know from personal experience, though, that whatever you can do to stay well ahead of the airplane probably enhances the safety of the flight. Whatever unexpected variables occur during the climb, there will be certain information at your fingertips and certain tasks that you won't have to complete or add to the bottom of your climb check list. In addition, if you are climbing out through weather, there will be more time to spend flying the airplane, setting up that initial rapport with the instruments, or establishing contact with departure.

I have often felt that preflight preparation, the steps that you take in inspecting and organizing and preparing your airplane, can set the tone for the entire flight. On those occasions where, for one reason or another, I have begun the flight with the "kick the tire, light the fire, knock on wood" approach, I have found that, more often than not, much of the flight is spent catching up with work that should have been done before the airplane left the ground. Where I begin, with method to my madness, a sound foundation from which to launch, the rest of the flight often follows along the same lines. Of course, preparation isn't a cure for all of the problems that may arise, but it certainly helps to head off silly oversights that can develop into problems during the course of a flight.

SECOND PART   Richard L. Collins

Some pilots use check lists meticulously and preflight the airplane as if it were time for an annual inspection. Others never use a list and follow the "kick the tires" theory of getting an airplane into operation. And the National Transportation Safety Board says that about 3 percent of the general aviation accidents are the result of an improper preflight inspection, which would presumably include the failure to use a methodical way of preparing the aircraft for flight, such as a check list.

Students, and the more meticulous among us, use the check list for the preflight and check every little thing on that list. But many pilots lapse into preflight inspections that cover the high spots, and in many cases we miss something. A reader called one day and asked me how many sump drains there are on my 210. I answered quickly. "Three, of course." He proceeded to tell me I was wrong, there were five, and the FAA was after his license because he had a fuel-contamination engine failure and didn't know there were five drains on the airplane. I went to the airport somewhat cowed, found the two drains on the belly, and atoned for 1,600 hours of flying sin by draining them thoroughly. Presumably, had I used the Cessna check list for preflights I would have noticed references to "fuel reservoir drain valves." Getting any water out of the fuel system is a key to a good preflight.

BUGGED

The pitot tube and static vents are things we check to make sure the airplane will be flying with a full set of instruments.

One pilot apparently missed the accumulation of mud-wasp deposits in the pitot tube of a Skyhawk. A takeoff was started, but when no airspeed indication was apparent the pilot aborted the takeoff, went off the end of the runway, and destroyed the airplane. Maybe the pilot was wise to abort the takeoff, maybe not, but the whole event could have been avoided with a thorough preflight. Another pilot substantially damaged a Cherokee with the same problem.

FUEL

There are frequent cases of pilots not making certain of the amount of fuel on board. And this check can't be a rote look into the tanks.

One instructor told me of a student who said the airplane was ready to go. Quite a bit of time had been spent on the preflight and the instructor had watched the student look into the tanks. When the master switch was turned on, though, the gas gauges read empty. Time out for the instructor to look into the tanks himself. They were empty. The student had, in his own mind, satisfied the requirement to check the fuel by looking into the tanks.

There have been enough cases of fuel caps being left off and fuel siphoning out to result in a requirement that newly certified airplanes have a system whereby fuel won't siphon out even if the cap is off or loose. Look at a late-model Mooney for an example of how this works. All the fuel will siphon out of some airplanes through a loose cap or if the cap isn't in-stalled. Aero Commander piston twins are such airplanes and a friend of mine, a consummate pilot, had to put his expertise to work on a highway landing after fuel exhaustion caused by siphoning fuel.

It is interesting, too, that in some of the accidents resulting from a takeoff with too little fuel, the pilot insists that someone stole fuel from the airplane after it was filled. That matters not, though. It is the pilot's responsibility to know how much is there. An airline Boeing 767 captain who didn't know how much fuel he had on board had to put his sailplane skill to work on the big Boeing one day after the fuel was exhausted far short of the destination. The report is not out at this writing, but the newspaper accounts said that a fuel-gauging system had problems and the amount of fuel was determined by manually measuring the level in the tanks. Only there was some metric-related mixup in transferring the measurement to the amount of fuel in the tanks and incorrect information was given to the captain.

Not only must the quantity be adequate, the fuel in the tanks must be the proper fuel for the airplane. After a rash of serious accidents involving jet fuel in piston-powered airplanes, a campaign was launched to educate the pilot population and to fix it so that jet fuel nozzles wouldn't fit into piston airplane tank fillers. But there have been cases of filling the avgas truck with jet fuel, so it is still mandatory to inspect the fuel. Smell it, rub it between your fingers (jet fuel is oily), and look at the color of the fuel. Look, too, at the sales slip to make sure it is for avgas. This is especially critical if flying a twin that has a look-alike turboprop sibling and doesn't have fuel restrictors. Watch out even more closely if the prop spinners are polished aluminum. At least one line person confessed that he put jet fuel in a Cessna 421 because it had "chrome spinners."

Oil is another matter, and checking the oil and the security of the cap is what counts. If the cap is off or loose, different things happen to different airplanes. I had a student who left the cap off a Continental-powered Skyhawk. No oil came back on the windshield, but he later said that the pressure instruments behaved oddly during the flight. The oil must have been flowing over the static port, but there was no way to tell after the fact. He was so embarrassed by the event that he cleaned the airplane before flying back home. In other airplanes, the oil might gush back over the windshield. One Cessna 210 was wrecked on takeoff because oil flowed back on the windshield and the pilot crashed while aborting the takeoff.

TAIL

Certain things need checking more closely than others. On my Cessna 210, I have found that the right horizontal stabilizer and elevator need extra special attention before every flight. This is the side with the trim tab, which results in higher forces on it. At the 4,500-hour mark that side of the tail had had a skin crack, and a lot of loose rivets had been replaced. All these items had been found during preflight inspections.

DOORS

Other preflight items that lead to accidents are doors. The cabin door will be handled with the in-cockpit check list, but the baggage door won't. And I know of one case in a twin where the pilot lost control of the airplane and crashed while returning to close a nose baggage compartment door. One with a happier ending involved the president of a company and his pilot. The president was going to another city to make a speech at a formal dinner, and the pilot neatly stowed the hang-up with the tux in the nose baggage compartment. After takeoff, the door came open and the tux went through the prop. The engine kept running, though a new tux, a substitute airplane, and probably another pilot eventually made the trip.

The preflight should always be thorough, but it goes without saying that the consequences of an unturned stone will be more serious on some flights than on others. A low-visibility IFR takeoff, for example, would be a bad place to have something happen that required a return and landing. The whole approach procedure would have to be flown, and this would be unnerving at best with your dirty clothes stuffed into an engine nacelle, or flapping around on the horizontal stabilizer.

HAND-PROPPING

If the battery is dead or the starter is shot, some pilots take it on themselves to hand-prop the airplane. Accidents occur when this is done without a qualified pilot at the controls, or with a person new to hand-propping on the outside. Usually the airplane just runs into something, but in at least one instance the airplane, with an unqualified person inside, actually roared away, took off, and crashed. In another, the airplane took off unmanned and flew quite a distance all by itself. An unqualified person inside or outside makes propping potentially lethal.

Back in the good old days, hand-propping was the only way to start a lot of airplanes. But there are not a lot of us left around who remember how to do this. And it isn't a safe thing to teach yourself.

ARRANGING THINGS

Although I've never seen it listed as an accident cause, a poor arrangement of charts and other items has most likely contributed to loss-of-control accidents soon after takeoff. An airplane cockpit is not the most spacious thing in the world—few of us have airplanes big enough for a chart table—and the paperwork associated with going flying can be considerable. This is especially true if IFR, or if VFR in an area where the navigational duties are complicated by restricted or regulated airspace. In preflight planning, the route should have been studied and appropriate frequencies highlighted or entered on a navigation log. Once in the airplane, the pilot need only position things where they are available for ready reference. There is nothing more useless than a map on the floor. By the same token, if it is a night flight, the flashlight needs to be handy. On an instrument flight, the approach plates for the departure airport should be immediately available should a return be dictated. A loss of control in flight accounts for almost a fourth of the fatal general aviation accidents; some diversion from the primary duty to fly the airplane has to figure in a lot of these. Anything that reduces diversions reduces risk.

CHECK LIST

Once the airplane is preflighted and everything is arranged, it is check list time. Some pilots use the manufacturer's list, others do their own by rearranging to make the checking flow across the cockpit. If you make your own, just be certain that all things on the original are there and that changing the sequence doesn't affect anything.

A Boeing 727 was once lost because the crew climbed into an icing layer with the pitot heat off. Turning it on was a pretakeoff check list item. The indicated airspeed started increasing (as it will do when the pitot freezes over) and in an attempt to control the erroneous airspeed, the pilot flying flew the 727 into a mighty zoom. The aircraft stalled, control was lost, and down it came. Pitot heat: On. That's pretty simple, but often it can be the simple things that get you. Much discussion of the Detroit MD-80 crash has centered on whether or not the flaps of that aircraft were in the takeoff position, and two foreign airlines have lost big Boeings on takeoff because of incorrect flap settings.

Controls free? The pilot of a Cessna 414 found, at lift-off time, that the wheel would not move back more than two inches. The takeoff was aborted, but the aircraft went off the end of the runway and was destroyed. The investigation revealed that an instrument had loosened from its mounting clamp and limited the aft travel. The pilot did state that he had run a controls check before takeoff. Another pilot tried to take off with one mag dead, unsuccessfully. Another did the deed after taking off with fuel, but with the selector on a tank without fuel.

And controls correct? This one is especially important after maintenance or when an airplane is new or has been modified. Piper lost a brand-new Navajo once, on its first test flight, because the ailerons had been hooked up backward. There is no way you could catch something like that and compensate for it once airborne. Most of us are pretty good about doing the "correct" part on the ailerons, but I must admit that I don't often look back to see what is going on at the tail. That is, I didn't look back until a good friend told me a scary story. He was flying a Husky. The airplane had been used for some air-to-air photography on the previous flight, and the front stick had been removed to give the photographer more room. When the power was advanced and the airplane accelerated, he said that the Husky just pitched nose-up steeply, climbed about 25 feet, and crashed. Somehow, the stick had been installed in reverse.

CABIN DOOR

Door latched? The records tell stories of pilots losing control of the airplane after a door came open and they hastened to return and land to close the door. It isn't a frequent occurrence, but in a recent year there were two fatal accidents related to this simple omission. And in flying we have to work at eliminating all the risk areas. If it happens twice a year and can be fixed with a simple thing like a check list, it is worth doing. And if a door ever does come open, the next thing to do is make a normal approach and landing. Even though it is noisy and there might be some vibration, the airplane should be flyable. (This is not true of some experimental or kit-built airplanes.)

Another door scenario involves the pilot who catches it

quick and decides to land on the remaining runway and close the door. A Bonanza pilot did this one day, only he forgot one thing. He had already started the landing gear up, so when he landed to close the door, he stayed for a while.

As important as arranging things in the cabin is the check list item on setting the avionics. Everything can be set for the first phase of flight before the airplane starts moving. And if the clearance comes through with a different route, it can be changed before takeoff. This minimizes fiddling with dials and gauges after takeoff. A possible diversion of attention is eliminated.

STARTING

"Clear prop." Every time I yell that I next wonder if I remembered to take the tow bar off the nose wheel. A prop slamming into a tow bar would probably never make the accident reports, but it would be embarrassing and expensive—definitely something to avoid. I have always wondered if the fact that I am not sure and often open the door and lean out to look (it has never been there) is a sign of a poor preflight inspection. I always resolve to do better.

Once the engine is running, a primary bit of preflight work is making sure the engine and accessories are running properly. There are also the instrument checks while taxiing, especially if going IFR flying, to make sure the information there is accurate.

There is no statistic on the number of engine or airframe problems in flight that followed a pilot taking off with some doubt about the equipment. But just on a hunch, I'd bet this is a factor in a lot of accidents—especially where the trip is an important one. The crew of a jet that was lost in an area of thunderstorms had reported their radar wasn't doing well. Did they know this before takeoff? If so, this would be a flight where there was some doubt about what would be a key piece of equipment before going.

More likely would be doubt about the engine. Does it sound right? Is the mag check really within tolerance? Does the prop exercise okay? Are all the readings normal? If the engine was hard to start, might that have been a sign that something is wrong?

Cold weather can bring special checking requirements, one of which is not as true today as before the days of high-quality multi-grade oil. Then, with a superficial preheat, you might get the engine started, run what seems a suitable warm-up period, and take off with the oil in the crankcase so cold and thick that the engine wouldn't get normal lubrication. There were some accidents related to this, but you'd think that the oil-pressure reading would not have been normal before take-off.

THE FINAL CHECK

If a check list is arranged and used properly, most of the checking is done before the airplane is in the number-one position for takeoff. There, a final double check of critical items might be run. Some call them "killer items," for good reason. Neglected, they have done just that. What they are depends on the airplane, but there are similarities on all airplanes. Anything that could be critical during or after takeoff and that might cause a power loss or a control loss, or that might have a deleterious effect on performance is a good place to start. A basic list: I can fly this successfully if the instruments, controls, fuel, trim, and seat are okay.

Instruments would mean that all the engine gauges are reading correctly and the flight instruments look okay. And there's a little potential trap in the artificial horizon that has caught more than one pilot. If you start the airplane, taxi it for repositioning, shut down, and restart before the gyro in the horizon has run down, strange things happen. The horizon spins back up, but not erect. It might show a 20- or 30-degree bank one way or the other. And it takes a few minutes for it to erect properly. A pilot who taxied rapidly after the second start, took off without looking at the horizon, and then needed that information, would be in for a rude awakening. That's why instruments is a killer item.

Controls we have already discussed. But it is important to do that second check, right before takeoff. A large jet was once lost because of an obstruction to control movement that was thought to have occurred while the aircraft was taxiing.

Fuel: If there is none or if the selector is in the wrong position, bad things can happen.

Trim is a big one because too much trim in the wrong direction can render an aircraft virtually unflyable. A large jet was once lost because of an attempted takeoff with landing trim still selected. And while we don't do a "trim correct" on most preflights, this is worth doing after an aircraft has been in for maintenance—especially if it has electric trim. There has been at least one case of an electric trim system being hooked up backward and the pilot losing control because of this. A final trim question would relate to the autopilot. It should be off for all takeoffs. If it were on when the pilot started applying pressure to lift off, the autopilot would start to trim against the pilot—nose down when the pilot pulled back—which is a characteristic of most autopilot/trim systems.

Seats have been known to slip backward on takeoff, causing a pilot to lose control of the airplane. There have been some serious accidents caused by slipping seats, and there is an airworthiness directive on light Cessnas requiring that the seat tracks and latches be up to snuff. To seats, I'd add safety belts, because if you did happen to have a problem, having the belt and shoulder strap tight would be comforting.

On some airplanes, flaps would be on the killer list. With a constant-speed prop, the prop control is part of it because there have been unsuccessful takeoffs when the pilot failed to place the prop control in the high RPM position.

THE PURPOSE OF ALL THIS

The importance of what we do before pulling out on the runway shouldn't be underestimated. Maybe it shows up as a cause of only a small percentage of accidents, but it has a strong influence on the flight, and lack of planning and proper preflight action has probably made at least a small contribution to big troubles later on a lot of flights. These are the easiest of all accidents to avoid. The purpose of preflight planning, the preflight inspection, and using the check list is to enable us to pull out onto the runway feeling comfortable that no stone has been left unturned and that everything that can be done to make the flight go smoothly has been done. Doing the groundwork involves very little hazard (unless you start swinging the propeller, walk into the trailing edge of the wing, or trip over something) but it is a big part of flying as safely as possible. The management of risks here is not as dynamic as it becomes once the throttle starts forward for takeoff, but it is a full partner. For those of us who are not full-time pilots, it is the bridge between whatever else we do (to be able to afford to fly) and approaching the operation of the airplane in a professional manner. Once you start down the runway, skill at law, medicine, business, or publishing becomes secondary. Taking off means becoming a full-time pilot until you tie the airplane down at the destination.

CHAPTER 3

The Takeoff

FIRST PART   Patrick E. Bradley

There's something about the roar of an airplane engine when you first apply takeoff power that brings all pilots to an extra high level of awareness. Maybe it's the sense of force as the airplane accelerates down the runway. Maybe it's the feeling of speed that you seldom experience at altitude. Whatever it is, takeoff is the first point during a flight when one really experiences the power and magic of the airplane—a clumsy ground machine is transformed into an airplane, summoning a grace and dignity which it often does not possess when rolling on the tarmac. For me, experiencing this transformation justifies the hours of tedious preparation. It is the payoff.

Regardless of the thrill and delight, or perhaps because of it, takeoff can also be a technically very challenging phase of flight. You're close to the ground, the engine is cranked up to full power (or close to it) and airplanes, light on their feet, are sensitive to whimsical gusts of wind and the treachery of ground obstacles. I treat the takeoff as a time of high potential risk, simply because the margin for error is small and even minor errors or malfunctions can leave you with few appealing options. During takeoff especially, it becomes critical to work at minimizing the potential for mishaps.

FINGER IN THE AIR

I suppose that my first consideration prior to takeoff is the direction of the wind. It seems so elementary, but at a controlled airport, where the departure runway is selected for you and where wind speed and direction information is dispensed over ATIS, it's easy to ignore the good old wind sock. Even at a controlled airport, if the wind sock indicates that the wind is running directly down the active runway, it would be well worth taking the matter up with the tower. More frequently, though, the direct headwind reported on ATIS may in fact have changed to a crosswind. It's also common for a light crosswind to have picked up sufficiently to call for a high degree of care.

At uncontrolled airports, it isn't at all uncommon for the active runway announced on the unicom to bear no relation to the direction from whence bloweth the wind. Sometimes, the unicom operator may not even be able to see the wind sock from the office of the FBO. Even if the unicom operator can see the wind sock, there is no guarantee that he will consult it. Often it's just easier to go with the flow and to repeat the runway announced by the last landing or departing airplane. Whatever the reason for the mistakes, they do happen, and it behooves us to check firsthand the direction and the speed of winds prior to takeoff. Where the runway is short, or where an aborted takeoff becomes necessary, or where it becomes necessary to use crosswind technique, the best policy is to determine the critical information firsthand, where possible.

INTERSECTIONS

Another pretakeoff consideration that many pilots must confront is whether to depart from an intersection. At Teterboro Airport, where I am based, and at many other airports, ground control will occasionally direct me to an intersection for departure. For a long time, I accepted the instruction (in the spirit of cooperation) without question, and certainly without considering the ramifications of what I was doing. One day at another airport, though, after having been given and accepting an intersection for departure, the pilot I was flying with questioned my automatic acceptance. "Why," he asked "increase the risk of the takeoff without any reason whatsoever?" He pointed out that, in the event of an aborted takeoff or an engine failure directly after takeoff, the distance that I so blithely surrendered moments before could mean the difference between a scare and a bent airplane. My immediate response to the other pilot's question was incredulity. The chance of an engine failure or the need to abort a takeoff was, at best, remote. How much of a chance was I taking? The pilot's response, though, was worth considering. "Even if the risk is remote," he pointed out, "it's not worth taking for no reason at all."

The pilot made an excellent point. Very few of the requests for a pilot to use an intersection departure amount to more than a minor convenience matter. In fact, the controllers may be trying to accommodate the pilot of the airplane by reducing the distance that he must taxi. Now I think before I accept an intersection departure. First, I never request one myself. If a controller asks me to take an intersection for departure, I ask what the distance is from the intersection to the end of the runway and whether it would be possible to get a full-length departure. If the intersection is just a hundred feet from the end of the runway, and if there are other airplanes lined up at the end of the runway, chances are I will accept the intersection. If the intersection is offered merely to reduce the distance I need to taxi, I'll take full length, thank you very much.

ROLLING

A lot takes place during the initial application of takeoff power, and though many of a pilot's reactions can be instinctive, there's still much to think about. First and foremost is the control of the airplane. While most of us have little difficulty controlling familiar airplanes during the takeoff roll, I learned from experience that it often pays to be wary of flights in new types, especially when they are more powerful than your usual steed. My experience occurred on takeoff from a small paved strip in Arkansas in a shiny new Bonanza. At the time, the Bonanza was new to me, but during the inbound flight I had come to feel quite at home with the airplane's excellent handling characteristics. I could see why the Bonanza had developed a reputation as a "pilot's airplane."

I was to take the left seat again for the return flight, and judging from the responsive nosewheel steering and controls, I expected a routine takeoff. After running through the final check list items, I applied full power with the palm of my hand on the vernier control. Looking back, it seems pretty clear that I was more than a little cavalier with the power. The Bonanza leaped forward with an unexpected roar, and within moments I felt as if I were holding on for dear life rather than flying the airplane. Despite the Bonanza's fine ground handling, I began to notice the airplane easing to the left, almost side-stepping, in a manner that I had never before experienced. I applied right rudder, but it didn't seem to halt the airplane's sideways progress. Through the entire takeoff roll, the airplane edged slowly but steadily to the left and toward the weeds of our relatively narrow runway. My attempts at control seemed entirely ineffective, and I was beginning to wonder whether I ought to abort the takeoff. Ultimately, I did not abort. But I can truthfully admit that the only thing that prevented me from taking a ride through a goldenrod field was the good luck of getting the airplane off the ground first.

For most of the flight back to Kansas I remained mystified by the airplane's behavior. Had the wind blown across the runway? Was there something wrong with the rudder? What was going on here? Looking back, I suspect that at least two factors had combined to make this takeoff a particularly exciting one. First, I was not accustomed to takeoffs in an airplane with the power of the Bonanza; consequently, I think that I underestimated the degree to which left-turning forces will grab hold of an airplane, particularly when you crank in the power with a bit too much zeal. I have since learned that a new airplane will take the earliest opportunity to illustrate its distinctiveness to a new pilot, and frequently this is on takeoff. I ought to have been gentler with the controls in the Bonanza, and I have since learned that even airplanes with fine handling characteristics can surprise a pilot with an unusual trick played in unusual circumstances. As in my case, nearly all surprises can be avoided with a little care.

A second factor that I ought to have considered was the runway. The airport, as I recall, was graced with a relatively short and narrow paved strip. Although the runway was not unlike the one that I learned on, and was certainly wide enough and long enough for airplanes much larger than the Bonanza, I had become accustomed to flying from the expansive strips of Teterboro Airport, my home base. A little shilly-shallying on either side of the centerline generally was not even noticed, much less cause for alarm. So who knows, maybe I had been drifting about on takeoff with all airplanes but just had not noticed previously. I doubt this, but I am now particularly careful to keep the airplane solidly on the runway centerline during takeoff roll regardless of the amount of elbow room the runway allows.

THE AIRPLANE'S PULSE

The takeoff roll is usually the first phase of the flight where it is possible to get a good idea of how the airplane's power plant and primary systems are operating. I was cautioned early in my instruction that, if your airplane is going to experience mechanical problems, chances are they will show themselves during the first few moments of flight. The engine is running at full power, the fuel is flowing at its highest rate and, in short, the airplane is putting out all it's got. The problem with airplane malfunctions in the first moments of flight is that the pilot's options are limited. What would be a mere emergency at 8,000 feet can become a catastrophe at 300 feet. There just isn't the time to think about what you are going to do.

For this reason alone, I view the takeoff roll as an initial test run prior to takeoff. During the roll, I have the opportunity to look at each of the engine gauges prior to breaking ground. Assuming that the airplane normally runs with all gauges in the green, it is probably worth working up an emergency procedure for the situation in which all of the gauges are not in the green. If I were still on the ground and the cylinder-head temperature were up in the red, I would abort the takeoff, unless there were some immediately apparent and resolvable answer to the problem, like closed cowl flaps. In IFR conditions, I wouldn't even need to think about the response; taking off into clouds with a known mechanical problem is just too great a risk to attempt.

WHAT'S UNUSUAL?

Another ground for aborting the takeoff is any roughness in the engine during the takeoff roll. If the engine is surging or coughing while on the runway, I can't think of many situations where I would leave the safety of terra firma. The chances that the problem would work itself out are far too remote to justify a possible off-airport landing. The problem that pilots sometimes have is deciding in the heat of the takeoff, when their minds are on such matters as aircraft control, whether the airplane is actually malfunctioning or whether it is simply clearing some carbon from a plug, or belching, or any number of other rationalizations that fall into the category of "whistling in the dark." Pilots who own their own airplanes or who are very familiar with the airplanes that they rent or borrow are at a decided advantage in this sort of situation. Again, they know the airplane's quirks and can readily judge when something is going wrong with the airplane or when it's just being finicky.

One airplane that I fly frequently sounds the alternator alarm even though the alternator is working perfectly. Whereas this would certainly be grounds for aborting a takeoff into instrument conditions, I generally will double-check the indication with the ammeter. By verifying that the alternator is, in fact, operating normally, and that the airplane is safe to fly, I've been able to avoid more than one aborted takeoff and delayed flight. Where there is an anomalous indication from even the most reliable, true-blue airplane, the safest course, runway permitting, is to call off the takeoff. Even where there may not be enough runway to avoid the weeds at the end of the tarmac, an overrun still might be preferable to takeoff where the engine sounds as if it's getting ready to call it quits.

HEADS UP

Prior to leaving the ground, much of a pilot's attention is focused inside of the airplane. I have always found that with airspeeds to peg, headings to follow, and check lists to complete, it is difficult to move my attention from inside the airplane to outside. One reason for this, I believe, is that most instructors place a greater emphasis on pegging airspeeds and headings than on checking the horizon for other airplanes. The first instructor I ever had who insisted on constant attention outside of the airplane was Duane Cole, the famed aerobatic showman.

I had traveled to the Fort Worth area to learn the intricacies of flight around three axes—you know, loops, Immelmanns, hammerhead stalls and the other tricks that make up the repertoire. Although I was there to learn, I naturally wanted to impress Mr. Cole with my control of the airplane and my finely honed mastery of stick-and-rudder basics. Before flying, we went over the cockpit layout, V-speeds and procedures for the Citabria, an airplane with which I was not familiar, and I was, of course, determined to establish the proper airspeed and attitude, and pretty much peg all of the numbers with the precision of an aerobatic maestro.

In my zeal to demonstrate my mastery, I overlooked the fact that to an aerobatic maestro having the right stuff means never staring at a cockpit instrument, especially during climbout. Rather than compliment me on my skills, Cole's first words told me to get my eyes outside of the cockpit. During takeoff, a primary concern of VFR and IFR pilots is to maintain a healthy distance from any other airplanes in the pattern. Whether you are departing from a controlled airport or an uncontrolled airport, the only effective way to do this is to look outside the airplane.

As Cole liked to point out, there is nothing on any of the cockpit gauges that is more important than avoiding collision with another airplane. Of course he was correct, but I had a difficult time flying without the instruments, even on a VFR flight. Looking back, I know that this was simply a matter of habit and technique. Cole sat behind me in the Citabria, but he had an uncanny ability to sense when my attentions were focused inside rather than outside the airplane. He later admitted to me that a shift to cockpit instruments was nearly always accompanied by sloppy flying.

STRIKING THE IFR BALANCE

Of course, there are some significant differences in initial climbout when under an IFR flight plan. Those differences are most pronounced during the zero-zero or low-visibility takeoff. The first really low-visibility takeoff that I ever made was from Houston Hobby Airport. A gummy fog had descended over the airport, and in some areas it was quite difficult to taxi, much less take off. Because of the limited visibility, the transition from visual to instrument flight began immediately upon applying takeoff power. Although I was able to see the centerline of the runway and used it to keep the airplane straight during the takeoff run, I also used the DG as a crosscheck to assure me that the airplane was straight. After rotation, rather than establish the climb attitude of the airplane with respect to the actual horizon, I used the artificial horizon as the primary instrument. And because we entered instrument conditions immediately, there was no duty to maintain separation from other aircraft.

After climbing to a safe altitude, the instrument takeoff becomes identical to any other actual IFR flight. I suspect, however, that an instrument takeoff involves substantial risks. While one generally has time to become accustomed to controlling the airplane prior to entering instrument conditions, the instrument takeoff requires the pilot to jump immediately into the fray. This can be challenging. Furthermore, the proximity of the airplane to the ground during an instrument takeoff leaves an extremely small margin for error. Quite literally, there is no room for error. For these reasons, I don't make a habit of embarking on very low visibility departures. For me, the risks just aren't worth it.

Between the no- or low-visibility departure and the VFR departure is the garden-variety instrument departure, where you will have at least 200- or 300-foot (probably much more) ceilings and at least a little time to transition into actual instrument flight. During these takeoffs, the pilot must maintain separation from other aircraft prior to entering cloud. He must also, however, accomplish all of the other tasks and duties incident to an IFR departure. For instance, it may be necessary to follow a complex SID or follow vectors issued by departure control. Unlike the VFR pilot, the IFR pilot must devote a certain amount of attention to duties inside the cockpit. Like the VFR pilot, however, he must also keep a close lookout for other airplanes, particularly other VFR flights whose position might well not be known to the tower or to approach. Because of the IFR pilot's mixed duties, the workload during the transition from takeoff to cruise can be quite heavy.

SECOND PART　Richard L. Collins

Advancing the power and starting down the runway moves us into the dynamic risk-management business. The plans are laid, well, we hope, and starting the takeoff roll puts the plan into action. The statistics here aren't too happy: Approximately 20 percent of accidents occur during takeoff and initial climb. Engines quitting on singles? Not really. Whether the aircraft is single engine, multiengine, turboprop, or turbojet, about 20 percent of the accidents that involve substantial or greater damage to an airplane occur on the roll or soon after. Time it next time you fly. From a standing start to 1,500 feet would take maybe three minutes, even in a poor climber. With 20 percent of the accidents in what must be a tiny percentage of the hours flown, there have to be lessons in the record.

Takeoff is a time when pilots are generally most alert and aware that they are in a critical phase of flight. While some pilots might become complacent after droning along for several hours, few are likely to be blasé about a takeoff. The crew of Concorde has worked all the numbers, and to them the takeoff is a special time.

Accelerating to 199 knots on the ground is not only a

thrill, it is a deed that quite apparently must be done with utmost precision. Every gauge, every warning light, every sensation, and every sight has something to do with whether they continue or abort the takeoff. The crew has to be ready for power contingencies—an engine failure, failure of reheat (afterburner) to kick in, unacceptable power output on one of the big engines, or any system problem would send them from the go mode to the stop mode unless V1, the decision speed, had been attained. They give every appearance of tending to serious business seriously, which is exactly what they are doing. At all times during takeoff, initial climb, and the rest of the flight, the crew has a trained reaction for anything that might happen. The lone pilot in a Cessna 152 can operate in the same manner.

BEGINNING

A pilot has a lot of things to do on takeoff other than steer down the runway. Part of learning to fly well is learning, on takeoff, to be aware of things both inside and outside of the cockpit simultaneously. At most other times, we can move our attention in and out. When cloud flying, concentration can all be on the inside. During the last part of a landing, concentration is all outside. On takeoff, though, when the power is coming up to maximum for the first time, the pilot needs to be sure it is coming to the desired value and all the accessories are coming along with it. This attention to instrumentation needs to continue in the climb. For the pilot of a piston twin that had been partially filled with jet fuel, instrumentation in the climb outlined that he had best get back down quickly. He could tell that engine operation was not normal and that both engines were affected. A quick look at the exhaust gas and cylinder head temperature gauges (I think I remember him saying the exhaust was colder than normal and the cylinders hotter) convinced him that conditions were anything but normal. He landed okay. This made me resolve to note the normal exhaust gas temperature for full power, and to check it immediately after power application for takeoff. The EGT gauge exhibits almost no lag, so if it isn't in the right place, the takeoff should come to a halt.

STEERING

With tricycle landing gear, loss of directional control on takeoff is not the factor it was when tailwheels were the norm. I remember an adventure the pilot of a corporate Model 18 twin Beech had one crosswindy day. The runway was north-south, the wind was west-northwest about 30 knots and it was gusty. The larger tailwheel airplanes usually had tailwheel locks: With the airplane in position for takeoff, the pilot would lock the tailwheel so it would stay straight. As this pilot lifted the tail in the run, the wind picked that moment to huff and puff. The 18 had relatively small rudders and vertical fins, not adequate for the crosswind in this case, and the pilot was not quick enough with differential power to keep the airplane from turning about 30 degrees into the wind. Fortunately there was grass out there that we used for Cub flying, and the Beech bumped across the grass until it had adequate speed for the crew to take it flying. Nothing damaged but one captain's ego. The passengers must have thought it interesting. If it had happened in less friendly surroundings, it could have become a major accident.

With modern airplanes, takeoff accidents come in several forms. One is the trip off the end of the runway because it isn't long enough or because the pilot made a belated attempt to abort the takeoff. Unless the airplane goes off the end into bad stuff, or off a cliff, or at high speed, the accidents are usually serious only to the airplane. On the other hand, if a pilot decides not to abort an impossible takeoff, the airplane will be accelerating to the very end.

INTERFACE: PREFLIGHT AND TAKEOFF

A lot of takeoff accidents, some of them serious, reflect the interface between preflight action and safety on the roll and liftoff.

A pilot flying an Aerostar flew into electrical wires and trees and then the ground shortly after takeoff on a night IFR flight. The investigation revealed that the elevator trim actuator rod was in a position that corresponds with full nose-down trim. A wire was disconnected and evidence showed that the wire had been subjected to high amperage. The Aerostar has electric trim only, and the pilot's operating handbook for this aircraft did not state that flight was prohibited with inoperative trim. It was demonstrated beyond a doubt that the airplane was manageable with full trim in either direction, but that would be a diversion a pilot might not handle well on a night IFR takeoff. If the trim was in the full nose-down position, it should have been apparent on the walk-around inspection.

Nobody was hurt, but the airplane was damaged substantially when the engine of a Cessna 150 quit at about 200 feet following takeoff. A landing was made in a plowed field and the aircraft flipped over on its back. The pilot said he calculated that there was enough fuel on board for the flight, but information gained from another source indicated that the airplane was last refueled more than five flying hours before the crash. In another 150, the student reported to the instructor that he noticed water in the fuel. No action was taken, and shortly after takeoff the engine quit. The airplane was landed in a parking lot, a car was struck, and there were serious injuries. Following the accident, traces of ice were found in the fuel system.

At times the action can take on an immediacy that would not be found on a normal flight.

A pilot flying a Cessna 210 at night shot a VOR approach to an airport that was reporting an indefinite ceiling with a mile visibility in fog. After landing, the pilot realized that he was too far down the runway to stop. He took off again; at 300 feet the engine quit and the aircraft crashed into trees. The pilot was seriously injured. Only about a pint of fuel was found in the fuel system and there was no evidence of spill in the crash area. The engine was subsequently test run and operated normally. Perhaps it is a little farfetched to use that one here, but the airplane was on the ground at one point and had the pilot made the decision not to go flying again, the accident might have been less serious.

HOMEBUILTS

There are an unusual number of homebuilts involved in takeoff and initial-climb accidents. A common thread here is unfamiliarity with the airplane.

A pilot who had recently purchased a homebuilt was seen

to pull up after takeoff, stall, spin, and hit the ground. Witnesses reported that the engine sounded like it was was running rough. On the pilot's first flight in the airplane a few weeks earlier, a groundloop followed the landing, the pilot's first in a tailwheel airplane, and the engine suffered sudden stoppage. There was no recorded maintenance and the accident flight was the first since the incident.

A pilot who had recently purchased a homebuilt pulled up into a steep climb right after takeoff. The climb lasted from 300 to 500 feet, where the airplane nosed over and dove into the ground.

Another homebuilt crashed on first flight after the pilot realized something was wrong soon after liftoff. The airplane simply would not climb. With a power line ahead, the pilot cut the power and crashed in a bean field. Investigation revealed that the center of gravity was ahead of the forward limit.

Still another first flight: The pilot planned to lift off the runway and let the aircraft settle back to the surface. It lifted off at a high angle of attack. Full forward elevator and a throttle reduction brought the aircraft to level flight about 20 or 30 feet over the runway. Then it started rolling, pitched nose down and crashed off to one side of the runway. The pilot was a student with no time in the make and model and no endorsement for the flight.

Even if nobody is hurt, first-flight accidents must take a toll of the builder. All that work for nothing. This is a difficult risk to manage, too, because often there is no way to get dual in a like airplane before the first flight. A homebuilder might also be a pilot who hasn't flown a lot recently because all his aviation time has been spent building. Perhaps the best way to manage the risk is to be aware of it and to take as many steps as possible to eliminate any doubt about the airplane's handling qualities or the pilot's test-flying skills before takeoff.

TAKING A LOOK

Another preflight action that relates to the takeoff is a simple visual and mental inspection of the conditions that exist for the takeoff. Had the pilot of a Comanche done this on a realistic basis one dark night, an accident could have been avoided. The pilot didn't have an instrument rating but had logged three hours of simulated instrument time prior to the accident. Perhaps this bolstered his courage. Reported conditions nearby were 100 obscured and a quarter of a mile visibility in fog. The pilot took off, entered a left turn and shortly flew into the ground in a nose-down left turn.

The pilot of a Cessna 152 was taking off north with a surface wind from the east at seven knots. There was apparently wind shear, with the wind stronger and out of the south just above the runway. The airplane reached 25 feet, where it entered an uncontrolled descent and crashed.

If careful thought is given to conditions, wind shear can often be anticipated. I was leaving Mercer County Airport in New Jersey one day and was assigned Runway 34 for departure. The surface wind was very light but was indicating west-northwest, so the runway was a logical one. After takeoff the airplane did not climb well and it was at 500 or 600 feet before I thought it had its act straight. The climb was into a strong southerly flow and climbing into an increasing tailwind can have a strong effect on performance. What was the clue that could have tipped me off to the wind shear? Listening to my friend Bill Korbel do the weather on WOR in New York should have been enough this morning. He had said, while I was shaving, that it was going to warm up rather drastically that day. For it to warm, the wind has to come from the south or southwest. And where the early morning surface wind might be from any direction, the wind above might be blowing from a different direction rather strongly. Every little item of information counts.

A final item relates to the runway, the load, and the temperature. Usually when there is an accident involving too much load and too little runway, the outcome should have been obvious before starting. The pilot of a Cherokee loaded four people into the airplane on a hot day. The fuel tanks were almost full, the uphill, 1,700-foot-long grass runway pointed to the northeast, and the surface wind was reported as 260 at eight in the NTSB report. You can imagine the result.

FURTHER ALONG

The further into takeoff and initial climb, the greater the risk, simply because the turf beneath becomes less friendly as the airplane moves away from the airport. You are getting into an area where the airplane isn't high enough for there to be a lot of choices if power is lost or a lot of altitude for recovery if control is lost.

One thing that helps manage risk is a continuous chain of thought about what is going on. The old saying about a pilot being "behind" the airplane relates to this. The thought processes in flying always have to be realtime, right up to the second, with this more important at certain times. If anything happens in initial climb, the time available to formulate a response is limited, so the best deal is to always have alternatives in mind. At some point, a landing back on the runway becomes impossible. Even though the alternatives become far less attractive at that point, they have to be considered. Whether flying a single or a twin, a pilot needs to think about where he would go or what he would do in a worst case. The record shows a high level of survivability in singles deposited in impromptu locations. Twins don't do as well on survivability, but they do have power left after one engine fails and offer the option of getting back to a runway, or, if the single-engine performance won't allow that, the choices of off-airport landing sites are wider. The key in a twin is in taking maximum advantage of the capabilities and, if trouble does come, in maintaining control until the airplane contacts whatever is there for a landing.

The pilot of an Aerostar was cleared to taxi to a 7,500-foot-long runway for departure; he requested a change to a 4,500-foot-long runway with a light quartering tailwind. Use of the shorter runway apparently involved less taxiing. The aircraft was observed using almost all the runway for the roll, after which it rotated abruptly and yawed left into a low-altitude left turn. Then the aircraft descended rapidly into trees and caught fire. The left prop was found in the feathered position. No evidence of internal engine failure was found, but a while before the accident the airplane was heard taking off with a series of backfires, after which work was done on the engine to correct the problem. The pilot's logbook didn't show any recent training in single-engine procedures.

TYPICAL

Unfortunately, that accident is what might be described as a typical twin takeoff accident. Even the smallest twins are complex airplanes that add another dimension—the potential for asymmetric power—to flying, and if a pilot doesn't take every possible action to minimize risk, the chances of a serious accident after an engine failure are increased dramatically. If a pilot doesn't always use the longest available runway, or uses airports with short runways, or if a pilot attempts or continues a takeoff if there is the slightest doubt about either engine, then the risk starts going out of sight. Load and density altitude enter into the picture. Occasionally, but not often, there's a twin accident where the pilot made the conservative choices but still crashed. In many twin takeoffs there is just a fleeting moment when, if an engine quits, even a good and conservative pilot would be at considerable risk. But this time is quite short, and even it can be minimized. For example, a Baron B55 at gross weight flying in standard conditions will accelerate to a speed 10 knots over the engine-out minimum control speed and then stop in less than 3,400 feet. That's with the test pilot flying; add 20 percent for less than ideal technique. If the runway is 4,100 feet long, any power problem before reaching a speed 10 knots over the minimum control speed might be contained within the confines of the runway if the pilot is quick. If it's hotter or higher than sea level, more runway will be required. This information is only helpful if the pilot has it in mind, and has a plan throughout the takeoff. Pulling out onto a runway and mindlessly launching works almost all the time, but almost isn't enough. A sad statistic has been around for a long time: The chance of being killed after one engine fails is four times greater in a twin than in a single. This is a slight reflection on the engine-out performance of the airplanes and a major reflection on the proficiency of the pilots who fly them.

SINGLE

The thought processes in a single takeoff are much the same as in a twin. Only the outcome is different. If, in a single, you are fortunate enough to have up front the engine that didn't quit in the twin, then the takeoff remains routine. If you are unfortunate enough to have the engine that did quit, then the task becomes more difficult. How difficult will become apparent if, after every takeoff, you keep tabs on the available places to go if the engine quit right now.

A Cessna 150's engine suffered an internal mechanical failure on the test flight after engine maintenance. The pilot attempted to return to the airport but was unable to, and the aircraft had to be landed in trees and brush. The NTSB investigation revealed that an incorrect part had been installed in the engine. A Cherokee Six lost power on the climbout and the aircraft was landed in small trees and brush away from the airport. In both these accidents only minor injuries were suffered, so the pilots managed the risk very well. The key was in picking the best place to go and maintaining control until it was reached.

There are accidents where the mechanical failure of an engine in a single leads to serious injury or death, but you have to go through stacks on stacks of accident reports to find one—especially one that involves a certified engine that was properly maintained. There are a lot, though, where there was no fuel, where the fuel was contaminated, or where the engine was suspect from the beginning.

LOSS OF CONTROL

Loss of control of an aircraft during initial climb is most often related to heavy loads, high-density altitude, or short runways when no engine problem is involved. Sometimes all three factors come into play. The loss of control occurs when the pilot stalls the airplane in an attempt to make it do the impossible. There are also some losses of control during initial climb in instrument conditions. Most involve pilots without instrument ratings, but a few pilots with instrument ratings operating on IFR flight plans let the airplane get away from them during initial climb.

Dark nights contribute to loss of control, especially where the area of initial climb is without ground lights, as is the case going out over water or desolate terrain. Even though there might not be any clouds, these are instrument conditions. The record has shown time and again that VFR flying at night is dangerous except on sparkling clear nights. There is really little mystery to a loss of control when a pilot who can't fly instruments takes off and either flies into clouds or into an area where there is no visual reference. The only mystery is in why the pilot attempted the flight in the first place.

On the other hand, why would an instrument pilot lose control in initial climb? It doesn't happen often, but it does happen, and the reasons are likely complex. Because the pilot is not often around to explain what happened, and the accident report seldom goes beyond the fact that the pilot very obviously lost control, we are left to explore reasons why this might happen.

One important factor might be confusion. That first few minutes in clouds is a challenging time for any pilot, as the old familiarity with the sights of instrument flying, the sounds of the airplane, and the sometimes strange sensations of the very beginning of a flight are experienced. Perhaps the air is turbulent where the pilot thought it would be smooth. Perhaps there is some wind shear that results in an unusual rate of climb, either better or worse than expected. Some change in a clearance could be confusing, or, if something was set incorrectly before takeoff, that could pull attention from the instrument flying.

Unfamiliarity with equipment can also cause confusion. Just because a pilot is current in one Cessna 210 does not mean that pilot is current in all Cessna 210s, because of the wide variety of equipment installed in the airplanes. Differences in autopilots, or a basic lack of understanding of the characteristics of autopilots, could cause problems. A while back I got a checkout in a Bonanza to use while my Cessna was in the shop. I have been flying Bonanzas almost since I started flying in 1951 and they are old shoe, but I still like to get those checkouts. The next day when I was launching on a trip in the airplane it was cloudy. Once off the ground and in the clouds I momentarily thought about turning the autopilot on. Bad thought, though, because I hadn't flown the particular King autopilot installed in the airplane very much and it hadn't been covered on the checkout. I waited until later, with the airplane on top of all the clouds, to teach myself how to operate the autopilot.

In that first few minutes of instrument flying, too, I reminded myself time and again that instrument flying in a Bonanza is different than in a 210. The Bonanza is delightfully responsive to the controls, meaning that any inadvertent control movement while looking at a chart will result in the airplane straying farther from the straight and narrow than would the 210 with the same inadvertent control movement. The nice flying qualities of the airplane actually make it a bit more demanding on instruments.

Another strong requirement became apparent as I was preparing for the flight. To avoid any confusion over what was where after takeoff, a good pretakeoff plan was required to work around the differences between this airplane and the one I fly most often. When a pilot just jumps into a relatively unfamiliar airplane and launches into clouds or a dark night, it is no mystery if a problem with aircraft control occurs soon after takeoff.

BIG ONES, TOO

Loss of control after takeoff is not limited to general aviation pilots flying light airplanes. The Northwest MD-80 at Detroit, the Continental DC-9 at Denver, and the AVAir Metro at Raleigh-Durham, in late 1987 and early 1988, were all loss-of-control accidents. The official findings on these are not out as this is being written, but press coverage of the initial investigations gave us a lot to think about.

Speculation was that the flaps of the MD-80 were not extended for takeoff. What does this have to do with a loss of control? The airplane got off the ground, but if the flaps were not extended it would have been hard to control at the speeds selected for a takeoff with the airplane in the proper configuration. If a pilot knows exactly why an airplane is behaving differently, he might be able to handle it. In the American DC-10 accident at Chicago some years ago, the left engine was physically lost from the airplane, damaging the hydraulic system. The leading edge flaps on the left wing retracted. But the crew did not know this—they didn't even know the engine had fallen off. In following the proper engine-out procedures, the airplane was slowed to a speed below the stalling speed of the left wing and control was lost. Had they flown faster, control might been maintained, but they didn't know the nature of the problem. Likewise, a pilot taking off with the flaps stowed instead of extended might have been able to pull it off, but only if he knew the flaps were stowed and knew of a procedure to fly the airplane away in this configuration. If a problem develops with the airplane just off the ground, there is little time and the demand is to make a quick and correct assessment of why things aren't going as they should. That is why playing "what if?" can pay big dividends in the risk-management business. There has to be a lesson in every crash, and our job is to learn that lesson.

At Denver, the Continental DC-9 possibly had ice on the wings. This is disputed by some, but the fact remains that control of the aircraft was lost immediately after takeoff. The pilot flying—in the right seat—was not experienced in the DC-9 and the weather was inclement. If there was just a little ice atop the wings, perhaps a little more on one wing than the other, it might have caused the airplane to roll in one direction or another right after liftoff. If a relatively inexperienced pilot were to overcontrol in roll, a pilot-induced roll oscillation could result. If the pilot in the left seat were not an experienced instructor in the type, it might be difficult for him to arrest increasing rolling moments. The FAA addressed this soon after the Denver crash by asking the airlines not to pair pilots with relatively little experience in the type being flown.

My son started flying in the left seat as soon as he was tall enough to see over the instrument panel. One day when we were leaving Asheville, North Carolina, with low visibility, I told him to slip into the right seat. He didn't like that; he wanted to fly, but I explained that it would be better to have the pilot with the most experience in low-visibility takeoffs flying.

In the AVAir Metro accident it was speculated that the pilot in the right seat was flying the airplane, and that while the pilot's experience level was good, it reportedly took three tries for her to pass a check flight, and a captain had written a critical memo after a flight. These items, in initial press reports, offer nothing conclusive but, again, they do show that one of the keys to managing risk is, with two pilots, to have the best of the two doing the difficult stuff.

How does this relate to those of us who fly without another pilot in the right seat? If we don't do it well, or don't have recent experience with it, best not do it at all.

Where the accident record shows a relatively substantial amount of trouble in takeoff and initial climb, there is little in the record to suggest that this is of necessity an unduly hazardous time. Rather, it is a time that is unforgiving of any lapses. To me, the takeoff has always been the most enjoyable time in flying, but it can be so only if done with the knowledge that everything that can be done to manage the proven risks has been done.

CHAPTER 4

En Route VFR

FIRST PART   Patrick E. Bradley

The en route phase of a VFR flight can be the most relaxed and enjoyable time that a pilot spends in his airplane. The bustle and crunch of takeoff and initial climbout are complete, and the airplane is established at the desired cruise altitude. With the proper heading chosen and the sectional in hand, there's not a whole lot more to do than keep the airplane straight and level and wish for better winds.

For a long time I felt that en route VFR flight was probably one of the lowest risk times in an airplane, and to some extent, I still believe that that's true. I also know from past experience, though, that the en route phase of VFR flight is the time when past oversights, shortcuts, and indiscretions come back to roost. For instance, was your preflight of the airplane up to snuff? You may find out en route, when you finally notice that the fuel filler cap that you neglected to check flew off, with most of that tank's fuel following close behind. Did you spend enough time checking the weather? Well, if not, you may learn during the en route phase how beautiful the weather can be at your departure point and how dreadful it can be at your destination, only a few hundred miles west. And did you plan your route as well as you should have? A flight of F-111s passing overhead may remind you not only that a military operating area straddles your route of flight, but that the area is hot.

So although the en route phase of VFR flight can often be a relaxed time, it also holds traps for the unwary. It is during the VFR phase of the flight that the pilot must not only fight off complacency, but make some of his most challenging judgment calls in response to changing conditions.

WEATHER: CHOOSING YOUR BATTLES

As most pilots learn early in their careers, the decision whether to continue a given flight is an ongoing process that is as dynamic and complex as changes in the prevailing weather conditions. Of course, we make our initial go/no-go decisions on the ground. But that's not the end of the process. The en route phase of a VFR flight will bring new conditions and new demands for weather judgments. In fact, the decisions that we make en route can be much more critical than those that we make on the ground, particularly when facing the classic declining weather scenario.

One of my first long VFR cross-country flights took me from Lincoln Park, New Jersey, to Tamiami Field, Miami, Florida, in a Cessna 150. Needless to say, the trip required numerous stops. It also required more weather-related decision making than I had struggled with prior to that time. Besides having to evaluate forecasts provided to me by flight service, it was necessary to evaluate the conditions that I encountered and assess my ability to deal with them. In short, I had to learn how to choose my battles wisely, because a defeat could be for real.

SLIPPERY SLOPE

One of the most important lessons I learned on the flight to Florida and back was that a pilot's worst enemy can be himself. On the trip back, we departed Tamiami in conditions that I described in my logbook as "cloudy, with scattered rainshowers." For about two hours, I dodged in and about the rainshowers with some success. Basically, I followed the main coastal highway running north and had little trouble navigating as long as I was able to stay out of the cloud. When fuel started running low, we stopped in Melbourne, Florida, topped the tanks, and again had to decide whether to continue the flight. Since I had succeeded in making the trip so far at about 1,000 feet, and since the weather seemed to be improving, I decided that it couldn't hurt to give the next leg a try. And looking back, I don't think that my reasoning was faulty. Although the weather at Daytona, our destination, was reported to be IFR, flight service had been reporting the same conditions for Melbourne, where the weather was certainly VFR and even seemed to be improving. Certainly there would be no harm in taking a look where the back door is wide open.

Looking back at my logbook for the attempted flight from Melbourne to Daytona, I see the entry "warm, rainshowers, deteriorating weather, turned back from Daytona." My logbook entry downplayed the experience. In fact, the rainshowers would have been described more accurately as thunderstorms. The "turned back from Daytona" part would have been more accurately stated as, "fled from certain doom in the nick of time." My ultimate destination for the flight was Titusville. I remembered that even without the logbook, because it was one of the two destinations where I kissed the ground when I got out of the airplane.

I recall the flight quite vividly. It involved a classic case of ignoring the indications of weather in front of me and continuing into conditions that I would not now attempt on an instrument flight plan. In short, I saw the weather ahead, but I was able to convince myself, somehow, that the black, ominous form on the horizon was merely an isolated thunderstorm, and that I could simply fly around it and continue on my way. I convinced myself that certain lighter areas around what was actually a line of thunderstorms would lead me to better weather. For some reason, I just couldn't bring myself to land the airplane, even though the view in front of me presaged completely unacceptable weather. I was on the slippery slope of knowing that I would have to stop at one point, but wanting to get farther than I actually could.

WHEN TO CRY "UNCLE"

To my credit, I did take some sensible precautions. I stayed over the main highway at all times. It became my lifeline to kinder, gentler conditions. I also periodically checked the conditions behind me to make sure that my route of escape would not be cut off. Unfortunately, I did not finally turn back until it was clear that the weather at my rearward retreat route was as bad as the conditions in front of me. When I got to the point where the rain was falling quite hard on the windscreen of the little 150 and the escape route had closed in behind me, I made the decision to turn back—and it was nothing short of a panicked decision.

By the time I turned back, the airplane was in pretty much solid instrument conditions. Recalling the instrument training that I had, I made a delicate 180-degree turn with reference to the instruments, attempting not to climb or descend or bank too steeply—all I wanted was a nice, slow turn away from the lightning and thunder. Fortunately, I was able to reverse course. Unfortunately, though, I had lost sight of my lifeline, the highway. Although forward visibility had deteriorated to nearly nothing, I looked down and was able to see a highway heading south. I began to follow the highway and began a slow descent to about 500 feet above the ground. Forward visibility was better down low, and, before long the conditions began to improve and my pulse returned. The first airport I came to that was VFR was Titusville, and I landed there quite happy to be still alive and determined not to overfly my capabilities again. I spent the rest of the day hanging around the airport and visiting the local alligator farms and souvenir stands. After spending the night, we were again anxious to be on our way.

GET ME DOWN

The next morning, the weather was mostly clear, with the exception of some scattered clouds at around 3,000 feet. The weather had not cleared entirely up north, but was forecast to be improving, so I struck off, hopeful that I would be able to make some headway against the uncooperative winds and weather.

Initially, at least, I was flying below the clouds. But as I progressed up the coast, the clouds began to descend and so did I. At some point, I decided that I would fly on top of the cloud layer rather than continue lower than I wanted under the bumpy belly of the clouds. I recall that the decision was innocent enough, since the layer was quite scattered and it would have been a simple matter to descend beneath the layer.

I was aware of the dangers of flying VFR on top of a layer of clouds, and kept a close tab on cloud separation and the opportunities to drop down below if necessary. About a half hour into the flight, it became clear that the benevolent white puffballs, previously content to drift about in no particular order, were beginning to form up in suspicious layer. I began to suspect that at some point I would have to either descend below the clouds and proceed or call it quits. Now, when I say I understood this, I mean it as an objective fact. I had much more trouble deciding how dense the layer would have to get before I descended back down where I belonged. Once again, I found myself skidding and clawing on the slippery slope. Unlike the previous day, the conditions on top of the clouds were wonderful. I saw the first sunshine of the entire trip, and the air was smooth and gentle. This was the type of en route flying that I dreamed of. Too bad I couldn't see the ground below.

DUCKING OUT

By the time I reached St. Augustine, the conditions were fast approaching the point where a decision would have to be made. There were still holes left in the overcast layer, though, so I continued on for another 15 or 20 miles—until it was obvious that the broken layer I was flying over previously was entirely overcast. There was not a lot of leeway left for discretion or interpretation. I had reached the point where I could not descend beneath the clouds without boring through them.

Since I had had my fill of instrument flying the day before, I again executed the faithful 180-degree turn back toward St. Augustine. Fortunately, there were still sufficient breaks in the cloud layer there to allow a VFR descent and an uneventful landing. I was fortunate, though. The cloud layer could easily have closed in behind me, leaving me in what is a common (and dangerous) bind for VFR pilots: above a solid layer with no place to go.

LESSONS

I learned a great deal about en route VFR flying during that flight from New Jersey to Florida in the 150. I suppose the main lesson I take with me is an improved understanding of the unpredictability of weather conditions and the need to consider this during the en route decision-making process. Although I made a number of mistakes during that trip, the one error that I scrupulously avoided was burning bridges. When the weather conditions reached the point where I would have to forgo a safe escape route, I landed.

WHERE AM I?

Unfortunately, there were times when, although I did not burn any bridges, I sometimes left them smoldering on the brink of conflagration. Those were my mistakes. I was fortunate that the airplane was operating properly and that I did not run into any navigating problems. At a number of points during the Florida trip, I would not have been able to handle a compound en route emergency had one arisen, and this is always playing a little too close to the edge.

I suppose that one of the most common problems encountered in the en route portion of a VFR flight is getting lost. These days, I file IFR for most flights, regardless of the weather. One of the reasons for this is so that I can stay in touch with the instrument system. The other reason is so that I don't get lost.

I never cease to be amazed, during a VFR flight using pilotage, how much attention it requires to fly from point A to point B without making a wrong turn. I got severely lost during one of my very first long cross-country flights. The route I was to follow was from Lincoln Park, New Jersey, to Albany, New York, to Griswold, Connecticut, and back to Lincoln Park. I recall that the flight from Lincoln Park to Albany was entirely uneventful. The weather was good, and there is an excellent highway, the New York State Thruway, that runs directly from northern New Jersey to Albany. I was feeling quite good about my navigating skills at the conclusion of this first leg of my longest cross-country flight to date.

The feeling was not to last, though. Although I had carefully laid out my route of flight for the leg from Albany to Griswold, I somehow got seriously turned around early on. I don't mean turned around literally, although I might as well have been. It was more like experiencing a sudden and complete confusion regarding my location in the universe. Although I was flying the proper heading, I could not pin down any landmarks. I was also preoccupied throughout the initial minutes of the flight with the control tower. I was still very intimidated by controlled airports, and no doubt this contributed to my confusion. Whatever the reasons, I followed roads, dialed in VOR frequencies, and craned my neck around the cockpit for what must have been thirty minutes or so without being able to get a good fix on where I was. Finally, I reached the end of my rope, admitted I was lost, and set about finding my way to the Atlantic coast.

What I did was climb a few thousand feet and dial in the frequency for the Madison VOR, which is just a few miles from Griswold. Much to my amazement, I was able to identify the VOR and received a nice strong signal. Next, I dialed in the proper bearing to take me direct to Griswold and flew it. I still had no idea where I was or how far I was from the VOR, but I flew there. I don't think that I would recommend this procedure, except in times of dire emergency, for several reasons. First, although I identified the VOR, I had no idea how far from it I was and how long it would take me to reach my destination. Second, for some reason I did not go to the trouble of identifying my position with a crossing VOR. It was simply bad piloting technique.

I am still not particularly good at navigating from one point to another using pilotage only. I tend to be a bit too cavalier, flying approximate headings in approximate directions to large landmarks. When I miss the landmark, I end up entirely lost, and have to begin the process of locating my position using the VOR bearings, which I have gotten much better at. The trouble with sloppy navigation is that you can get lost. And the trouble with getting lost is that you can stumble into poor weather conditions or restricted areas. You can also end up taking much longer than expected to reach your destination. It may even take longer than your airplane's

endurance. And finally, it complicates the procedures for dealing with other potential en route problems. A pilot ought
always to have a reasonably good idea of where the closest
airport is along his route in the event of mechanical failures.
If I had begun to experience engine problems on my flight
from Albany to Griswold, I would simply have had to stumble
around until I found an airport or made an off-airport landing.
In addition, it is difficult to avail yourself of the services of
controllers or flight service when you don't know where you
are.

Looking back, it becomes obvious to me that the en route
portion of a VFR flight does hold challenges for pilots and is
not to be underrated in terms of its demands. Although there
is generally more time to think through problems during the
en route portion of a flight, poor responses to the problems
can result in dangers as serious as those in any other phase of
flight.

SECOND PART   Richard L. Collins

In recent times the airlines have lost very few airplanes in
the en route phase of flight. Most of their problems have come
on departures and arrivals, takeoffs and landings. In general
aviation, a fourth of the fatal accidents occur in the cruise
phase of flight. When accidents happen in the cruise phase,
they tend to be more serious than accidents that happen at
other times. Eight percent less, 17 percent of total (including
non-fatal) accidents happen in cruise; the higher fatal-accident
number poses some interesting questions. Why, if there is an
accident, is the risk of serious injury or worse more likely in
cruise flight than, for example, on takeoff? Why, as you con-

sider more complex airplanes, do twins, turboprops, and jets have lower involvement in cruise accidents? Jets are lowest, singles are highest. Weather is the first thing that comes to mind, and when that number is found in the National Transportation Safety Board's records, it is apparent that when it comes to fatal accidents, weather is a culprit. What is called an "inflight encounter with weather" occurs before 25 percent of total fatal en route accidents in singles, 19 percent in twins, 16 percent in turboprops, and before very few of the jet accidents.

DRONING ALONG

While doing some of the research for this book, I was in the process of moving from my old job at *Flying* to my next job, at AOPA. There was a move to be made, from New Jersey to Frederick, Maryland. Until the move was made, I used my 210 to commute, almost on a daily basis, for over a month. As I did this, I gave a lot of thought to why the risk in cruise might be higher and how it might best be managed. The relationship to weather has to be a number-one factor, at least as far as serious accidents are concerned. But isn't this a risk that can be managed? Of course, the answer is that it can be, but managing it might mean that the airplane loses some utility.

A couple of flights in May, when there was a stationary low off the northeast coast, provided food for thought on this.

The first was an early-morning flight from Trenton to Frederick. The weather that I called up from CompuServe appeared innocuous. The lowest clouds around were at 3,100 feet, only one station was reporting light rain, and visibilities were averaging 5 to 9 miles. The terminal forecasts were for VFR, with conditions improving. No mention of thunderstorms until late in the day. The radar at Naval Air Station Patuxent in Maryland showed thunderstorms more than 100 miles south, and Patuxent is well south of the route I was flying. The area forecast was for good VFR. The Weather Channel agreed. Would I have flown it VFR? There's no way that I would have planned to do it that way because of a basic distrust of morning forecasts. As one weather sage once said, clouds have a habit of forming or dissipating at sunrise. However, if the FSS had lost my flight plan or an indefinite delay was in the offing, there's also no way I could say I wouldn't have considered making the trip VFR.

I wasn't far into my IFR flight before it was apparent that the weather was much worse than forecast. The air at 6,000 feet was troubled. Rain, moderate at times, was falling. I was working a lot harder than I thought I would be working. Later, flying at 4,000 feet, there were clouds well below, and scud could be seen, practically in the treetops, through breaks. The rain was heavy in spots, and as I maneuvered for the ILS at Frederick, I deviated around a cell of moderate rain that looked decidedly unfriendly. A colleague who lives near where the deviation occurred said there was one roll of thunder that morning and indeed some dots did appear on my Stormscope.

SCUD RUN

In retrospect I thought I had done a reasonable job of managing any risks posed by weather worse than forecast. This was done primarily by using the IFR system. We all do have to fly with the realization that what you see, not what is forecast, is what you get. This day, though, some commuter airline pilots definitely had their jobs made more interesting by conditions worse than forecast. Because of the amount of traffic in the New York–Washington corridor, IFR routings can be roundabout and altitudes not always of your choosing. So a lot of the commuters fly VFR when possible. Some were out VFR this morning, and the voices of the crews sounded anxious as they sought "traffic advisories." As hard as it was raining and as scuzzy as the low-level weather looked, what they probably wanted was some separation as they moved through the area of clouds and rain. One reported flying at 1,500 in a nineteen-passenger turboprop. Scud-running with fares. That couldn't be classified as good risk management. The forecast was wrong, but at some point that should have become obvious, and they should have retreated to an airport with good conditions. But this illustrates an area where pilots are weak at risk management. If VFR, and if the reported weather at the destination is okay, the temptation to continue is strong. Much is made of making good go/no-go decisions; in VFR flying this is better thought of as start/continue, with the latter evaluated on a continuous basis.

A FEW DAYS LATER

I thought about this again a few days later. The weather was low and it was forecast to be low. It was actually a bit better than forecast; even so, nobody in their right mind would have been flying VFR. As I moved along in rain and clouds, with some occasional bumps, I wondered about the relatively high incidence of accidents in cruise. I was flying at 5,000 feet, pretty far from trouble. Though thunderstorms were in the forecast, the tops in the area were reported as uniform at 16,000 feet. The primary apparent risk would have been from mechanical problems, but the ceilings beneath were good enough to allow some time to select a landing site in case of power failure, and there was a procedure to follow for any system failure. There is always risk, but this flight seemed like a reasonable deal to me. It would have been impossible VFR, though at times there were periods of VFR conditions. North of Philadelphia, the airplane broke out clear of clouds at 4,000 feet, with only some scud below. A real sucker hole for the VFR pilot, because in a few miles the showery clouds were back in force.

CLEAR DIVISION

There is a clear division of risk in VFR cruise. A power or other failure can cause the flight to wind up coming to a stop somewhere other than at the planned location. The pilot's inability to deal with weather can do the same. The risk to life is far lower when the airplane's inability to continue causes the problem. In one sample, about 70 percent of the accidents that began to happen as the airplane was in cruise flight related to a power loss or to mechanical problems. Less than 10 percent of these resulted in serious injuries or worse. Virtually all weather-related accidents are serious.

A first key element of airplane-related risk management is to make sure there is fuel on board and that it is getting to the engine. Almost half of the accidents following a power or mechanical problem involve fuel exhaustion or fuel-system mismanagement. Whether power is lost because something breaks or because the gas is all gone, the ensuing risk is similar. Conservative fuel planning reduces risk substantially.

REAL FAILURES

Anything mechanical might break, and when this happens in an airplane, the pilot moves into the serious risk-management business. The pilots who so skillfully landed that Aloha 737 after 20 feet of the fuselage top blew off and those who landed a 737 in a field after both engines quit set a high standard for the rest of us. They did all the right things and the outcome following the failure was certainly a good one. Twins or singles, we don't do as well.

The heavier the airplane, the greater the risk in an off-airport landing. In fact, most of the serious accidents after power failure involve high-performance singles and light twins. People successfully park airplanes like Skyhawks and Warriors in some of the craziest places without serious injury. Up the ante and the risk increases. In the sample that we have been using, every one of the serious forced-landing accidents came after a mechanical problem; half involved singles and half light twins. Almost all the fuel-exhaustion accidents involved two-place or basic four-place airplanes, and nobody got hurt. That is not to cast these thoughts in stone. There are plenty of successful forced landings in complex airplanes, and there are unsuccessful ones in simple airplanes. But the heavier the airplane and the higher the stalling speed, the more complex the pilot's job when it comes time to land somewhere other than on an airport. The items of technique are selecting the best spot, flying to that spot, maintaining control of the airplane until it comes in contact with something, and flying at the slowest safe speed. After initial contact it becomes a matter of how well the belt/harness system holds you in place.

AT THE SHOP

Managing the risks posed by mechanical or engine failure starts at the shop. As the general aviation fleet ages, we do have to spend more bucks on maintenance. This is especially critical for the high-performance singles and light twins, and maintaining one of these properly can pose a dilemma. Major work can come to a substantial percentage of the total value of the airplane. But neglecting maintenance is dangerous.

WEATHER

The most serious en route VFR threat comes from weather. About 17 percent of the total cruise accidents are weather-related, and in this sample all but one were fatal. In it the pilot, flying VFR, was, according to the NTSB, unable to divert around numerous thunderstorms. He elected to make a precautionary landing. The surface was soft and the aircraft nosed over. That result was a lot better than the others, which included everything from two-place through light twins. The reason so many of the VFR weather accidents are fatal is related to the fact that the pilot continues until the battle is completely lost. The end comes when the airplane winds up in clouds and the pilot is unable to control it, or when the pilot flies the airplane into the ground. Though some people survive accidents like this, the hit speed is usually too high for survival unless some lucky set of circumstances spreads the stop over a substantial distance and allows the cabin of the airplane to remain relatively intact.

WHY?

There are a lot of possible reasons that weather accidents remain a big part of the serious accident picture. One relates to training. Most dual cross-country is done in excellent weather in flight training. Then when the pilot earns a private license he is let loose in a never-never land of VFR flying where the legal minimum is as low as clear of clouds and 1-mile visibility. Weather is reported only at airports, along with a relatively few mountain passes or ridgelines, but even in areas where there are a lot of reporting stations, pilots get caught. There were two tragic accidents in a relatively short period of time near Washington, D.C. Both pilots were flying VFR, both were relatively far from home. Both apparently flew into clouds.

Flying in marginal VFR conditions is one of the most demanding forms of flying. There is nothing to tell what the weather ahead is like, nothing, that is, other than what the pilot sees. A constant determination that continued visual flight is possible has to be made. It is far more demanding and dangerous than IFR flying, yet it is not taught. Pilots learn to do it by surviving a few encounters, and the very fact that it worked might then urge some on to bigger and better things. A lot of the accidents involve rough terrain. Pilots using VOR for VFR navigation hit so many hills near VOR stations mounted on hilltops that the names of most were changed to include the word *mountain* to give a hint. Page VOR became

Rich Mountain, for example. Warning broadcasts were added to some, but nothing can alter the fact that a pilot who has no experience or training in this type of flying is ill-equipped to do it.

SCUD RUN LESSONS?

In discussions of low visibility VFR accidents, the next question is always whether or not people should be taught the techniques of flying visually in marginal weather conditions. Teach it, and that might be viewed as an endorsement of scud-running. Back in the bad old days I was a pretty fair scud-runner, having been taught by an expert. But he also taught me to fly needle, ball, and airspeed, which was the limit on what we had on the panel. He instilled a belief that keeping the airplane under control and in the air was the key to success. If it got into a cloud, okay, you can fly instruments, so turn around. This was socially acceptable in that day, when there were few airplanes flying IFR and this was being done in uncontrolled airspace. And the practitioners of this art realized that when it became impossible to fly visually, a complete transition had to be made. Maybe the simplicity of it helped, too. There was nobody to call. There was really nothing to do but concentrate on three instruments, the turn and bank, the clock, and the vertical speed. Standard rate turn for one minute while not descending. That points you in the direction from which you came. It wouldn't get you where you were going, but it would keep you alive. Times have changed, and today the emphasis has to be put on flying IFR when the weather is the least scuzzy and limiting VFR to days when the forecasts at least call for good VFR.

For the bad times, when the forecasts are wrong, teaching the VFR relationship with weather completely lacks definition. The FAA has never been able to prescribe training requirements that address problem areas, and they probably never will be able to do so. That leaves students and instructors to improvise. And unless a pilot develops and follows some hard rules on VFR flying in marginal weather, it is best to stick to excellent VFR conditions. Even then, there can be bad moments caused by missed forecasts, as related earlier in this chapter. VFR cross-country in what is defined as marginal VFR, a 3,000-foot ceiling and 5 miles visibility or less, is with added risk over what is there on a clear day. As the ceiling and visibility decrease from that value, the risk increases even more. At 1,000 on the ceiling and 3 on the visibility, the risk is extremely high, and it goes out of sight below those values. Multiply risk by four at night, which will be covered in Chapter 9.

EQUIPMENT

There is some equipment available that helps in marginal VFR flying. Loran, for example, works at low altitude, and some sets give the minimum safe altitude for the area in which the airplane is flying. But loran is best used as a backup for the old reliable map-and-highway system. One great loran feature, found on many sets, gives the bearing and distance to close-by airports along with information on those airports. If you are flying VFR and feeling a little lost and a lot confused, with strong questions about continuing, punching a button or two and finding the location of the nearest Coke machine with a runway is like magic.

Even things that are usually thought of as IFR tools can be a big help in VFR weather avoidance. I put radar to good use on the first day of the air traffic controllers' strike. No clearance was available for the leg ahead, and the weather was marginal VFR. I collected the sectionals and took off down a highway. The weather was barely okay; then I noticed an area of rain ahead on the radar. As marginal as conditions were, I knew that rain would cut the visibility below that which would be acceptable and lower clouds would likely form in the rain area. The only reasonable deal was to retreat to an airport that had just been overflown. The only way to reduce the risk was to stop. There are as many VFR airplanes lost in thunderstorms every year as IFR airplanes, so a weather radar or Stormscope might be considered of equal value on both types of flights.

ON THE OTHER HAND

There might be a flip side to the equipment question. Because so many of the airplanes flown VFR are actually well equipped for IFR flight, does that lull pilots into a false sense of security? Back in the good old days when we flew without radios and instruments, we knew that if the weather got bad we had to land. There was little information on the panel. Seeing was it. Now every pilot has a smattering of instrument training and most airplanes have the necessary instruments to fly without visual reference. If the wrong thing is done, though, it matters not how much equipment is in the airplane. A pilot flying VFR in the Rockies in a pressurized twin might have felt that he had all the cards: a well-equipped and capable airplane plus an instrument rating to use if necessary. It is possible that he bought the twin because he didn't want to fly a single in the mountains. There was a line of weather along the way that, according to the NTSB report, was advertised, but the pilot had apparently not gotten this information. It was a short flight, about 100 miles, and about 40 miles along the way the pilot flew into an area of low ceilings, fog, and mixed rain and snow. The airplane impacted terrain at 7,500 feet in mountainous terrain. As a matter of reference, the minimum en route altitude on the airway between the two points is 14,000 feet.

A surprising number of instrument-rated pilots are lost when flying VFR in fully equipped airplanes, which makes you wonder in each case why the pilot didn't just fly IFR. The answer is that there are times and places where VFR appears a better deal. Perhaps the pilot flying this twin felt there would be ice and turbulence in the clouds and that he could stay beneath and maneuver around terrain at a low altitude. It didn't work, and in reality the things that make inadvisable an IFR flight often make impossible a successful VFR flight, regardless of the airplane, the equipment, or the pilot's ratings.

COMPARED WITH JETS

The virtual lack of en route VFR problems in business jets and airliners is related to a number of things. They don't have the problem of forced landings, which handles that risk. They tend to fly higher, above some of the weather, and carry weather avoidance equipment. But the simple fact is that airline jets fly IFR all the time and business jets do almost all the time. So you would not expect them to have VFR problems, but they don't have en route IFR problems very often either, so there is something to learn there.

There is nothing holy about IFR except that it forces the pilot to have a plan, to follow procedures, and the plan doesn't fall apart when clouds are in the way. When we strike out VFR cross-country, the risk can be dramatically reduced by a plan that is similar to what we do for an IFR flight. Similar, but because there are more variables in VFR than IFR, the plan both takes more effort and has to consider more elements.

When IFR, the published minimum altitudes on the charts take care of obstacle and terrain clearance. A VFR minimum altitude has to be calculated in conjunction with the sectional charts and might be considered as needing to be about the same value as an IFR minimum: 1,000 feet above the highest terrain or obstacle within 5 miles of the course to be flown; 2,000 feet in mountainous terrain. Or if flying airways with IFR charts on board, the published minimum works. The zinger on VFR comes when you have to deviate from the planned route because of weather. Then a new minimum has to be calculated, and that is not easy in flight.

MINIMUMS

When IFR, we deal with minimums all the time. There are minimums for straight-in approaches, minimums for circling approaches, minimum sector or safe altitudes, minimum vectoring altitudes—all designed to keep the airplane out of the weeds until it gets to a point where visual maneuvering to the runway is possible. A weakness in VFR flying is probably found in a reluctance to adhere to some predetermined minimum safe VFR altitude that is as important as any IFR minimum.

There used to be an old axiom in scud-running about flying

as low as possible because the visibility gets better the lower you go, presumably because the higher you fly the nearer you are to the cloud bases. But pilots flying by this rule of thumb have been caught by trees draped with scud. There simply comes a time when you can't fly low enough to maintain enough visibility to successfully fly the airplane visually. The risk-management technique thus becomes predetermining a minimum safe altitude and flying that altitude. If at any time it appears doubtful that visual flight can be maintained at that altitude, then a retreat or landing at a nearby airport is the alternative.

ALTERNATE

In IFR flying we have to have an alternate airport to go to in the event the destination folds or closes. The alternate rule is not flexible, and few IFR pilots ever go to the filed alternate when unable to land at the destination. Because of variations in forecasts there is usually a better deal by the time the flight gets that far along, and a new alternate is chosen. In VFR flying, the same is true. The best alternate changes continuously during a flight, and the selection should be on a continuous basis.

ROUTE OF FLIGHT

IFR routings are dictated more by computers than by pilots or controllers, but VFR routes are left to pilots, which is good if we do the job on picking the best route. Terrain and obstacles figure in this; so do airports along the way. The best route is the one with the highest ceiling, the best visibility, the lowest terrain, and the greatest selection of airports.

It is often tempting to plan something that is a combination of IFR and VFR, which might be called RFR for "radio flight rules." Using the navaids and talking to controllers for advisories is preferred by many VFR pilots, but it has to be done with recognition of the fact that it is still VFR. When flying in the Middle West one stormy day IFR, I overheard a conversation between a controller and a pilot who had been working the RFR system pretty hard, to the point of asking for vectors around a thunderstorm. The controller did his best, but the pilot apparently wound up in an area of turbulence and rain. He became quite excited and all of us on the frequency shut up so the controller could do what he could to help the pilot fly to the nearest better weather. I was fearful that we were all about to be witnesses to something that would go in the record books as yet another "continued VFR into adverse weather" episode. But in a few minutes the pilot announced in a relieved tone of voice that he was "out of the storm" and could see pretty well. Then he asked the controller if he couldn't have kept him out of that weather. That is where he parted company with reality. Being VFR, it was his job to keep out of the weather. The controller's role was to give him what information he had available, as time allowed. Nothing more.

REGULATED AIRSPACE

Something that is complicating VFR navigation and that can force a VFR pilot to fly in air that might not be as friendly as desired is the proliferation of regulated airspace around the country. Airport radar service areas, TCAs, and the new Mode C requirements are forcing or will force pilots to plan routes that avoid these areas. As that becomes part of the VFR task, we have to be aware that the weather avoidance flexibility of VFR is diminished. Zigging and zagging is a big part of VFR flying in areas where showers are causing restricted visibility, but if there is an ARSA over there you might not be able to zig or zag. This will heighten the need for a good plan before takeoff. These areas are established because the FAA feels that they will minimize the risk of midair collision. It is the pilot's job to manage the additional risk they might create in other areas.

VFR cross-country flying is a great natural asset as well as one of the finer personal freedoms. It has to be protected, and one way to do this is to use it carefully. When a newspaper story reports, "The plane crashed after the pilot radioed and reported poor visibility," the suggestion to the lay public is that this asset and freedom is not being used in a proper manner.

ADVISORIES

I once wrote that the best way to fly VFR is to squawk altitude, code 1200, say nothing, and steer around areas of high traffic. This created a lot of controversy. Many pilots wrote in that I was being snobbish by suggesting that the system is only for pilots flying IFR. Most adamantly defended their right to "use" the system when VFR. The exchanges were interesting and to this day I feel that the procedure suggested is the best way to preserve the freedom of VFR, which is a different way of flying than IFR. I practice what I preach, too. One day when I was flying from Trenton to Frederick, the ground controller at Trenton reported that he was having a terrible time getting clearances out of Philly. And two of us had just flown from Frederick to Trenton and the Baltimore controller was incredibly busy. He didn't even have time to give advisories to IFR traffic.

The weather was okay, so there was no additional risk involved in flying the trip VFR. The controllers were all swamped, so there would be no reduction in risk through traffic advisories. It was clearly a time to steer well around Philly and Baltimore's airspace, fly without talking, and keep the old vigilance for other traffic at top form. I did monitor the approach and departure control frequencies to stay abreast of the traffic flows.

THE FUTURE OF VFR

The increase in regulated airspace does raise questions about the future of VFR. It will indeed become more complicated, but it will also remain a most important part of the system for a long time. A form of VFR contributes greatly to airport capacity when the weather is good. Visual separation is used at the busiest airports and, for example, enables a place like Washington National to handle almost 130 operations an hour on a clear day, where 60 is the limit in instrument meteorological conditions. And there is no way in busy areas for the system to accommodate all the traffic that wants to go from here to there when the weather is reasonably good. The two things that threaten VFR cross-country the most are close or actual encounters with airline aircraft, and weather. To allow the first to substantially alter the pattern of VFR flying would be a mistake, because the best air for VFR is, fortunately, not the air that is frequented by airline jets. The weather part is highly personal. Bellyache as some do about weather reporting and forecasting, it is pretty good now and is not likely to improve a lot more. Weather is dynamic and can't be perfectly forecast or reported. It is a "what you see is what you get" deal, and this part of the problem will respond only to pilot education and training.

CHAPTER 5

En Route IFR

FIRST PART   Patrick E. Bradley

There are both substantial differences and substantial similarities in the handling of en route IFR and VFR flight. In both cases, special challenges will present themselves. During any given flight, the pilot may have to diagnose, evaluate, and respond to anything from poor weather to mysterious mechanical anomalies. But in the case of en route instrument flying, there is also the added challenge and benefit of being part of an intricate "system" of IFR aircraft. Though I don't have statistical proof, I suspect that the pilots who have the best success during IFR en route flight—those who can respond easily to the challenges of weather, mechanical malfunction, or other mishaps—are also those who fully understand and are best able to use the "system" to their benefit.

IF YOU'RE BORED, YOU'VE FORGOTTEN SOMETHING

I remember initial instrument training. My instructor began the lessons with drills, mainly. First we would practice flying with reference only to the instruments. Later we would begin practicing approaches. I would fly ILS after ILS and then, for variety, switch to VOR or NDB approaches. After a few months of this, I began to yearn for cross-country flights. I wanted the opportunity to see what a real instrument flight would be like. And yes, I wanted the opportunity to log some hours without having to pay for them in cash and sweat.

Well, the time finally came when we began to practice planning and executing actual instrument flights. The first one was quite short, from Syracuse to Utica, New York, but I still looked forward to a few moments to lock onto the airway heading and kick back a bit. My instructor had different plans. As soon as we were established on the airway, my instructor began to quiz me:

"Okay," he would say, "what's the plan?"

"What do you mean?" I responded, a little irritated at having to think during my rest period.

"I mean, what is your next step?" he snapped. "What are you going to do next?"

"I'm going to change over to the Utica VOR at the midway point," I answered, though not without having to check the chart first.

"Good," my instructor answered. "And when will that be?"

"I'm not sure," I said. We did not have a DME in the airplane, and I had not calculated the groundspeed.

"Well, figure it out," growled my instructor, beginning to become irritated, "and when you have, let me know."

Sweat began to bead up on my brow, and before I had quite completed the calculations my instructor chimed in again.

"What's our approach going to be at the destination?" he asked.

"Here we go again," I thought, perspiration beginning to drip down my back. "It just doesn't get any easier."

STAYING IN THE SYSTEM

It's true, those initial cross-country instrument flights were so short that they were as challenging, from the perspective of cockpit management, as a lesson consisting of multiple approaches and go-arounds. I understand now that the purpose of the incessant questioning and quizzing by my instructor was to show me the importance of remaining an active participant in the IFR en route system even when I was not communicating with ATC or directly involved with the system.

Even on our longer flights, it was extremely important to my instructor that I have my next three or four steps planned out in advance. I should know where I was going, when I would get there, what I would do when I got there, who I would speak to when I got there and what I would tell them. After nailing down these basics, it would be time to check the next level of information. How much fuel did I have and what was the fuel burn for the flight so far? How fast was I traveling and what was the speed and direction of the wind? Was this in keeping with the forecast wind? If not, would this affect the weather?

No matter how well prepared I was for a flight, and no matter how efficient I became in the cockpit, and no matter how facile I became with the flight calculator, my instructor was able to keep me on the edge at all times. And I suppose that this was all part of one basic, underlying lesson: The en route phase of a flight is not the time to kick back, even if you can afford the time. Good piloting technique, according to my instructor (and who could disagree?), does not permit sloughing off in the cockpit. Even if the immediately necessary tasks don't demand a heightened level of awareness, it's still good technique to keep the juices flowing with tasks that are less critical but still helpful to good piloting.

KNOW YOUR LOCATION

One of a pilot's most obvious but oft overlooked duties in the cockpit is to know where he is at all times. Now, if nearly all of your flying is in one particular area over a single route, this is a fairly straightforward task. If, on the other hand, you are flying in an area of the country with which you are unfamiliar, on a route that you haven't taken before, it is entirely possible to find yourself flying a bearing between two frequencies without much idea of where you are with respect to the rest of the world.

Of course, there isn't any virtue, from the perspective of piloting technique, to knowing the name and history of the hamlet you happen to be droning over at any given time. Frequently, though, convective sigmets and other advisories are provided with respect to location names, and it can become critical to know your own location with respect to other previously strange areas. Knowing your location precisely, then, becomes more than just a trick for remaining alert during the en route portion of a flight, it becomes a critical factor in participating in the IFR en route system.

The importance of location awareness was underscored for me one day on a short flight from Mercer County Airport to Teterboro Airport, in central and northern New Jersey respectively. Although the weather was clear at Trenton, my departure point, it was obvious just from looking to the north that the cumulus, friendly-looking in southern New Jersey, were in the midst of a towering act up north. A talk with flight service confirmed that there was, in fact, a line of thunderstorms moving through the Teterboro area at the time. They were expected to be through shortly, though, and were not thought to present much of a factor for my flight.

As it turned out, the clouds did not move through as quickly as expected. Still, the thunderstorms, at least where I was, were widely enough scattered that I thought that I could circumnavigate them without much trouble. As I approached Teterboro, however, the picture began to change. Specifically, the scattered "stick ups" had convened for an orgy of lightning and rain over New York City and, you guessed it, Teterboro Airport. New York Approach confirmed my picture, but with characteristic helpfulness (when it really counts) offered some options.

I had been approaching from the southwest. Without my asking, approach diverted me to the northwest, "Direct to Stillwater and then direct Sparta" VORs. Amended clearances on short notice always tend to throw me, but in this case I was familiar with the location of the navaids, their direction with respect to me, and even the frequencies. That always helps. A moment or two later, approach asked whether I would like direct to Broadway and then Sparta instead. The savings in distance was just a few miles and I took approach up on its offer, but trundling along in the bumpy air that afternoon, I was glad that I didn't need to begin researching my en route charts during that short but extremely active flight. I was fortunate during this flight that I was able to participate smoothly as a part of the IFR system. Controllers appreciate it, I think, and I also believe that it contributes to the safety of a flight. Where the pilot is sharp and aware, he can more readily operate within the system to complete his flight successfully.

HELLO OUT THERE

While it is important for an instrument pilot to see himself as part of the IFR system, I suspect that there is real risk in abdicating one's own responsibility for a flight to the system itself. Again, this becomes most apparent during situations where weather has become a factor in the completion of a flight. On many occasions I have heard pilots literally handing over responsibility for the completion of a flight to controllers. Understandably, the controllers are not in any position to accept responsibility for the flight and, while offering what help they can, the primary responsibility for the flight must remain with the pilot. Frequently pilots, myself included, are confronted with the balancing act of getting as much help from the system as possible without giving up the flight to someone who doesn't want it and can't manage it as well as the pilot. I become embroiled in this question most frequently where thunderstorm avoidance is the order of the day.

As most pilots know, ATC's radar will "paint" precipitation. The only problem is that some controllers apparently are willing to give information on the basis of their radar and some are not. I recall one flight from upstate New York to New Jersey where the upstate controller apparently had either an extremely effective radar capability or a crystal ball. Without my even having to ask (which I'm not above), the controller gave me vectors around and about precipitation that he was painting along my route. In fact, the controller would make 10-degree corrections in my route where it looked as if I was getting close to significant weather. Although I was in cloud for most of the flight, I encountered almost no precipitation or turbulence.

When I was switched to another approach controller, the vectors ended and I was relegated to the airway. At one point, when I began to encounter some precipitation, I queried the controller regarding the weather along the airway. The controller snapped that he did not see anything, "but that they couldn't effectively pick up precipitation with their radar." I'm still not sure what capabilities ATC has in this respect, but I know that, in the final analysis, it is extremely hazardous to undertake a flight with the expectation that ATC will somehow magically guide you through the tough spots. On an instrument flight plan, we are all part of a larger system and should be able to operate within it. This does not mean, though, that we somehow hitch the airplane onto a track and follow the car in front of us.

EMERGENCIES EN ROUTE

Another situation in which pilots need to evaluate their relationship with the en route system is when an emergency or a potential emergency arises. The FARs require that we inform ATC in the event of an avionics malfunction. And the FARs allow pilots to deviate from the regulations in the event of an emergency to the extent necessary to meet the emergency. But beyond that, I'm not sure that there is much in the way of guidance controlling the relationship between the system and the pilot. Again, I expect that this is an area where the pilot must be aware of the services that the system can offer him and what it can't offer him. That the ability to work within the instrument system can be helpful in the event of an en route emergency, I have no doubt. I also suspect, however, that failure to understand the limitations of the system has led to the loss of aircraft and lives.

TAKING CONTROL

I learned an extremely valuable lesson regarding en route emergencies during a flight from Cornelia Fort Airport in Nashville to a final, unplanned destination of Bloomington, Indiana. I was in the left seat of my coauthor's Cessna P210 and he was, of course, alert and in the right seat. The flight was proceeding normally when, about forty-five minutes into the flight, I sensed a slight hesitation in the drone of the engine. I say sensed, because the noise wasn't really audible. It was just a brief syncopation in an otherwise steady rhythm. I looked over to the right seat and saw that Dick had also noticed the blip. We both examined the engine instruments, noting no discrepancies. We both eased back in our seats, hoping it was nothing, but suspecting that the story had just begun.

Five minutes later it came again—the blip. It was momentary but slightly more pronounced. With this, we began to make contingency plans. The nearest airport with services was Bloomington, about ten or fifteen minutes away. At this time Dick had taken the mike and was informing approach of our change in plans. Although we were given a clearance to descend, that idea was nixed immediately. From the point at which we decided that there was a problem and that an unscheduled landing was necessary, we maintained altitude.

Although the tower controller considered the procedure highly unorthodox, Dick had settled on a plan that made a lot of sense. We flew direct to Bloomington at about 10,000 feet and stayed there until directly over the field. Our greatest concern was that, upon power reduction, the engine would just pack it in, leaving us with only one option: gliding. When we got over the airport, I reduced the airspeed and began a spiral over the approach end of the active runway until we reached about 2,000 feet above the ground. We were still quite high, but continued to set up a final leg on which, if the engine failed at any time, we could still make a landing on the tarmac. On final, the gear and flaps went down to slow the airplane. Still, we could have landed at any time if the engine had quit.

Interestingly, this approach, though unusual, did not result in much disruption at the airport. In fact, though we had informed approach and the tower of our situation, the tower was able to clear landings and takeoffs until we began our spiral pattern.

KEEPING THE RIGHT SIDE UP

The final en route IFR occurrence that I suspect may constitute a risk may have nothing to do with the weather, mechanical malfunctions, or with the IFR system. Unfortunately, I also think it is the one that IFR pilots can do the most to avoid: loss of control due to disorientation.

I have experienced times, flying in actual IFR conditions or under the hood, when everything seems off balance. Usually the feeling is a momentary one, and it's possible to overcome with a little concentration, but I have wondered what would happen if circumstances conspired to create a real emergency. Consider the situation where the pilot of a complex single, flying in actual conditions, encounters some turbulence. Assume also that the pilot has just received an amended clearance. He begins a turn to the left as he looks down to study his en route chart. He looks up quickly as he begins to feel the g-forces of a diving left turn.

With the proper training and practice, it should be possible for the pilot who finds himself in such a position to recover fairly rapidly. But this, I suppose, is the critical factor. Would the pilot have learned and practiced the procedure of leveling the wings and then slowly raising the nose of the airplane? Would the pilot, disoriented, find it impossible even to determine whether the airplane was in a climb or a dive, a left or a right turn. Again, the risk exists, and the only certain means of avoiding the danger is either to never find yourself in an unusual attitude in instrument conditions, or to practice the procedures to escape the condition.

SECOND PART   Richard L. Collins

In theory, the en route portion of an IFR flight should be a low-risk form of travel. In the U.S., progress is monitored on radar virtually everywhere. There's a double check on navigation as well as altitude if the airplane is equipped with an altitude-reporting transponder. An autopilot is installed in most airplanes used for IFR flying, so even a pilot flying alone has some backup. And there are times when the drone of the airplane moving through the murk can be mesmerizing. It seems so peaceful. More than once the thought has occured that the airplane seems suspended, not moving, like a simulator. But it is moving, rapidly, and perhaps en route complacency is the reason we lose a substantial number of general aviation airplanes en route, IFR. What are the factors? Weather is the first that comes to mind. Ice and thunderstorms. Every year close to ten airplanes flying IFR are lost to each. Some years more, some years less. There's more to weather than well-defined storms and ice, though, and the majority of the accidents occur in what might be deemed benign weather. I learned more about en route weather in a seven-year period when I lived in Little Rock, Arkansas, than at any other time. The airplane business was booming at the time, and while I spent a lot of time going to other places, I made many trips between Little Rock and Wichita. New models of old airplanes were coming out on almost a continuous basis, and I got to go fly them and write about the experience. In so doing, I made about 400 flights between the two cities, with as many in the bad-weather seasons as in the good. Tornadoes were spotted and once, when flying in clouds, traffic was called at 12 o'clock, opposite direction, out of 13,000, a National Guard fighter. The controller added that the pilot had just ejected. Naturally, I asked for a vector.

The weather lessons came from the juxtaposition between the route and the spawning ground of low-pressure storm systems. A substantial number of the trips were flown in a Skyhawk, virtually always IFR, and I worked hard at keeping the risk low. At the time, I felt that the greatest risk was in the en route portion of the flights, even though it was almost always flown IFR. This was probably due to the nature of the weather and the basic nature of my airplane. It was a mistaken assumption. The approach is actually riskier, as we'll explore in a later chapter.

My method of managing risk was to segment the flight into parts, with an ILS approach defining decision time. My airplane was based at the North Little Rock Airport, close to the National Weather Service office. I had no Stormscope or radar at the time, and the drill was to stop by the weather office and examine the radar before launch. If it looked okay as far as Fort Smith, I'd begin the trip. Before reaching Fort Smith, I would try to assemble a picture of conditions as far as Tulsa. Before Tulsa, I'd decide on continuing to Wichita. It worked, and the history of reliability on this run was good. Occasionally I'd have to scrub a trip because of a line of storms, ice, or wind that was so strong there would have been no fuel reserve. One day I leveled off and found the groundspeed to be under 60 knots. That meant that it would take five hours of flying to complete the trip, plus at least one stop. I turned around and went home.

FUEL

Because of the strong relationship between the wind and the cruising speed of the airplane, fuel was always a factor when there was a headwind. More than once I had to stop for fuel on the 300-mile trip, even though my Hawk had the big 48-gallon tanks. Engines won't run on air and using all the fuel is as foolish when IFR as when VFR. A surprising number of pilots do it, too. In a representative sample of IFR en route accidents, a quarter were caused by the pilots using all their fuel. While this has always appeared the easiest of all risks to manage, there are times when events can pressure a pilot into trying to fly for too long before landing.

Consider this narrative from an NTSB accident report: "Pilot departed Bowling Green with a listed 5.0 hours fuel on board. After 3 hours and 35 minutes he arrived over destination after exhausting fuel in the right tank about 30 minutes prior. He states that the other tank was about half full at the time. Fifteen minutes after right tank exhaustion the pilot requested his first weather update at destination. It was at minimums. After arriving over the destination the expect further clearance time was about 25 minutes later. At the EFC the pilot was cleared to approach control and told to expect further clearance one hour later. The pilot indicated that he could not hold that long. He requested that approach control 'leap frog' him past the other traffic. Approach denied and the pilot requested diversion to another airport. He was cleared to Valdosta but was told that approach gave him two other choices, stay in the pattern or declare an emergency and he would be worked in. Pilot requested priority instead of emergency and was denied. Pilot was cleared for an ILS approach.

At 1821 the pilot radioed that the engine just quit. He then radioed the tower that he had hit some wires and was down off the airport but was okay. Total flight time about 4 hours and 40 minutes." The NTSB contended that the pilot erred in many areas, but it appeared that he had some help in using up all the fuel. And consider that this private pilot with just over 300 hours maintained control of the aircraft and landed without hurting anybody—at night with a 200-foot ceiling and a mile visibility.

That wasn't an en route accident, but if we are to learn an en route lesson, it is to stop if there is any doubt about fuel. While this pilot did arrive over the destination with an hour and five minutes of fuel on board, there are times and places where this isn't enough.

IFR GLIDERS

What is the record on IFR gliders, airplanes that have had to be landed power-off at a random location because power was no longer available? Is this a big risk in IFR flying? Not really. Long periods of time have elapsed without a single serious accident falling into this category. That doesn't mean there is no risk, though. It takes little imagination to recognize that an engine failure while flying in clouds, especially at night, would leave you wondering about the immediate future.

RECORD

When there is an accident during en route IFR flying, the accident is more likely to be serious than, say, a landing accident, just as we saw for VFR. The impact speeds are higher and, often, the terrain less friendly. In an average sample, just under half the IFR en route accidents involved serious injuries or worse. The failure of something while en route, for whatever reason, is linked to almost three-fourths of the IFR accidents, though these accidents are not predominantly serious. While involvement in a serious accident might seem to be primarily the fault of the pilot and not the airplane, some of the serious accidents might be linked to equipment failure. However, the condition of the airplane after the fact precludes any determination that a specific item of equipment failed. In jets, cockpit voice recorders will likely be required, as on airline jets, and this will help remove the mystery from some accidents in that type of airplane.

One oft-touted guard against failures is to fly jets, Part 25 airplanes, that meet the same standards as airliners. As is always true, however, things can and do fail regardless of how redundant a human may feel he has made a system.

The NTSB's narrative of a business-jet crash illustrates this point: "As the aircraft was climbing through 19,000 feet at night the number two generator light came on. The flight crew noted there was no output from the number two generator and it would not reset. Then they checked the number one generator voltage and noted it was 14 to 15 volts. The crew reduced the electrical load; however, about five minutes later, the batteries became discharged and there was a total loss of electrical power. Using a flashlight, the crew diverted to the Chester Country Airport, which had a 4,600 foot runway. The gear was extended with the emergency system. The elevator trim was inoperative so both pilots applied back pressure to the yoke to overcome the nose-down tendency. After landing, about one-fourth of the way down the runway, the crew tried to use the thrust reversers, but the reversers were inoperative. Subsequently the aircraft continued off the side and beyond the end of the runway, hit a wooden beam and a snowbank, then came to rest in a ditch. An investigation revealed a shaft failure of the number two generator and worn brushes in the number one generator. With total electrical failure the following were also inoperative: wing flaps, antiskid, captain's airspeed indicator and altimeter, nosewheel steering, cockpit lighting." While the airplane was substantially damaged, the NTSB reported no serious injuries, so the landing has to be rated a job well done.

LOGIC

While I was flying along with another pilot, on an IFR flight plan but operating in visual conditions, the discussion turned to the risks involved in this type of flying. We agreed that the failure of something would increase the risk, but unless it were the failure of an item of primary structure, such as a wing, or the failure of something that resulted in an uncontrollable fire, we should be able to minimize the risk and park the airplane somewhere without a high risk of personal injury. Another risk that was discussed was the chance of a midair collision with a VFR airplane, something that has happened in en route airspace but is still relatively rare. The chance of a midair with another IFR airplane is a remote possibility.

Failure of the engine in a single is the thing we think of most, because it would transform a serene flight into one where you had a few minutes—how many depending on altitude—to apply all the principles of basic airmanship to getting down safely. There are times when the risk would be very high and times when it should be easily manageable. The times are fairly obvious. The worst case would be at night, over mountainous terrain with the ridges obscured. The best would be with a comfortable ceiling and the plains of Kansas beneath. When the relatively small amount of time spent flying in the higher risk condition is considered, maybe the risk is worth taking in return for utility. Maybe it is not. That is an individual decision that has to be made on the basis of knowing you will crash if the engine quits. How well you manage the crash and where it occurs will be the determinant of personal injury. Probably the best way for a pilot to rate a risk is to consider how he feels while taking the risk. If he is uncomfortable about doing it while doing it, the risk is probably not worth taking.

HOW TO

Something that often isn't taught in single-engine instrument flying is the power-off glide. It might be argued that we could figure that out rather quickly in time of need, but it is still probably worth some practice. The goal in any IFR landing in a random location should be a touchdown at minimum possible speed and lowest possible sink rate while maintaining control of the airplane. The best aircraft configuration will vary with the type, and our deliberations on this are rather like those you might have on ditching—something else you never practice to completion. It is one of those things that we can and should think through very carefully, so if the time ever comes there will be no question about how to handle the impromptu arrival.

The first step in risk management is to see if there is an airport nearby. Many of the new loran sets have a nearest-airport feature that will suddenly be worth far more than the total purchase price of the unit. The second relates to knowledge of the airplane. How far will it glide? If the number isn't in your mind, it will be hard to do the best possible job of managing the risk. For a 210, it's a mile and a half glide for each 1,000 feet high. For a Bonanza, it's 1.7. If I am at 10,000 feet in my 210 and there is an airport within 15 miles, I have a shot at it, depending on wind aloft. Going to Oshkosh for the air show, I cross Lake Michigan at or above 16,000 feet to always be within gliding distance of shore, thus minimizing the risk from a ditching.

If there is no airport and the landing is to be in a random location, how far you glide before landing doesn't matter. But I still would keep the airplane clean in order to glide for as long as possible while working to restore power. If the failure is a massive mechanical one or the result of dry fuel tanks, this won't be too important.

Another airplane item concerns instruments. What will be working after an engine failure? Electric instruments should still be going unless fire burned through wires. If the prop is still turning, some air will be available for instruments powered by that source. If the suction (or pressure) gauge shows an acceptable reading, those instruments should be okay.

The likely surface wind is important, as is the orientation of any ridges in the area. Into the wind and parallel to the ridges is the way to go. I think if the wind were perpendicular to the ridges, I'd base the heading on the ridges rather than the wind.

A couple of thousand feet above the highest possible touchdown, I would configure the airplane for the event. My preference would be the landing gear down and, in any airplane, the flaps setting that gives the best balance between a stalling speed reduction and drag. The speed is important because the slower you hit, the better the chances. The drag is important because the attitude at which you hit and the rate of descent can also affect chances. If it is foggy, or if the ridges are obscured, you might have to fly the airplane into whatever is there at the attitude and speed selected for the glide, so these items should be carefully considered—and practiced.

SCREWBALL

Some might suggest that it would take a real screwball to think about all that and then go flying over fog or obscured terrain in a single. Maybe so, but I would rather think things through in advance. And the decisions are not often clear-cut. On flights across the mountains of Pennsylvania, there has often been fog in the valleys that was not forecast. Would the risk best be managed by landing in the foggy valley or on the clear ridge? At the first sight of the foggy valleys, are you going to return to base and park the airplane, or are you going to continue with knowledge that the risk blipped upward a mite?

UNSUCCESSFUL

Though most of the IFR forced landings in singles are not fatal, some are.

From an NTSB report: "Pilot experienced loss of power during cruise flight at 6,000 feet. ATC vectored aircraft toward Daviess County Airport, approximately 10 miles away. Pilot reported aircraft on fire. Witnesses saw it in a left bank turn then 'nose dive into ground.' Post-crash examination of engine revealed number three cylinder separated from crankcase. Further examination revealed the throughbolts/nuts were undertorqued. The number two and number four cylinders were top overhauled in July, 1981. [The accident occurred in 1986.] Metallurgical examination of bolts/nuts revealed fatigue failures and 'working' of number three cylinder for a long period of time."

The airplane was a Mooney, a good glider, and the night was a bright one, so the airport ten miles away was within reach. The NTSB findings of probable cause suggested that panic was a factor, and that the pilot lost control of the aircraft and a stall/spin ensued. No mention was made of the extent of any fire, but certainly the failure described would result in smoke entering the cockpit even if there were no out-of-control fire in the engine compartment.

The NTSB's mention of panic should make all of us pause. That is a very real possibility for anyone and is best addressed by having thought through every scenario in advance. By thinking it through we develop a procedure for anything. With a well-defined course of action, the old brain is less likely to slip over the fine line between self-control and disabling panic.

MOTHER NATURE

While stuff breaking or a pilot using all the fuel is the number one cause of en route problems, the other ones are more likely guaranteed serious. These most often relate to ice, thunderstorms, other severe en route weather, or the pilot simply losing control of the airplane.

I remember one particular flight that illustrates this. It was on my fifty-first birthday and I wrote in my log, "very bumpy trip." If anything, that was an understatement. I did relish a big tailwind going home to New Jersey from Huntington, West Virginia. Trouble was, there was a jet stream core aloft and turbulence up where the wind was blowing was so severe that nobody would go up there. The airliners were all flying low. The trip started in daylight and the clouds were purely scary looking, though to begin with the air wasn't rough at low altitude.

After it got dark and the air got bumpy, I flew along working quite hard and thinking that perhaps this wasn't the best way in the world to celebrate one's birthday. The airborne weather radar and the Stormscope showed no convective activity, though an airliner lifting off from Harrisburg, Pennsylvania, asked for a deviation around what he described as "a cell." Nothing more negative from him. The only other airplane on the frequency for a rather long period of time was an Army helicopter. I thought about the pilot flying the helicopter in those bumps and decided that my lot in life at the moment wasn't all that bad. In fact, once I convinced myself that the level of turbulence wasn't likely to increase, the flight became an enjoyable challenge. The risk was there if the engine decided to pack it in, but that didn't prey on my mind. Later, when I flew out under the overcast the view was pretty, as it always is in a heavily populated area at night with an overcast and the city lights reflecting. When I landed, I didn't feel like the risk of the flight had been particularly high.

THUNDER

There are still some old-timers around who will regale you with tales of flying though thunderstorms. What they don't tell you is that it is a terrible mistake to make. If an airplane, especially a light airplane, winds up in a thunderstorm, the outcome is doubtful—especially if the storm is a strong one.

I flew into one a lot of years ago, in a Beech Twin Bonanza. That was a terribly stout airplane with excellent handling qualities. I could not have picked a better airplane in which to do the deed, which was accidental, not on purpose. The weather briefer didn't mention that there might be a storm out there and there was no traffic control or weather radar at the time. But I still had a clue. The sky ahead was dark. A check of the ADF revealed extensive static. That combination suggested that the clouds ahead might be more than benign. Fly on, young (twenty-three) fool. My boss, a fine gentleman named Ben Hogan (not the golfer, but occasionally we got exceptional FBO service because of the name), was in the back, and he had told me many times to feel free to can a trip if the weather was doubtful. I carried on into the dark cloud ahead.

The ride was a wild one. I called the controller once and told him that I could not even begin to hold altitude. The thought of turning around entered my mind, but I remembered from teaching Army and Air Force pilots instrument flying that the theoretical best way out is straight ahead. To this day I remember the details of the moment, and the fact that even though my belt was tight, I was bouncing up and down in the seat so much that it was hard to see the instruments. I quickly decided that all would be forsaken save the artificial horizon. The drill was to keep the airplane right side up, period. That it made Mr. Hogan nervous was quickly evident. He seldom flew in the airplane without some Jack Daniel's close at hand and the aroma drifted forward every time he took a pull on the bottle. Do this right, Richard, and you can buy yourself a bottle of that good stuff on the way home and have your own talk with Uncle Jack.

It probably took no more than ten minutes to fly through that storm. The paint on the airplane was worse for the wear—we had to repaint all the leading edges—but everything else was okay. Mr. Hogan requested that I not do that again, and I told him not to worry, I wouldn't. And I haven't. Knock on wood.

WHAT HAPPENS?

When a light airplane is lost in a thunderstorm, chances are it is a result of a loss of control rather than turbulence breaking the airplane. There are some recorded cases of the latter, but basically airplanes are pretty strong and can withstand a terrible pounding as long as the airspeed is kept within limits. In some storm-related accidents, it is clear that the pilot entered an area of turbulence and made a hasty decision to turn around. It is easier to lose control in a turn than in straight flight, and once the nose is down and the bank steep, school is out. Storm flying and losses of control are not something we can practice, and once a pilot crosses the line into either, the outcome is nothing more than a big question mark.

LOSS OF CONTROL

In a previous Macmillan book, *The Perfect Flight*, I went into losses of control and the dynamics of a spiral dive at some length. I am as convinced now as then that once an airplane is in a fully developed spiral, a recovery is unlikely. The challenge is not to lose control. What factors lead to losses of control? Certainly thunderstorms are prime causes. But garden-variety turbulence, distractions, and the failure of instruments or instrument power systems have to be added to the list. So must the failure of the pilot to come to grips with the demands of instrument flying.

Any time an airplane is operating in clouds, or in any condition where the pilot does not have a strong visual reference, the risk blips upward. We are depending on the relationship between the pilot and the instruments (probably including an autopilot), and the ability of the pilot to not make a mistake. While the time might seem a serene one if there is no turbulence, an impossible situation is not many seconds away should something go awry. The pilot has to either hand fly the airplane with precision or monitor the autopilot and take manual control of the airplane should the autopilot fail. The latter doesn't happen often, but when it does, the pilot has to perform flawlessly.

STORMY DAY

I had an interesting look at the pressures that en route instrument flying can bring to bear on a pilot one day when a warm front was located along or across a 350-mile round-trip flight. The pilot flying my airplane had limited instrument-flying experience, had done initial training for the rating, and flew the airplane very well when clear of clouds, which was the case most of the way on the outbound leg. I did notice that this visual flying was with extensive reference to the instruments.

Near the destination he got into some bumpy clouds during the descent. I could tell that the beginnings of spatial disorientation were there because he had a strong tendency to turn to the right and you could almost feel him twisting in the seat trying to make the airplane turn left. In fact, it was almost more than he could do to correct the heading back to the left. I was doing all the talking and radio setting, so his only chore was handling the airplane. Despite the difficulties, the pilot was very much in control of the airplane. There were no big swoops and dips as long as we were in the clouds. It was when he got to a mixture of clouds and clear air, busting through turbulent cloud bases, in and out, that he got a really bad case of the leans and I had to help out to avoid an altitude excursion in excess of the limit.

When we got ready to go home, I offered him the left seat again. Reluctantly, he took it. While we were taxiing out, the ground controller called with a convective sigmet that affected our route of flight, and I could tell he didn't like that at all. I requested a change in routing to avoid the affected area, and we were soon off and at Flight Level 190, a higher altitude than would normally be used for a 350-mile trip. But hope springs eternal: maybe we could stay on top at that altitude. The warm front was to our right and we initially deviated to the north to avoid that portion of the weather that was showing on our radar, on the Stormscope, and on the controller's radar.

Eventually we had to turn and fly through the warm front. When we did, the portion of the flight that followed was a good example of how you have to perform, all by yourself, when you commit an airplane to a flight through an area of weather. You might prejudge it as a pussycat; how it turns out can often be a crapshoot.

NO ECHOES

The controller was a good, friendly sort and gave a good description of what he saw on the radar. This corresponded with our on-board information. One thing was clear: It would take a lot more than 19,000 feet to top all the clouds.

When flying into clouds in an area where there is convective activity, I always psych myself up for turbulence. Even though the radar and Stormscope show nothing, I rig for rough running, with tight belts and the airspeed on 130, the turbulent air penetration speed for my airplane. Then there is a little lecture to self about flying in such conditions being a lonesome but challenging way to spend time. The air in this warm front wasn't particularly rough, but I could tell that my colleague in the left seat was having problems. He was clearly not comfortable, and when I would make reference to an altitude or heading deviation he would respond with "Yes, I see," but his actions were slow to match words. It was an obvious case of overload and I wound up flying most of the trip home from the right seat.

EXAMPLE?

Why is that a valid example of pressure and how, once you commit to instrument flying, the immersion is total? The pilot wasn't instrument rated, or heavily trained, for that matter. But at the time he was a private pilot with several hundred hours and a desire to get an instrument rating. Even with a keeper in the right seat, he was apparently overwhelmed by bumpy clouds. In no case did we fly where there was any inclement weather according to radar or the Stormscope. Those who try to classify IFR as hard or easy would not have called this hard IFR, yet it was hard enough for this pilot at this time. That is why the definitions do a lousy service to pilots flying IFR. Instrument flying is what you make of it and nothing more.

This flight illustrated to me once again the big difference between visual and instrument flying. The pilot did an excellent job of flying the airplane when he had visual reference, even though he did refer to the instruments a lot to reinforce the correctness of what he was doing. When he was flying visually, trouble was at arm's length and he knew it. When he was in the clouds, trouble was close and he knew it. When he becomes an instrument pilot, he will be better for the experience.

KEYS

If there is a key to staying in control, it is in an understanding of weather. A pilot simply has to know that what is ahead is okay to fly through in the airplane that is strapped to his bottom. If flying is with a "I think I can make it" attitude, the risk is very high. Everyone has heard pilots ask for vectors through the lightest area of weather, as shown on a controller's radar. It's time to cringe when they do that, because the air can be incredibly wet and bumpy in areas that do not show as heavy precipitation on air traffic control radar. And once a pilot is in a convective area, minutes seem like hours. The next question after the request for a vector through weather is usually "How much longer before I am out of this?" It is usually only a few more miles, but those are the longest miles you will ever fly. And the risk is high. The best way to deal with thunderstorms is to avoid areas of precipitation, even if it means flying hundreds of miles out of the way, or to land and wait for conditions to change.

Ice is a much simpler problem as long as the pilot is willing to accept the only solution that keeps risk as low as possible. When an airplane flies from no ice into ice, the no-ice air is still back there. Everything is cool as long as the airplane is extricated from the icing condition. Even with de- or anti-ice gear, the drill is to get the airplane out of the icing condition. No exceptions. We all play silly mental games when ice starts to form, but these do nothing more than increase the risk. I'll fly five more minutes and if it doesn't go away, I'll do something. The time is now, not then. Patience does a lot of positive things in flying, but it doesn't work on ice.

En route IFR can and should be a low-risk time in our flying. As much as in any other area, this is up to the pilot.

CHAPTER 6

Arriving VFR

FIRST PART   Patrick E. Bradley

I have noticed that some pilots have a special ability to identify an airport from a distance. I've seen it lots of times. You'll be about 30 nautical miles from the airport and the other pilot will nudge you, or indicate:

"There's the airport, over there to the right."

"Where?" I ask.

"Over there. Don't you see the clearing? And now you can see the hangars next to the runway."

I, of course, remain baffled throughout. It's not a matter of eyesight, because I have nearly 20/20 vision. I suspect that it is more a talent for translating the terrain and landmarks in front of the airplane onto the sectional chart at a low altitude. Focusing on the small lake and following it to the rise on the left side of the railroad track, and then going from there to the clearing with the single grass strip is a talent that I will never have. And this is just one of the reasons that I find VFR arrivals quite difficult. There are lots of other reasons, so many that, given the choice, I will often opt to fly IFR into a new field in a busy, congested area. Although the IFR system presents its own challenges, I sometimes find them more manageable. When you're flying IFR, you can always request the approach that will bring you pretty close to the threshold while keeping you away from the terrain. When arriving VFR, you are all alone out there.

INITIAL DESCENT

Being all alone in the world has its advantages, particularly in the timing of each phase of the arrival. For instance, it is possible, when flying VFR, to give yourself just the right amount of time to complete your descent from altitude and slow the airplane prior to entering the pattern. Exercising complete control over the descent entails some additional responsibilities, too. First and foremost is obstacle clearance. It's an extremely important consideration in the best of weather. In marginal conditions, staying clear of mountains and antennas becomes critical.

I recall returning one day to Tompkins County Airport in Ithaca, New York, from the southeast. I was flying VFR that day when, looking back, it probably would have been wiser to have filed an IFR flight plan. The ceiling was 2,500 feet broken to overcast, which put me about 1,000 feet above the terrain. The clearances became slightly more questionable in and about the hills southeast of the airport. I was flying a road that I had followed on a number of occasions that would take me directly to the airport and, being relatively familiar with the terrain, I knew that I had ample room to clear the highest in the area.

Just about 10 nautical miles from the airport, I was about to call the tower to inform them of my intention to land. At that moment, a passenger seated in the right seat of the cockpit next to me grabbed my arm and pointed off to the left. A few hundred feet in front of us was a tower extending up to about 2,300 feet. Although we would have cleared the obstruction with a hundred feet to spare, there is something unnerving about seeing an extension of the earth reach up to greet you, its strobe eyes winking you on. Along this same road were two or three other towers extending two or three hundred feet above the hilltops, and almost precisely at the pattern altitude of the airport. A pilot unfamiliar with the terrain around the airport could easily make the mistake of descending to the pattern altitude too early and find himself impaled on a microwave tower.

I'm also always amazed at the proximity of the 700-foot tower 2 miles from the approach end of Runway 01 at Teterboro, my present home base. Ironically, Teterboro tower frequently requests that pilots report the tower inbound for the traffic pattern. Although the pattern altitude is 1,000 feet, pity the pilot who begins descending a bit soon. Three hundred feet, nearly the length of a football field, seems a great deal less when playing chicken with a broadcast antenna.

When I am flying in a mountainous area in the West or the East, I almost always have my guard extended. The vastness of the mountains and the unpredictability of the terrain and the record of VFR pilots in the mountains illustrate the importance of paying close attention to your descent and approach to the airport traffic pattern. More recently, though, I have begun to realize that even the flattest areas and the moderately hilly areas can be deceptive and dangerous. It's easy to complacently expect that 500 to 1,000 feet above flat terrain will keep you clear of any man-made hazards. Usually this is true; I just can't help thinking about the rest of the time.

LEARNING THE PATTERN
FOR THE PATTERN

One of the problems that I often encounter during VFR arrivals at an uncontrolled airport is sorting out the proper runway and pattern to use prior to entering the pattern. The problem with determining the proper runway to use is that, frequently, the winds may be from such direction that, in the case of a crosswind or light wind, the proper runway to use becomes a judgment call. At other times, the proper runway to use might be obvious according to the wind sock, but the unicom is announcing the other runway. Or else, traffic remaining in the pattern may simply continue to use one runway even though the winds have changed.

Besides the obvious problems associated with landing or departing with a tailwind, there is also the problem of confusion among pilots in the pattern. A pilot acquaintance of mine recently told me of an experience that he had at an airport where the wind sock was placed where the unicom operator could not see it. In the morning, the unicom operator would take a look at the sock and would decide the proper runway to use on the basis of the winds at that time. Unless the operator was able to go around and look at the sock later in the day, he would simply use the runway that the morning's winds indicated.

My acquaintance told me that on the day of his visit he overflew the airport to look at the wind sock and then called unicom to see which runway they were calling. Sure enough, the runway advisory issued by unicom was opposite that of the prevailing wind. The pilot called the unicom operator and informed him that the sock was standing nearly straight, indicating the opposite runway. "Oh," the operator said, "then we'll switch runways. I don't think there's anyone else in the pattern now anyway." A call to the FAA got the wind sock moved to the top of a hangar in a hurry, but this is not an uncommon example of the difficulties that pilots encounter at uncontrolled airports and one of the circumstances that increases the midair and near-miss occurrences.

Although it is impossible to expect absolute order at an uncontrolled airport, there are certain rules that I had drummed into my head while studying for my private certificate at Lincoln Park Airport, a field that is not only uncontrolled, but which boasts a nonstandard pattern for landings to the north. Perhaps one of the most important and most commonly ignored arrival practices is that entries should be made at a 45-degree angle to the midfield point on the downwind leg. The reason for this, like most other pattern customs, is so that other folks in the pattern know where to look for you and vice versa. It also lends some order to the flow of traffic in the pattern.

I recall one sunny and very busy Sunday afternoon at Lincoln Park. The weather was excellent, the winds were calm, and everyone decided to head for the airport to fly locally for a while. Needless to say, the pattern was a-hoppin', and tempers were a-flarin'. Standing near the fuel pump waiting to get topped off, I saw a man in dark sunglasses approach a pilot getting out of his Cessna 172.

"Do you know that you cut me off in the pattern?" the man in the sunglasses said, fists clenched. "I had to go around."

"I'm sorry," the pilot of the 172 stammered. "I didn't see you. Where were you?"

With this, the pilot wearing the sunglasses said gravely, "I made a straight-in. Don't you check for arriving traffic before turning final?" The pilot of the 172 just stared in abject disbelief. He didn't say a word. He just finished tying the airplane down and walked away as the pilot in the sunglasses shouted epithets.

Another rule that all of my instructors have held inviolate is the necessity of announcing your position when entering and progressing through the traffic pattern. Although unicom frequencies are often jammed with useless chatter, there are few better ways to lend some degree of order to a traffic pattern than to tell the pilots who really care where you are and where you're going. Announcing your position makes it possible for other pilots to determine how many aircraft are in front of them for landing and to pinpoint the position of each. It also tells inbound aircraft what runway is in use and how busy the airport traffic pattern is. Of course, I have heard of pilots who refuse to announce their position in the pattern because "I don't have to," or because "this is an uncontrolled airport." Uncontrolled needn't mean "out of control," though, and generally it doesn't.

IVORY TOWER

VFR arrivals at a controlled airport have some similarities to and a lot of differences from operations at uncontrolled airports. Although I fly out of a controlled airport now, I'm not sure that it's any safer than the uncontrolled airport that I started at. The first major difference between the controlled and uncontrolled airport is obvious: there is a man sitting in an ivory tower at the controlled airport, and he is master of all that he surveys. First, you've got to talk to the man if you're landing on his field. Second, you've pretty much got to do what the man tells you unless you can convince him otherwise or unless what he asks you to do is unsafe.

Looking at the risks involved in an arrival to a controlled airport, I suspect that they are not a great deal different from those involved in arriving at an uncontrolled airport: No controller is going to prevent you from running into terrain or an obstruction. This isn't his responsibility, even if he had the resources available to prevent such occurrences. Also, a controller is not responsible for providing separation from other VFR aircraft in the pattern, although he may help you to maintain that separation. I think one of the greatest dangers associated with arrivals at a controlled airport is the misconception among arriving VFR pilots that the controller can do what he cannot. Someone once described the role of a tower controller with respect to VFR arrivals as that of a gatekeeper. He will allow you into the traffic area, sometimes he will keep you out of the traffic area, and, almost always, he will tell you where to go.

KNOW THE DRILL

When arriving VFR at a busy controlled airport, it is critical to get all of the information that you can regarding your arrival and factors that could affect it. One way of obtaining information is to check the airport diagram in the J-Aid or in an airport guide. If you've got instrument approach plates, you can get even more detailed information about the layout of the airport runways, the length of the runways, frequencies, local obstructions, and perhaps even some cues on the type of pattern that you will be flying. Usually this would be some-

thing to cover during the preflight-planning phase of the flight
While en route, it is essential to obtain the airport ATIS information. The ATIS will tell you what runways are being
used, the wind, and any other information regarding the airport, like where the construction is taking place and where the
deer are romping on that particular day. For pilots who really
want to cover all of the bases, it is also helpful to know the
VFR arrival procedures. They're almost always established, at
least for busier airports in metropolitan areas. They can, however, be difficult to get your hands on. For example, at Teterboro Airport there are a number of specified arrival
checkpoints and approach routes favored by controllers, but
they are not published.

Of course, knowledge of specific VFR arrival procedures
is not required to land at a controlled airport. Controllers will
issue instructions for sequencing into the pattern whether you
are following standard airport procedures or not. At peak
hours, though, pilots unfamiliar with the drill at the airport
may be asked to wait outside of the airport traffic area simply
because they will need more detailed instructions for entering
and proceeding through the traffic pattern. A good way of
finding out whether the airport operates with special procedures, at least according to the folks at Teterboro, is to call
the tower on the phone and ask.

LISTEN CLOSELY

From my own experience, and from the experience of listening to other pilots entering the pattern at an airport, I think
that one of the most commonly made and potentially dan-

gerous mistakes made at an airport is failure to communicate clearly prior to and upon arrival at the airport. The first piece of information that the tower needs from an arriving aircraft is some idea of where the airplane is at the time of the call. The more precise you are, the better the controller can issue instructions for a quick and hassle-free arrival.

When I'm arriving at Teterboro, I always report at one of the checkpoints that I know the tower personnel are familiar with. By doing this, they know exactly where I am as opposed to estimating what I may mean by "northwest" or "west" of the airport. If I'm arriving at a strange airport, though, and I'm not familiar with the landmarks there I try to give the wer warning of my arrival at least 10 to 15 nautical miles from the airport. I also let them know that I've got the ATIS information. The reason I like to give lots of advance notice of my arrival is as much for my own convenience as the tower's. Ten or 20 nautical miles usually leaves enough time for the tower to issue an instruction and for me either to understand and begin to execute the instruction or to get a clarification. One of the scariest situations I think you can run into during a VFR arrival is when you are not entirely sure of what the tower wants you to do before entering the pattern.

One example of this came when I was flying out of Lincoln Park Airport in New Jersey and had occasion to pick someone up at Teterboro Airport, about 20 nautical miles away. Although I had landed at controlled airports on lots of occasions before, I had not landed at Teterboro previously and was somewhat intimidated by the volume of airplanes in the pattern and the proximity of the airport to Manhattan and the New York TCA. Prior to landing at the airport I studied the New York TCA chart closely and decided what altitudes and directions of flight I would use to avoid any incursions into the "off limits" areas, and the flight, as far as navigation went, was no problem.

There were problems, though, when it came to entering the pattern. I called the tower shortly after departing Lincoln Park and getting the latest ATIS information. Because of the heavy traffic, tower was issuing instructions in a rapid-fire staccato that didn't invite repetition or added niceties. I called in, tersely providing my N-number, location, altitude, and intentions. I was approaching from the northwest, was aware that Runway 06 was in use, and was expecting that the tower would give me a left base to Runway 06 or perhaps a left downwind entry. The response of the tower was: "Roger 49J, reportoverheadrightdownwindrunway06."

Unfamiliar with the fairly common procedure at Teterboro of crossing over the midpoint of the airport runways for the right downwind leg, I couldn't comprehend what the controller wanted me to do. Even worse, I was too intimidated by the whole ordeal to ask for a clarification of the instruction. I could hear the controller issuing the same instruction to other arriving aircraft, and I understood the words. I just couldn't believe that the tower would instruct aircraft to fly a pattern across the middle of the airport onto a downwind leg when they could just fly a left downwind or base. I had never experienced such a thing, and the instruction just wouldn't register.

At first, I thought that the controller misunderstood my direction of flight. I thought that he wanted me to report midfield for a right downwind for Runway 06. In fact, this is what he wanted me to do. I couldn't for the life of me figure out how I was supposed to get onto a right downwind for Runway 06 without crossing over the airport. As for crossing over the middle of the airport, I just didn't think that this was something that was done. Rapidly approaching the airport, I tried a different tack. I called the tower and noted that I was now 5 nautical miles *northwest*, and "would it be possible to get a *left* downwind for Runway 06."

The controller's response was unequivocal: "Negative," he said. "Reportoverheadrightdownwindrunway06."

Now two miles from the airport, I was still unsure of what I was going to do. If I called the controller again, he was going to blow his top. But if I started flying over the middle of a busy airport in broad daylight I could end up losing my license. I just had to come out with it:

"Tower, 49J. Do you mean that you want me to fly over the middle of the field to get onto the right downwind?" The tower's reply, ever terse, although beginning to sound a bit haggard: "Yes, 49J affirmative, just fly over the runways and turn right."

"That wasn't so bad," I thought.

SECOND PART   Richard L. Collins

As we take off and head out for somewhere, the options expand rapidly. The sky is a big place, and we can fly in many directions at many altitudes. But toward the end of the flight we have to make the peanut butter and bread come out even if the airplane is to touch softly, at the proper speed, in the first third of the runway of our choice. The wide range of options goes completely away, leaving us only one good option, to fly the airplane precisely to the spot. The flying is lower, so obstructions become more of a factor. The arrival is demanding of precision, whether it is IFR or VFR. And while the takeoff is an identifiable high area of risk, the VFR approach isn't without its problems. About 10 percent of the accidents occur in this phase of flight, including go-arounds, which are usually the result of a badly executed arrival. For the purpose of this discussion the arrival begins when the airplane leaves cruising altitude and ends when the landing begins, over the runway threshold. If the landing is a balked one, it goes on to include the go-around caused by an improper arrival.

Everything that can happen probably has happened in VFR arrivals. Airliners have hit TV antennas; airplanes have flown into mountains the pilots were unaware of, especially at night; airplanes have been flown into the ground; and there is a long list of simple losses of control—spin-ins, if you will.

THE PLAN

It is fairly clear from studying arrival accidents that there is one primary method of risk management: the plan.

An arriving pilot, talking with approach control, started a gradual descent for a night landing while a normal distance from the airport. Trouble was, there were mountains out there and the airplane hit one of them. A well-laid plan would have made the pilot aware of terrain; the FAA now adds to the plan with a low-altitude alert program in its computer. If flying VFR with sectional charts, a survey needs to be made of the arrival area. If IFR charts are on board, minimum en route and minimum safe altitudes are available.

A key to managing the arrival plan is keeping up with where the airplane is in space and in relation to terrain and the airport. A pilot who isn't constantly aware of altitude and flying miles left to the traffic pattern simply doesn't have a concept of whether or not the airplane will reach pattern altitude just before entering the pattern. Loran C, which most of us have embraced as the best navigational development since the map, will quietly tell us how far it is to the airport, offering an important arrival planning aid.

HOW FAR?

How far out should a descent begin? There are many rules of thumb; the one that I like best is quite simple. Start the descent 5 miles out for each 1,000 feet that you have to descend. At 150 knots groundspeed, 500 feet per minute is required to descend 1,000 feet in 5 miles. (Speed 150 equals 2½ miles per minute, 5 miles in two minutes; 1,000 divided by 2 equals 500.) You can work in any direction from this, with each 30 knots groundspeed requiring a change of 100 feet per minute: 120 equals 400 fpm, 180 equals 600 fpm, 450 equals 1,500 fpm. On VFR flights, where the time of beginning a descent is usually up to the pilot, this works well. On an IFR flight, or where the descent might have to start at a time other than that chosen by the pilot because of terrain or whatever, this system at least tells you where you are in relation to a plan. If closer than 5 miles per thousand, for example, you know that you have to descend at a rate in excess of that reflected by this rule of thumb. Closer to the airport, the descent becomes steeper because it is basically done at the same or greater descent rate but at a lower true airspeed. A crutch here can come from any ILS approach plate, with a glideslope defining a good approach slope. Most glideslopes are at about 1,700 or 1,800 feet when approximately 5 miles from the airport. If the airplane is higher than that when 5 miles away, you know that the descent has to be at a rate greater than that used for an ILS.

DIVERSIONS

It is our job to keep other factors from interfering with an arrival plan, but occasionally it happens and the arrival takes on added importance. From an NTSB narrative: "At the end of a 5.3 hour flight, the pilot entered the traffic pattern and was high on base and final approach. He elected to go around but the engine lost power due to fuel exhaustion at about 200 feet agl, just past the departure end of the runway. The pilot attempted to return to the runway. The airplane entered a steep left turn in a nose-high attitude, then pitched down and hit the ground before the pilot had a chance to recover."

I was passing by a southern terminal airport one day and overheard a discussion between a corporate turboprop pilot and a center controller. The pilot (this was before the days of FAA vindictiveness toward pilots) freely admitted to the controller that he had flown in from the West Coast and was quite short of fuel. He wanted to stay at Flight Level 210 until he was over, or at least within gliding distance of, the airport. Bad, very bad practice, but this pilot was trying to patch up his initial bad plan and incredibly poor decision making with a new plan that at least had a chance of working. We should all consider what might happen if the, or an, engine failed at any time during a flight. But a pilot approaching with low fuel has multiplied the chance of the engine failing by many thousands of times and has forced upon himself a critical risk-management challenge.

IS IT OKAY?

The arrival plan also has to consider weather and airport factors. On some arrivals, the only correct action might be to divert to a different airport. A business jet was lost on a VFR arrival after the pilot canceled IFR 8 miles from the airport to continue on a visual approach and landing. From the NTSB narrative: "Witnesses stated a strong thunderstorm had just passed over the airport. Wind information issued to the pilot by unicom was west at 20 knots. Witnesses observed the aircraft approach Runway 31 and execute a go-around before touchdown. The aircraft circled left to a Runway 6 (almost direct downwind) approach. Touchdown occurred almost two-thirds down the 3,100-foot-long runway. The engines were heard to spool up to high power (no thrust reversers) but the aircraft did not become airborne."

This occurred in the daytime and it was so clearly impossible that you would hope the crew was not aware of the fact that the runway they approached the last time was both quite short for a jet and downwind. The weather could have been such that the circle to that runway was better from a thunderstorm avoidance standpoint, but the wind was reported out of the west and there's no business jet built that can take a 20-knot downwind component on a 3,100-foot runway. During arrival, an airfield survey can make a pilot aware of the length of all the runways in the event the one chosen doesn't work out.

Wind has to be part of the airfield survey for pattern planning as well as landing because a crosswind affects phases other than the actual landing. For example, if the wind is blowing the aircraft toward the runway when it is on downwind leg, that means there will be a tailwind on base leg. Unless a wide pattern is flown, there will be a strong tendency to overshoot the turn onto final. If the pilot tries to salvage the arrival with a steeper turn onto final, the risk of accidentally stalling the aircraft increases. Considering how wind will affect the arrival is just part of the plan.

WEATHER

A survey of the weather is also important, and often what you can see, whether VFR or IFR, tells a lot about the advisability of an approach.

Approaching Little Rock, Arkansas, one day with a strong need to be there, I spent a lot of time studying convective activity in the vicinity of the airport. It was playing as a thunderstorm on both the radar and the Stormscope. The activity had passed over the airport with no increase in surface wind recorded at the airport as it passed. As I neared the field, the radar return placed the activity on the localizer, about 3 miles from the airport. But the bases of the clouds were much higher than my altitude as I came up on the final approach fix. The decision was made to fly on through because I was flying a light airplane to a 7,173-foot-long runway and could afford to pile on all the extra knots that I wanted in the bank to manage any wind-shear encounter. The approach wasn't bad, though there was some shear and a few bumps. After landing, I recalled another approach to that same runway. On the other one, I was a passenger in a Boeing 727. The aircraft was configured for landing, and the captain continued the approach past the final approach fix. Then came a great burst of power and a turn to the right, away from the airport. The captain announced that "It doesn't look quite right so we are going to wait a while." The timing of his decision might be faulted, but it was none the less a good decision.

One other factor has to be considered. I mentioned that I had a strong need to be in Little Rock. The captain of the airliner had no personal need to land, and his missing the approach at Little Rock would have no bearing on the next paycheck. It is probably in the arrival that the pressure to be there peaks. The trip has been flown and the destination is at hand. Anyone who says there is no temptation to take a chance in such a case doesn't haul all the normal human emotions around with him. But if risk is to be managed, this has to be managed.

SHORT FIELDS

In flying to relatively short airports, we accept more risk than when flying to acres of federally funded pavement; it is in the arrival that the stage is set to best manage the risks. And while you can think about this all you want while sitting in front of the fire at home, the full risk-management job can't be done until you are there, approaching the airport, with full knowledge of the existing conditions.

I used to fly a lot out of a short, 1,400-foot-long strip at Fordyce, Arkansas. The strip was aligned 03/210 and did not have clear approaches. I would start planning the arrival when miles out, gathering wind information to decide whether or not it would indeed be possible to land there. A direct crosswind of more than a few knots meant no landing. If there was no wind, a landing was possible only if the air was smooth and there was little or no possibility of wind shear on the approach. Depending on the airplane, the landing could not be attempted unless the weight was quite light. Most general aviation pilots don't test the brakes for firmness before landing, but I sure did before landing on that strip. When ten miles out, I had to feel that the risks were in mind and were manageable before I would continue inbound for a landing.

As the arrival at this diminutive airport unfolded, everything had to be perfect or the arrival would be aborted. The speed on final, the sight picture of the runway, and the descent rate were either bang-on or the drill was to go away. No second chances. If I couldn't get it right the first time, I'd go away. We all talk about stabilized approaches—speed and descent bang-on—and this little airport taught me more about them than any other. We might, in light airplanes, be able to fly unstabilized approaches, especially at big airports where they want speed maintained on final, but when we get to the smaller airports we have no choice other than to fly well-stabilized approaches.

I used that airport for a number of years without incident. The only time I got close to the airport with the intent of landing and then aborted the arrival was early in my use of it. There was a crosswind, but I thought I could handle it. On final, though, the perceived groundspeed and the amount of drift presented a clearly impossible situation.

RUNWAY SELECTION

An important part of managing the risk of a VFR arrival is picking the best runway when the surface wind is anything more than light, and especially when it is a crosswind. At smaller airfields, the choice is often left entirely to the pilot and must be made based on what we see and feel. This doesn't mean it is fraught with peril, only that it must be done carefully.

A primary reason for careful runway selection is that go-arounds can become quite hazardous at short fields, especially if they are begun late. The best direction for landing, based on wind and obstructions, needs to be picked, because trial and error in low-level turbulence is a bad deal. Then, if a correct approach is flown to the selected runway and the landing appears inadvisable when the airplane is on a half-mile final, the choice of an airport (not a direction of landing) was a bad one and it's time to go to an airport with a longer runway or a more favorable wind direction.

I tend to remember flights. One, years ago, on a TWA Boeing 707, stands out when contemplating this subject. The new, large airport at Kansas City had not yet been built and we were landing at what is now Kansas City Downtown Airport, where the north-south runway is 7,001 feet long. It was wintertime and a howling cold front had passed through, so there was strong and gusty crosswind for a landing to the north, and there would be a tailwind on left base. Throw in the buildings of downtown Kansas City to maneuver around, and the lads up front had their work cut out for them. It was a close circle, not a long stabilized final.

As the airplane was maneuvered around for landing, it was apparent that the crew was in a real wrestling match with the conditions. Large control deflections were being used, and while the wings would pass through level, they didn't stay level for long. On final the perception of groundspeed from my passenger seat was quite high. The levee passed beneath, you could hear the power start to be reduced, and the airplane felt squirmy. I could not help but wonder if this was really a good idea. Then the power came back up, all of it, and the crew started configuring the 707 for the go-around. We went to a divert airport (Wichita) with a runway more nearly aligned with the wind. I was glad they decided to cull Kansas City, but felt they could have made an earlier decision. The airplane really had the blind staggers on the go-around. After that, a 707 was draped over one of the levees at Kansas City during a landing that couldn't be contained within the confines of the airport.

Judging wind isn't always easy, especially when there are obstructions around an airport and when there is a crosswind. A strong direct crosswind poses the greatest challenge when picking a direction in which to land, because strong winds are never steady in direction or velocity. There are no absolutes on wind on runways because of the effect of terrain or obstructions, but sailors are pretty aware of the fact that in gusty conditions (in the Northern Hemisphere) the wind shifts (veers) clockwise when speed increases in a gust and does the reverse (backs) when the velocity decreases. While that is a nugget a pilot might store, the rule of thumb is likely fractured by those buildings or trees beside the runway.

DECISION TIME

When we took off, the decision was made that the destination airport is of adequate length. During the arrival, the decision has to be made again, based on current conditions.

One big factor in the decision to continue an approach has to be speed. It is easy enough to calculate a proper speed for arrival over the runway threshold. The industry standard for a reference speed on approach is 1.3 times the stalling speed for the selected configuration, or, in the case of a short-field landing, some show 1.2 Vso as the approach speed. If anything, pilots overdo this, adding extra speed because the air is rough or because the airplane just doesn't feel right. But we need to think of marginal airports as requiring a certain approach speed. If we don't want to fly that speed, we can't use that airport. And marginal airports had best be defined. It is up to the individual, but in a play on the transport category requirements, where extra margins are required, some pilots use a minimum runway length of 160 percent of the distance shown in the pilot's operating handbook to clear a 50-foot obstacle, land, and stop. If the book says it takes 1,500 feet to get down and stopped from 50 feet, then the minimum required runway length would be 2,400 feet. If the stalling speed is 60 knots, then the reference speed on final would be 78. Some POHs show 1.2 Vso for a short field, which would be 72 knots. Whatever, the required runway lengths are based on the speeds shown, so we can't count on the length if we don't fly the speed.

When considering speed we need to do a little simple arithmetic to understand why extra speed adds risk to a short-field approach. If the suggested speed is 70 and we approach the runway at 80 and there is no wind, the airplane is traveling at a groundspeed of 135 feet per second. If the float while the airplane is decelerating lasts for six seconds, not long, almost 800 feet of extra runway will be used. Where this is used in risk management is on final approach. Say, for example, that the wind is strong and the air incredibly turbulent. The airspeed is often difficult to maintain near a precise value under such conditions, and many find it a good practice to use a power setting and attitude that results in the lowest excursion of the airspeed being the reference speed. But when considering runway length, the highest excursion has to be used, because that is where the airspeed might be at the threshold. If that excursion is 10 knots over Vref, then the required runway length would have to be appropriately longer.

FEELS BETTER

The business about staying away from smaller airports when the wind is strong and across the runway is enhanced by the fact that if a runway is short, it is probably narrow, leaving no margin for error in drift management. I think that most pilots feel a lot better landing with a strong crosswind on a large open area with a wide runway than at a short strip—and for good reason. Risk management is a matter of margins.

POWER OFF?

If a power-off approach is made every time, that means that the runway will be reached even if the engine fails. And back in the good old days we all flew power-off approaches in light airplanes all the time. "Dragging it in" was reserved for short fields, where the use of a little power could make for a more precise arrival. It also serves, on most airplanes, to lower the stalling speed somewhat, enabling a slightly lower approach speed. With heavier singles and light twins, though, most pilots evolved into approaches with a little power, to make for a shallower approach slope and a better controlled flare before landing. In a heavy single, this has to be done with the knowledge that an engine failure would result in a touch-down short of the runway. But then we fly the whole trip with knowledge that an engine failure will result in a touchdown somewhere other than the desired point.

HUMAN FACTOR

One human factor, fatigue, looms large on many arrivals, VFR or IFR, and we have to have a plan to deal with it. The simplistic "don't fly when you are tired" just does not work. A pilot might feel fresh at the beginning of a flight and bushed at the end. If you toil all day and then fly home, there's no way to be as fresh for the arrival as when you hit the floor running in the morning. Also, the change from mundane work to something as enjoyable and challenging as flying might provide a big boost—at first. Later in the flight might come a letdown. Much has recently been made about airline pilots going to sleep in their seats on long hauls, and there is ap-propriate controversy over two-man crews on long-haul airline aircraft. At least they have two pilots, minimum; we often fly with only one.

Dealing with fatigue is a decidedly lonely business. Only the pilot-in-command can decide whether or not, at the be-ginning of a flight, the personal battery has enough charge to last until the airplane reaches the destination. Some of us oc-casionally suffer from the nod-offs, others do not. It has been my personal experience that the older you get, the less likely you are to suffer from an inability to stay away from an im-promptu catnap. Or maybe it's just that you tend to get more sleep as you age, thus being less prone to fatigue.

Regardless of whether it is a 747 arriving in Tokyo after

a non-stop from New York, or a Bonanza arriving at El Dorado after a non-stop from Topeka, if the person in charge of the airplane is tired, he has to be aware of that fact and take special precautions on arrival. The precautions have to revolve around mental work, because a busy mind is less likely to condone a nod-off, and the mental busywork can be used to catch the mistakes of a tired old brain. And that's the way such an approach has to be approached—carefully. Mistakes will be made and the procedure has to be there to catch those mistakes.

SERIOUS

The types of mistakes that are made because of fatigue are often not major ones—but they can multiply. Tired pilots more often than not make numerical mistakes. A misset navigational radio or altimeter is common—not immediately critical while en route but potentially serious during an arrival. The procedure for catching such mistakes has to be the old double check. Everything that is done has to be double- or triple-checked. Look at it, set it, look at it again, and check the setting. Such things as forgetting to switch to a fuller tank for landing can become all-important. Check lists are a good barrier against fatigue-induced errors.

Then there are mistakes or lapses in flying technique. Most of us are able to psych ourselves up for an arrival and landing, regardless of fatigue, but there is no question that some of the sharpness is gone. For a couple of years I flew with a NASA flight recorder in my airplane, gathering data for them on the stresses applied to a light pressurized airplane. The good man who read the tapes every month could spot every night landing by the g-forces on touchdown. Were the harder hits a result of poor night-landing technique, or were they a result of the pilot being more fatigued? I would bet on a little bit of both.

EVERY BENEFIT

On a tired approach, we can also work to stack the deck in our favor. Shooting an ILS, for example, gives the advantage of glideslope guidance. A runway with a VASI is a second best, especially if you arrange for a nice, long final on which to stabilize approach speed and rate of descent.

I flew out of Mercer County Airport at Trenton, New Jersey starting thirty years ago, so I probably know it better than any other and have made more late evening arrivals there than anywhere else. And I can remember times when, in retrospect, I did poorly at minimizing the risk in an arrival. One night with good ceiling and visibility but some rain, I circled to land on Runway 34. And I circled close despite the smokestack on a close base leg. It would have been much better to fly a longer final. Another time, at dusk, I flew the ILS approach to Runway 6 and had to maneuver around for a landing on Runway 16 because of a strong southeasterly flow. The air was bumpy, I kept the pattern close, and the arrival wasn't as pretty as I like. A straight-in Rnav approach to Runway 16 would have given all the stepdown fixes and altitudes. Even when VFR, the advantage is often in following an IFR procedure, mainly because it gives safe altitudes for all the different phases of the approach.

TOTAL

In total, the key to VFR arrivals is indeed planning. An awareness of the risks helps with the plan and, in studying the record, a primary risk to life on a botched arrival comes on a go-around, especially at a short field. Forewarned should be forearmed when on final with doubts in mind.

CHAPTER 7

Arriving IFR

FIRST PART   Patrick E. Bradley

There are few phases of flight that I find more technically or strategically challenging than the instrument arrival, and I suspect that, in terms of risk, the instrument arrival probably rates pretty high, too. Oddly enough, though, I'd bet that instrument arrivals aren't challenging for the same reasons that they are risky. Arrivals are challenging because they call on all of a pilot's flying skills and the results correlate quite closely with the pilot's performance during the arrival. In other words, there's a lot to do, and it's easy to see how well you performed each task.

I think that instrument arrivals are risky for somewhat different reasons. Arrivals bring a pilot into close proximity with the ground in situations where adherence to specific, well-defined rules is the only thing that stands between the pilot and the obstruction a few hundred feet below the glideslope. But this is only part of the reason. It's easy to say that the pilot broke a rule and then he crashed. It is much more difficult to understand why he would break the rule and why these breaches occur frequently during instrument arrival. I think that the best pilots in the world can break rules during an instrument arrival because of the nature of the arrival.

ARE WE THERE YET?

For the longest time I thought an instrument arrival began at the initial approach point, or when you are cleared for the approach. I believed that this was where you and the airplane were locked into the system and were inbound for the big landing. In fact, I think that I remember Collins asking me one day, "When does the arrival [or maybe he said "approach"] phase of the flight begin?" Obviously he had picked up on the fact that my approaches generally began at the words "cleared for the approach" with a flurry of papers and charts taking flight as if someone had just opened the door to the airplane. The fingers of one hand would begin to fly to avionics knobs and OBS knob and every other type of knob, while the fingers of the other hand simultaneously clutched the control wheel with two fingers and riffled the pages of my approach plates with the other two.

To tell the truth, I hadn't given the question a lot of thought (which apparently gave rise to Collins's question in the first place), but since Collins had on his trick-question face, I thought that I should try to figure out the puzzle (which shouldn't have been a puzzle). My initial thought was that the approach phase of the flight begins when you are on a published segment of the approach. But, thinking a little harder, when did I first get into the approach mode in terms of preparing the airplane for the approach? Well, that would probably be when I reached the initial approach altitude. And that was probably my answer. Now, having thought much more about the question, I think that the arrival phase of the flight comes much earlier. Probably around the time when you first start thinking about getting lower.

CAN WE PULEEEZE HAVE LOWER?

When flying in the Flight Levels in a piston-powered airplane, getting lower can be a major ordeal. A pilot is often confronted with the task of descending at as high a rate as possible while keeping the engine warm. Unless you want to put the gear down prior to every descent (which is a practice akin to slicing roast beef with a hacksaw—something one resorts to only in the direst emergency) the descent requires planning, cajoling, and a smooth touch. I use Collins's benchmark rate-of-descent profile for calculating when I would ideally like to begin a descent. By allowing 5 miles for every 1,000 feet of altitude (at 150 knots) I will be able to descend at 500 feet per minute, a nice, comfortable descent rate for passengers and the airplane. Unfortunately, if you are flying at FL 180, it would be necessary to begin the descent at about 90 nautical miles from the destination, and controllers frequently aren't ready to let you start down so far out. Thus, if I don't begin down until 45 nautical miles out, I know that I'll have to make 1,000 feet per minute or better to get down in time.

In any case, my ideal point for starting down often starts the approach phase of my flight. If I'm flying lower, it will often begin when I start trying to get the ATIS—about 50 nautical miles out. I guess that the arrival phase of a flight for me is just a time when you start attempting to prepare the cockpit, and map the route to the approach in your head. One primary concern when flying at higher altitudes is just getting down. I have found that controllers often don't realize how long it takes for a piston airplane to descend at a comfortable rate. The upshot of a delayed descent is a pilot and airplane blasting into the approach at a distressingly high rate. Instead of concentrating on the other pre-approach tasks, which are rushing by at a frightening rate, the pilot is attempting to slow the airplane down and descend in time for the approach. Usually at this point I'll begin to notice the beads of sweat forming, because I've been through the scenario so many times. If you don't have the airplane at an appropriate speed and altitude before starting on the initial approach point, you might as well scrub the approach right there. I usually will succeed in making approach's altitude restriction, but in the process the airplane will be so hot and the cockpit in such a state of disarray that the approach will be catch-up from the start. The answer? I think there are two parts. First, it is crucial to have speed and altitude where you want them before reaching the initial approach point. It is only by adhering to this rule that I have been able to begin an approach with a fighting chance. The second half of the rule is to begin preparations for the approach when the arrival phase begins.

SETTING THE STAGE

When I begin my descent, or when I'm 50 nautical miles or so from the airport, I will begin to set the stage and the cockpit for the upcoming approach. Like the airplane's configuration, the cockpit preparations should be squared away as much as possible before beginning the critical phase of the arrival. I try to take my last opportunity to pull and review the approach plate at a less than frantic pace, and I will look for any idiosyncratic characteristics of the approach. If I can begin to set in frequencies, I'll often begin that task so that I can check again later for all of the mistakes that I know that I'll make along the way. In any case, all of the frequencies should be set—to the extent they can be—prior to beginning any phase of the published approach.

In addition to setting the frequencies, I also try to use the initial part of the arrival phase to refresh my memory regarding the setup of the approach and the lay of the land in and about the approach. Presumably I have gotten the ATIS information and I have a good idea which approach I'll be flying. So what's the inbound heading? Are there any doglegs? What are the minimums for the approach? The inbound heading and the minimums for the approach are two items that must be committed to memory before starting the approach.

APPROACH: THE FINAL STEP

Ideally, by the time the approach begins the arrival should be complete except for the flying. I recall that during some of my refresher sessions at FlightSafety, the instructor would illustrate the point in the simulator by taking away the approach charts as the approach began. It wasn't a dirty trick, because we never would have looked at the approach plate. We had the inbound, the minimums, and the first step of the missed approach committed to memory. The piece of paper was superfluous.

The act of taking away the piece of paper has symbolic

significance for me, though. It shows that the approach, the final step of the arrival, should be a fairly simple technical task. Throughout the arrival phase of the flight, I find that I perform best if I am able to compartmentalize tasks and concerns. For example, once the frequencies have been set and checked, that concern can be filed away unless something happens where it becomes a concern again. The same practice works with every single flying task until, when you are on the inbound leg of the approach, there is relatively little to think about except your status on the approach.

I find that when my flying skills are up to snuff, the VOR or NDB or ILS approach becomes the straightforward conclusion to the arrival procedure.

COMPLICATIONS

If arrivals are so simple, then why do I believe they're so risky? Well, first, I don't mean to give the impression that arrivals are simple. It's just that the factors that make them risky often have little to do with the technical demands of flying an IFR approach. As in all aspects of flying, I think that the factors that increase the risks are often related more to preparation, the pilot, and his decision making than to the technical aspects of flying an airplane.

ARRIVAL WEATHER

From time to time, we confront the situation where the weather at the destination is such that the approach may be questionable from the start. On the one hand, my usual approach to weather is, "Well, let's take a look and see whether it's as bad as they say." The tendency is to proceed with the approach unless you've got thunderstorms on the inbound leg of the approach. In fact, thunderstorms in the vicinity of the airport make the decision a simple one. There are so few opportunities for avoiding cells while flying an approach that there really is no choice but to scrub this arrival and shoot for another. There are lots of situations that don't amount to thunderstorms on the approach, though, but still raise the question of whether the approach should continue.

BELOW MINIMUMS

What is one to do when confronted with a destination reporting conditions below minimums? I expect that making this decision can be a high-risk element of an IFR arrival, because there are so many variables to consider.

I recall facing this decision one rainy day en route to Trenton Airport in Trenton, New Jersey. I was flying with Collins on a practice flight of sorts. We initially wanted to see how well I would perform in actual instrument conditions (I had just recently gotten my instrument rating) and it later became an exercise in missed approach procedures. In any event, we were confronted with a situation where we knew that the destination conditions were below minimums while still en route to the airport. We had several options to consider.

The first option, of course, was to fly the approach and to see what the real conditions were. Ceilings can frequently lift and descend, and in a condition where the visibility is acceptable, you may be fortunate enough to encounter conditions well above minimums despite the weather report. If the visibility is below minimums, then it is a different story, the approach is out. But where you have a variable ceiling, many pilots will opt to fly the approach. We had several other factors in our favor as well. In addition to having visibility, we also considered what other pilots were experiencing on the approach. We were pleased to learn that an aircraft had just made the approach at Trenton, and conditions seemed to be improving. At least that was our hope. Another factor in our favor was the presence of two pilots. We had flown together quite a bit prior to this flight, and we knew how to work together. For me, having an experienced eye in the right seat meant a lot, and the possibility of a critical fatigue-induced mistake taking place was significantly reduced. Another factor in our favor was our familiarity with the approach. We were landing at the airplane's home base, using an approach that I had flown many times before.

SCRUBBED

With all of these factors in our favor, we decided to fly the approach. None of these factors changed the reality that, when we reached minimums, the airport was nowhere in sight. The approach was scrubbed and we opted to go to an airport reporting more amenable conditions. Missing an approach is not a particularly enjoyable experience, though. Flying an actual approach to minimums in poor conditions and following that with an additional procedure, the missed approach, is physically fatiguing. I'm always concerned with how well I will be able to perform on the next approach. In addition, a missed approach always leads to another unavoidable question: "What are your intentions?" You find yourself in the position of having to reenter the system and make decisions regarding your new destination. Hopefully most of these decisions have been made prior to beginning the approach, but now the time has come to make them with finality and to carry them out for real.

In retrospect, I think that flying an approach to an airport reporting sub-minimum conditions is a high-risk proposition without at least as many pro-landing factors as we had at Trenton. The worst concern, of course, is that for whatever reason, you will continue the approach below the minimums. There could be the unexpectedness of the missed approach, indecisiveness, or the firm conviction that "things will open up just a few feet lower." Unfortunately, things often do not open up in "just a few feet." And often, even if they do, the airplane is in no position to execute a landing on the runway anyway.

There has been only one solo situation where I continued an approach to an airport reporting visibility below minimums. That was on a flight to Martha's Vineyard Airport. Frequently, the airport will report below-minimums conditions in fog for a long time after the fog lifts or burns off. In addition, about five other airplanes had completed the approach in the last half hour, reporting that the actual conditions were quite good. I made the approach. That's the sort of confidence level I need, though, before risking a miss.

POOPED

Another factor that I think significantly increases the risk of the arrival phase of a flight is the pilot's fatigue level. Every instrument pilot learns very early in the course of his instruction that mistakes just sometimes happen when you're tired.

The mistakes may not be big ones, and you may even have enough back-up checks that you catch them before they get more serious. There is no doubt in my mind, though, that I don't fly as well when I'm tired. And the arrival phase of the flight always comes at the very end.

It's unrealistic to expect that you'll always be able to fly when you're feeling super. But it is also silly to put yourself in the position where serious fatigue becomes a factor in the completion of the flight. If the planning of the flight is going to require a night departure into instrument conditions after a morning flight and a day full of meetings, it might be wiser to spend the night and depart earlier in the morning.

KNOW THYSELF

Not surprisingly, many of the factors that increase the risks of the arrival phase of the flight are as much a product of the pilot's ability to make decisions as of his ability to physically fly the airplane. The arrival phase of the flight involves decisions regarding everything from whether one should even begin the approach to a particular airport to whether one should descend "just a few feet lower" on the ILS (although this should not even be a consideration). And it seems that it is in making these decisions that good pilots can show incredibly poor judgment.

I suppose that the demands of the arrival phase of the flight are a product not only of the need to perform like a pilot, but to exercise judgment like a pilot. We spend a lot of time learning, practicing, and discussing the performance aspects of arrivals. I tend to think we could reduce a lot of the risks by thinking more about the judgment and decision-making demands of the arrival.

SECOND PART   Richard L. Collins

Pilots flying IFR think about a lot of things, including engine and systems failures, thunderstorms, and ice. But the biggest risk in IFR flying is found in the approach. At times some of the other factors we worry over play a role, but more often than not IFR approach accidents are simply premature arrivals. This is a key area of risk management, because accidents that occur during IFR approaches are often fatal. Accidents resulting in fatal or serious injuries outnumber those producing minor or no injuries by almost two to one in the IFR approach phase of flight. They also have no respect for experience. In a sample of twenty IFR accidents, twelve of the pilots had four-figure experience, two were into five figures, and the lowest time listed was 275 hours. The lowest-time pilot did not have an instrument rating but was on an IFR flight plan flying an approach. There is a strong lesson about experience in the NTSB's probable-cause narrative about an accident involving a pilot with over 20,000 hours: "Aircraft struck trees 2 miles from runway at 15 feet a.g.l. The approach was conducted in heavy fog conditions. The pilot had descended below approach minimums on several occasions in the past." The lesson is that some pilots get away with going below minimums some of the time but, regardless of the pilot's experience, it can be a deadly business.

The airplanes involved in IFR approach accidents tell us something about ourselves as pilots. Eleven were singles (six retractables and five fixed-gear), seven were piston twins, and two were turbines, both turboprops. In informal surveys, it has been seen that singles, piston twins, and turbines all fly about equal hours of IFR each year. Because none of the single-engine approach accidents in the sample were related to any characteristic unique to singles, we have to go to the left front seat for an explanation. Even though more complex airplanes are more demanding on an approach, twin pilots do a better job of IFR approaches and pilots of turbines do a lot better job on IFR approaches than do pilots flying singles. The two-pilot requirement on jets and the general participation in high-quality recurrent training by all turbine pilots have to play a role—more of a role than experience, because most of the single pilots had well over 1,000 hours. Logic would suggest that the single should have a better approach record, because of its relative simplicity. There is less to do and lower speeds mean you have more time for thinking and planning. But it is an area where the risk isn't being managed.

COMPLACENCY

Could it be that single pilots have more accidents on approaches because, in assessing risk, they think about the wrong things? If the alternator, vacuum, or engine keep working, is there nothing to it? Certainly there are a lot of pilots out there who think that mechanical failures are the number one hazard. And they are a hazard but, in actual practice, flying into something when too low on approach is the culprit on twice as many single IFR accidents as is a failure of something in or on the airplane.

On approach, we all fly with a little devil on our shoulder

that makes a continuous suggestion about going a little lower for a better view. Sweeping that little fellow away is the key. Anyone who doesn't admit to being tempted, or to actually doing it if many approaches have been made, is likely fibbing. Pilots are probably more likely to go lower at home base, or at an airport with which they are familiar. I remember once musing through my logbook and coming to the realization that every trip I had canceled, and every diversion I had made, was on an outbound trip. Sliding for home plate, I had made it every time. Certainly I had to ask myself if that was an indication of a double standard.

One grungy day my destination was Auburn, Alabama. Our son was flying the airplane and we were making a VOR approach because their localizer was not yet installed. He missed the first approach clean, but at the proper time I thought I saw enough to have continued and landed. So I followed the very bad practice of going back for another shot at the approach. This time, I made the approach and the decision that the airport was indeed visible through the murk and descended toward it. I turned out to be correct, but my son said, "I'm glad I didn't do that." In retrospect, he was correct. Maybe I met the letter of the law, but that was all.

It made me recall an RNAV approach to Beech Field in Wichita. Beech used to have a lot of red, white, and blue paint on their buildings, a symbol of the company's patriotism. It was a murky day, with a north wind, and the approach was being shot to the north. Even though the area nav said I had a distance to go, the sight of red, white, and blue ahead prompted me to start down, thinking it was the building adjacent to the approach end of the runway. It only took a second to realize that the red, white, and blue was on a lumber yard or something like one, not by a runway, but that is just another example of how we will grasp for straws when looking for a runway. On approach, we tend to be programmed to descend when really the mind should be set on a missed approach.

SAFE HAVEN

Up to the minimum descent altitude on a nonprecision approach or the decision height on a precision approach, there is a procedure to follow. And there is a procedure to follow for a missed approach. But once the pilot elects to leave the lowest altitude shown on the approach, based on a sighting, the crisp IFR procedures crumble and it becomes a VFR scud run to the airport. On an ILS approach, the glideslope guidance is still there, but if you watch pilots fly ILS approaches, many go below the glideslope as soon as the runway is sighted, presumably because it is visual. And while a lot of us say that we prefer ILS approaches and don't particularly like to do it without a glideslope, there is no reason for one approach to be more risky than the other. All that's necessary is to follow the procedure and the rule about not leaving the MDA until and unless the runway is in sight. In fact, over half the IFR approach accidents were on ILS approaches in the sample studied, so the risk is apparently not removed by the availability of vertical guidance.

WHY ILS?

It isn't particularly logical for the ILS to be the site of most IFR approach accidents. What are we doing out there? Some NTSB reports shed light on this.

Cessna 172: "After failing to see the runway on his first ILS approach in weather reported at IFR minimums for landing, the pilot was radar vectored for a second approach. According to controllers the approach appeared to be normal until the aircraft's radar target disappeared off the scope approximately 2 miles from the runway. Ground rescue found the aircraft impacted in a fog-shrouded ridge, in the vicinity of where it disappeared from radar."

Piper Warrior: "During arrival, the aircraft was vectored to intercept the ILS runway 27 localizer before reaching the Munci initial approach fix, which was 21.5 miles from the runway. The ATC controller told the pilot to maintain 4,000 feet until on the localizer, then cleared him for the approach. From the initial approach fix the minimum altitude on the approach was 3,700 feet until intercepting the ILS glideslope at the Picture Rocks NDB (final approach fix). The NDB was 9.4 miles from the airport. The outer marker was 4.8 miles from the runway. As the pilot continued, he reported that his instruments showed he was on the glideslope at 2,700 feet, but that he was still headed inbound toward the NDB. The controller warned that the aircraft should be at 3,700 feet until reaching the NDB and repeated the altimeter setting. Moments thereafter, the controller lost contact with the aircraft. It crashed near the top of a hill on wooded terrain at an elevation of about 2,400 feet, approximately 9 miles before reaching the NDB. An examination revealed the aircraft navigational equipment was properly set. No preimpact malfunction or failure was found. The ILS system was flight checked and found to operate normally."

Beech 33: "During vectors for an ILS Runway 23 approach, the pilot allowed the aircraft to get 400 feet below the assigned altitude of 3,700 feet. The controller queried the pilot about his altitude and the pilot replied that he had gotten a little low but was returning to the assigned altitude after intercepting the localizer. The pilot was cleared for the approach and told to contact the tower. As the aircraft was on final approach, the tower controller noted that it was right of course and advised the pilot. The pilot acknowledged, but moments later the ELT activated as the aircraft hit trees on the crown of a hill and crashed. Initial impact was in level flight at an altitude of about 1,700 feet msl. The airport elevation was 1,519. The decision height for the approach was 1,718 feet. During the investigation, no preimpact malfunction was found concerning the aircraft or navigational equipment that would have resulted in the accident. About one minute before the accident another pilot, who had just completed the approach, reported that he had broken out of the clouds at weather minimums."

Piper Seneca: "The private pilot had been cleared for 27R ILS approach and was on the localizer at 1,600 feet when the controller noticed the aircraft north of the localizer course and in a right turn headed east. The controller queried the pilot as to his heading and the pilot replied, 'east, which way to go?' The flight was then given a turn so as to avoid another aircraft on the approach which the accident aircraft was approaching head-on. The pilot never acknowledged any further radio transmissions and shortly thereafter the aircraft dropped off radar and crashed into the Atlantic Ocean in 800 feet of water. The newly rated multiengine pilot had been advised by his CFI not to conduct any night IFR or flight into heavy IFR conditions until he gained more IFR experience. The weather conditions were night IFR with rain, heavy turbulence and thunderstorms in the area. Neither the aircraft nor occupants were recovered from the ocean."

COMPLETE MIX

In those four accidents we see a pretty complete range of mistakes, from general confusion to what appears to be a navigational error and premature descent. The tendency among pilots appears to be to err on the low side on approaches, where the high side is the safe side. On an ILS there is very little margin, especially as the approach unfolds. That final decision height is but 200 feet above the ground in most cases, so the clearance above obstructions is quite literally minimum. Wandering off to one side or the other doesn't work either. For the ILS to serve its purpose the pilot has to be willing and able to match the precision of the approach with a like amount of precision in flying.

COMMON THREADS

There are several common threads found in any study of IFR accidents. One will be fully explored in a following chapter but must also be discussed here. In our sample, three-fourths of the IFR accidents occurred at night. This very clearly outlines an area of high risk. Why so, if IFR approaches are procedural?

In the narratives quoted, picked at random, some of the pilots had apparent difficulty flying the airplane well. This would be enhanced at night simply because chart reading is more difficult and the instrument panel is not illuminated as well as by day.

Examples of the difficulty of night IFR are easy to find. One that I particularly recall involved a glitch as well as darkness. I was flying high and the alternator quit working at about the time I began the descent for landing. It seemed prudent to continue, running only the required lights and a nav-com. The controller agreed that I could even turn the transponder off. The only problem was in panel lighting. Post lights like I have use a lot of electricity, and I wanted to leave them off. Sure, I had a briefcase full of flashlights, but it takes one hand to hold a light, one to fly, one to turn the pages in the book, and one to work the power. The result was fine, thanks to the fact that it was a clear night. Had it been one of those legendary dark and stormy nights that people write about, I would have had to work a lot harder.

An FAA survey shows that 4 percent of the hours flown are in instrument meteorological conditions at night and 10 percent are IMC day, so if three-fourths of the IFR airplanes are lost in IMC night conditions, the higher degree of care required is obvious.

UNCERTAINTY

Another common thread relates to flying technique. In the accidents related earlier, some of the pilots clearly had trouble maintaining control of their aircraft. Perhaps they were not certain of what they were doing. When your brain goes into "coast" because it becomes overloaded, it is difficult to fly well. Which places the removal of uncertainty as one of the keys to risk management. That is true during all phases of IFR flying; it is especially true during an approach.

If you think back to some approaches, you will probably find one or more that stand out as being laced with uncertainty or confusion. One I remember was to Hartsfield at Atlanta. The controller vacillated about whether I was to shoot the ILS to Runway 26 Right or 27 Left. I could see his problem: He was trying to work a slower airplane in among a lot of faster ones. There were a lot of rainshowers in the area, with pilots requesting deviations, which further complicated his chore. The final decision was for 26 Right. He gave a heading and I tuned up the ILS. There was a moment of confusion when I noted that the heading of 300 degrees was taking me away from the localizer. At least the needle was off to the left. Had I tuned the wrong frequency? What was going on? Then the controller told me to turn left to 240, to intercept the localizer, "cleared for the approach, please keep your speed up as long as possible, sir." I never did know whether the 300 heading was given in error, or to keep me north of the localizer for as long as possible because of simultaneous approaches on the other runway. The rest of the approach, though, was not as well flown as it should have been because it does take a few minutes for a confused mind to recover.

WORSE THAN FORECAST

Another time we can find ourselves with a self-imposed disadvantage is when the weather is worse than forecast. Launch with the idea that the weather will be good for arrival, but get there and find it at 200½, and what appeared easy from a distance goes up in the level of difficulty. Being basically distrustful of all forecasts, I like to think that this doesn't bother me—but it does. There can be an unhealthy pressure on such an approach, especially if the options have become limited because of busted forecasts. Say everything in the area is hovering around minimums and you are shooting an ILS to the very bottom limit. If the runway is not in sight at the decision height, does the thought process go into a missed approach, or does it dwell on the fact that it might not be any better at another airport, so why not keep descending in the hope that this one will work? Very dangerous business any time you fly an approach with the thought, "This one has to work."

ELEMENTS

The job of thinking through an approach in advance and leading the airplane down the lines prescribed on the chart is clearly defined right up to the point where the decision is made. To that we have to add a study and understanding of the weather cross-section that has to be dealt with on the approach. The nature of the restriction to visibility, for example, can tell us a lot about what it will be like right at the last. With ground fog, the visibility will likely deteriorate close to the ground. It can also be patchy. The tower might be fogged in and the end of the runway clear. Or vice versa. I landed one foggy day at an uncontrolled airport run by a very conservative old gentleman. At least it was foggy on the transient ramp. The runway had been clear and in sunshine for the landing. But the FBO was upset about someone landing in the fog; I always wondered if he drove out on the runway to see if it was really as clear out there as I said it was. With fog, you do have to hedge your bets. The approach lights might be in sight, but a thin layer of fog might obscure the runway, making a safe landing impossible.

Fog is almost always forecast to lift at some time during a day, but the forecast is no guarantee. In the winter, when the sun is low in the sky all day, forecasting the time fog might lift is more difficult. Throw in some higher cloud cover that keeps the sun from warming the layer of fog, and it might stay around all day. With widespread fog the only real approach salvation is in having enough fuel to fly out of the foggy area. A pilot who depends on a forecast of lifting fog will eventually be faced with the dilemma of not having an airport with minimums within reach.

RAIN AND SNOW

Rain adds its own set of circumstances. A visual illusion caused by rain streaming back over the windshield makes the approach look higher than it actually is. The temptation would be to go too low. Low scud, almost down in the trees, often is around when it is raining, and a report of a good ceiling might not hold in the approach area. If the rain has just started and the ceiling is reported good, the next report might be of a low ceiling—clouds forming because of relatively warm rain falling into cooler air. Whenever it is raining, just don't be surprised if there are clouds at or below 500 feet. Snow also might give the illusion of being higher than is actually the case. It is hard to see through, and with heavy snow the visibility might be cut more than in rain, though snow won't streak the windshield like rain does. One added possible last-minute hazard is blowing snow. It can quickly reduce runway visibility to an unsafe low level even though the general weather is fine.

WIND SHEAR

All the recent emphasis on wind shear has added an element of mystery to a rather simple subject. The wind has always changed with altitude and distance when there is a weather disturbance—a thunderstorm, low center or front—or when there is a high-speed jet core aloft. When we are flying en route this relates to turbulence and groundspeed. The National Weather Service uses a change in velocity of 40 knots over 150 miles or 10 knots over 1,000 feet vertically as the guideline for forecasting severe clear-air turbulence. When such changes in wind exist, the air moving at different speeds is disturbed. If you could see it, the air would roll and tumble. Of more interest on approaches is the fact that 3 to 5 knots per 1,000 feet can result in light turbulence; 6 to 9 might give moderate turbulence.

In flying an approach precisely, we have to acknowledge that the wind will likely change during the descent and the air might not be smooth. If, for example, the surface wind is calm or light, but you are really cooking with a strong tailwind at 2,000 feet, you know that a lot of things will change before you land. The passage isn't likely to be a smooth one. The changing wind will affect the amount of power that will be required to track the glideslope. A decreasing tailwind makes an airplane trend high; a decreasing headwind makes it want to go low. A pilot shooting an approach through a thunder-shower gets a great mixture of this; it has proved lethal.

We are taught that stabilized approaches are the way to go, and certainly if the speed and power are stabilized when the airplane starts down the glideslope, the approach will be easier. The wind, though, is not likely stabilized so changes will be required as the wind shifts on the approach, and as the velocity changes. If we think through the changes that are likely to occur in advance, they will be easier to deal with.

ACTUAL APPROACH

I have always been a great proponent of talking to yourself on an approach. Earlier in this chapter we explored how much better two-crew turbines do than singles when it comes to approach accidents. If we work ourselves like a crew of two, perhaps we can swipe some of their advantage. The best way to do this is to make all the same altitude and performance parameter callouts used by crews and do a running commentary on the approach. If you are talking to yourself, you are not likely to fixate on something. If you are worried about your passengers thinking you are nuts, try this: Explain the approach to the passenger as it unfolds. Do tell him to zip his lip—no questions—and you'll do a narrative so he will understand what is happening. In light airplanes, good callouts are 500 and 100 feet above all altitudes used in the approach, plus the target altitude itself, localizer and glideslope "alive" or starting to move toward center, navigational deviations of one dot, and, on final, periodic calls of airspeed and sink rate. Add to this a commentary on the approach. Chiding yourself does indeed help.

MYRTLE

The weather was forecast good for a midmorning arrival at Myrtle Beach, South Carolina. The en route weather, though, had been substantially worse than forecast, so I wasn't surprised when the controller told me that the Myrtle Beach weather was 400 obscured, three-quarters of a mile visibility in fog. There was a lot of fuel in the tanks, and better places were easily within reach if the approach did not work. It would be an ILS to Runway 23. Following a usual procedure, 75 nautical miles to go on the loran signaled time to study the approach plate, set the ADF on the locator, activate the marker receiver, and preselect the frequencies to be used for the approach and missed approach, should one become necessary. The fuel selector was put on the tank best for landing.

The controller this day cleared us down to 2,000 feet early enough for us to reach that altitude and have a little level time before reaching the final approach fix. It is possible to make "dive bomber" approaches successfully, but there is no question that this blips the risk up at least a little. Spending a few minutes level is what you might call "quality time," moments used to psych yourself up for the event that is about to begin.

The glideslope is at about 2,000 feet at the locator; this gives a way to check the accuracy of the glideslope. The inbound bearing is 232 and the decision height 231 feet.

"Four Zero Romeo Charlie, fly a heading of 200 to intercept the localizer. Maintain 2,000 until intercepting, cleared for the ILS approach to Runway 23."

The ILS had already been tuned and identified and, as I have always done, the audio was left on to let the beeping of the ILS continue softly in the background. Back in the bad old days before we had a lot of avionics, all the towers could talk to you over the ILS frequency and that was what we'd use for listening when on the approach. If the airport had ground-controlled approach capability, they would monitor ILS approaches and call you if you strayed. Finally, with it beeping you know it is still playing.

"Okay, sport, two miles from the final approach fix, level at two, on the localizer . . . there's the marker and the ADF reversal, on glidepath, it checks, gear and approach flaps down, power set to 15 inches. There will be a decreasing headwind on this approach that'll make it want to go low, so bring the power up to 16 inches. The localizer is half a dot to the left, not moving rapidly, turn 5 degrees left. Glideslope is good. Speed is 110 knots, in the full-flaps range, hold the rest of the flaps until visual. Localizer is centered, turn a few degrees back to the right. One ten on the speed, sinking five (500 feet per minute), 500 feet to go. Back to the right a hair, little high on the glidepath, power back to 15 inches. Hair to the left, 110 on the speed, sinking five, 100 feet to go, approach lights in sight, full flaps." The approach had worked okay and even the landing was not bad.

Taxiing in, I reflected on the approach. It was one that I had shot a number of times in the past, so there was some familiarity. But my real question, and the question of all who regularly read accident reports related to risk, is: Why, in such a procedural area of flight, does the record suggest that the risk is very high? Why don't we do as well doing that as we do arriving on a sparkling clear day? The only answer is that we can, provided the things that lead to accidents are understood and avoided.

CHAPTER 8

Landing

FIRST PART　Patrick E. Bradley

Landing an airplane is frequently viewed by non-aviators as the most dangerous phase of an airplane flight. The airplane is close to the ground, traveling at high speed, and the pilot must align the airplane so that it sets down on the end of a seemingly minuscule strip of pavement. The thought of this was nearly enough to put me off taking my first flying lesson. At the airport where I started flying, people would come from miles away just to sit outside of the FBO and watch airplanes land—I was one of them. On final, the airplanes always seemed to flinch up, down, and from side to side in involuntary spasms. Then, when the airplanes were about to land, there would be a long floating spell, during which it seemed the airplane would never settle. Or there were the other landings, where the pilots wouldn't begin the float until banging the airplane on its main gear first. Yes, landings certainly appeared to be a handful for the pilot and, although I never viewed any mishaps, I saw a pretty risky few moments for the pilots and his passengers.

Since learning how to land myself, my opinions of the event (and I would still call some of my landings events) have changed. Although some landings can appear quite dramatic, and may even seem pretty exciting from inside the cockpit, I suspect that the landing phase of a flight is one of the safest from the perspective of loss of life. Although the airplane is low to the ground, a normal landing also has the airplane at fairly low speeds. And assuming there is no complete loss of control, it seems difficult to imagine how one could do much more than damage the airplane. Yet, it would be wrong of me to suggest that there are no risks involved with the landing phase of a flight. I would be willing to bet that they arise from the pilot's failure to understand that the success of landing is a product of the approach preceeding the landing.

STABILIZE

I am ashamed to admit that I was a pilot for many years before I learned that the only way to achieve a good landing was to first set up something called a stabilized approach. The notion of a stabilized approach is simple. As soon as possible after turning final, you want to have the proper power setting, the proper attitude, the proper direction, and the proper speed established and stabilized. Although it sounds simple, it requires the sort of judgment and airplane sense that I have yet to perfect with any consistency.

The problem is that outside variables on the final will be working constantly and vigilantly to destabilize the approach. For example, there are changes in wind velocity, there are updrafts and downdrafts, and there are shears. All of them will affect the airplane's approach, and we never know precisely when to expect them. In addition, pilots introduce destabilizing forces from within the cockpit. We jerk the controls and readjust the power to such a degree that it becomes impossible to establish anything remotely resembling a stabilized approach. In the end, it is a pilot's ability to avoid self-induced disruptions while evaluating and responding to the outside forces that will determine whether he will win the holy grail of aviation: a smooth landing.

POWER: LAY OFF

I remember that one of the most common criticisms of my landings made by my instructor was that I "goosed" the power. I never really knew what he meant by that comment. On final approach, I would reduce the power when the airspeed got high and I would increase the power when the airspeed got low. It wasn't until about five years later, after I got my instrument rating and when I was studying for my commercial rating, that my instructor took me out and woodshedded me for that move. I didn't understand very clearly that, for a given power setting and descent rate, you will get the same airspeed every time. Basically, I didn't know that, once you have a stabilized approach, there is no need to touch the throttle on an airplane.

The result of my lack of understanding was that I never established a stabilized approach. I couldn't. Every time the approach stabilized itself, I would change the power setting, which would result in a change in the descent rate. Then, to increase or decrease the descent rate, I would lean on or rare back on the control wheel. This would in turn change the airspeed. And guess what I would do then? As a result, maintaining a relatively constant descent rate and airspeed required continual rapid control inputs that would have been entirely unnecessary if I understood the role and use of the controls.

These days, I begin with a predetermined power level that I set at the end of the downwind or during the base leg of the pattern, when I begin descending. The power setting will yield the target landing speed with full flaps and about 500 to 600 feet per minute descent every time, without fail. Thus, if I turn final at the proper altitude, I only need to deal with a correction for wind. The airplane will descend at the proper rate and at the proper airspeed. Over the fence, I pull off the power and just let the airspeed bleed off as I begin the flare. This will result in the perfect landing. Unfortunately, not many of my landings could be termed perfect.

EYEBALLING A GLIDEPATH

Often, the reason my landings don't always proceed (and end) as smoothly as I would like is that I don't always do such a good job of judging my desired glidepath early on in the approach. The result is predictable; usually I'll end up high on short final with the prospect of having to salvage the approach and landing. To compensate, it will be necessary to lose altitude, which I will trade for airspeed. If I succeed in readjusting the glidepath early enough, the additional speed will bleed off, and I'll be back on a stabilized approach before landing. If I don't, and this often seems to be the case, then I'll land fast, and long, and the airplane may well bounce up and down a few times in my effort to make it stick to the ground before it's ready.

I've heard numerous theories on the best way to determine

whether you're low or high on the ideal glideslope. Unfortunately, I've never been able to find one that's foolproof for me. The most common method I've heard for judging an approach path is to select your desired landing point and note its position with respect to the windshield. Ideally, the pilot freezes that picture and maintains the relationship between the landing point and the windshield. If the landing point begins to move upward with respect to the windshield, then you may undershoot the point and will need power. If the point begins to move lower with respect to the windshield, then you will overshoot the point, and it becomes necessary to decrease power. When you find the airplane attitude and power setting that results in no movement of the landing point, you have a stabilized approach and you hope for no changes in the wind. If there are, you make the minor adjustments necessary for speed and descent rate.

POWERLESS

But what happens when there is no power with which to make the adjustments? This, of course, is the power-off landing. Although most students recall the power-off landing as a drill necessary for the flight exams, the actual application is for a landing made necessary by an engine failure. The difficulty of making a power-off landing should never be underestimated, even by pilots who take some sort of bizarre pleasure in practicing this sort of thing.

One of the reasons the power-off landing is more difficult than most pilots think is because we practice it improperly. I recall in particular when I was practicing power-off landings in preparation for my commercial flight test: I was practicing in a Piper Arrow, and I generally practiced at Tompkins County Airport in Ithaca, New York. I had a great deal of difficulty with the first few landings. I didn't have a good sense of how the Arrow glided with power off. I stayed in the pattern while practicing, so it took just a few attempts before I was able to estimate the point in the pattern at which I should reduce the throttle to idle. Once I got that point nailed down, the task became significantly simpler. During my next lesson, I was able to thrill and delight my instructor with my facility in power-off landings.

What I failed to realize, though, was that I had created a recipe for power-off landings that would work at only one airport for only one runway. If I ever had an engine failure at that particular point, I'd be completely prepared and quite confident during the ensuing emergency landing. If the engine failure ever occurred in any other place, I would be in a world of hurt. This became obvious when my instructor, probably for the purpose of showing me the problem with my power-off landing technique, took me to a different airport to practice power-off landings. He made the task fairly simple. We were in the pattern, and I knew the winds. All I had to do was select the point at which the power would come back to idle.

As you would expect, I tried to fly an approach and select a point that I thought matched my target point back at Tompkins County. It didn't take long to see that things just weren't quite the same. Though I selected the same point in the pattern to reduce the power, I obviously wasn't the same distance from the runway. I ended up seriously short on the approach and was forced to accept the ultimate indignity of having to add power to make a landing where I wouldn't end up pulling weeds out of the brake shoes. As my instructor aptly illustrated that day, when judging a power-off landing, it's essential to judge distances with respect to the total picture, and not with respect to artificial landmarks.

GLIDE STYLES

The first trick in making a power-off landing is figuring out how far your airplane will glide from a given altitude. The first place to look is the airplane's manual, but it will give glide distances in miles per 1,000 feet of altitude; this never helped me much, since I had problems judging distances on the ground from up in the sky. A better method is to learn from experience how far the airplane will glide.

Recently I flew an Archer after having spent most of my time in a rented 182 and Cessna 210. During the checkout in the airplane, the check pilot asked me to tell him when, during the approach to the airport, I thought that the airplane could make the runway with the power reduced to idle. We were flying at about pattern altitude, and I selected a distance based on my best estimate given my past experience. Humoring me, the check pilot suggested that I pull back the power, and I did. I selected a point on the end of the runway as my reference point and set up the airplane's best glide speed. In a few seconds it became obvious that the airplane would never make the runway. The reference point, instead of staying at the same point with respect to the horizon, began to move higher, closer to the horizon than when I started. If this had been a real emergency, I would have had to choose another landing point about two miles closer to the airplane. After a few more power-off approaches, I overcame my usual tendency of overestimating the distance that an airplane will glide. Much of the trick is a matter of experience with a given airplane. But just to make sure, I usually estimate how far I think the airplane will glide and divide that in half.

GUSTS ACROSS THE BOW

One of the variables most detrimental to the ideal, stabilized approach is the crosswind. Crosswinds come in several different varieties with varying degrees of severity and scariness. Perhaps the easiest to deal with is the garden-variety steady breeze across the bow. Adjusting the approach simply requires a crab into the wind to compensate for the wind's tendency to blow the airplane off course. Just prior to landing (usually right over the fence) I dip one wing into the wind, straighten the airplane and plan on touching down first on the main gear on the windward side of the airplane.

Landing with a steady crosswind is a fairly simple matter. It becomes a good deal more dicey when the crosswind comes in the gusting variety. Landing the airplane becomes a matter of usually minor and sometimes dramatic adjustments fairly close to the ground, and I've seen even the most steeled instructors seriously on edge during landings performed by their students in gusty crosswinds. I suppose this is because it is easy to overcorrect for gusts just because they tend to take you by surprise. On the other hand, failing to react decisively to a heavy gust can put you in a serious position. One means I have used to avoid overcontrolling is to be particularly careful not to fixate on the point just in front of the airplane during the landing flare. While it is usually best to avoid much of a flare during gusty crosswind conditions, I find that orienting myself with respect to the far end of the runway is often helpful.

I have found that jolting gusts may not have all that much effect with respect to moving the airplane and do not warrant abrupt responses. As with nearly all other aspects of flying, jerky control inputs are almost never necessary.

IFR TRANSITION

Some of my worst landings have come at the conclusion of instrument flights, and I've thought for a while about why that should be. One reason, I think, is the transition from ILS mode to landing mode. During an ILS, I will seldom have more than one notch of flaps. Depending on when you break out of the clouds, it may be difficult to apply full flaps and stabilize the approach prior to landing the airplane. To avoid this problem, I generally will not even bother to apply more flaps unless I can see the runway at 600 feet or so.

Another reason for my substandard post-approach landings is degraded depth perception. I think when you have spent an entire flight focused on instruments a foot or two in front of you, it is difficult to readjust your focus to the big picture outside of the airplane. After breaking out of cloud on an approach, I usually make a deliberate effort to readjust my gaze to the outside of the airplane and to the far end of the runway, so that my sense of perspective will be more acute than if I follow what seems to be the natural instinct of staring at the nose of the airplane during the final landing flare.

Again, the most important factors in landing after an instrument approach are the same for landing after a VFR flight. Maintaining the glideslope and the proper speed are essential. Just as in a VFR flight, the most difficult phase of a landing occurs before the airplane ever crosses the runway threshold.

SECOND PART   Richard L. Collins

To a lot of pilots, landing is the most challenging and most fun maneuver in flying. Fun? Yes, otherwise why would we go out and shoot landings for an hour or more? The simple fact is that making a good landing does a lot for you, and the chance of making an absolutely perfect landing increases with repetition. Passengers love our perfect landings, but a nonpilot would probably suggest that landings are more risky than a lot of other things in flying. Perhaps that is because, as pilots, we seem to take them quite seriously and appear to be working as hard here as at any other time in a flight.

What are the risks? There are three distinct areas to consider. One is the normal landing, where any accident would involve poor pilot technique in placing the airplane on the ground. Another is the overrun, where the pilot's management of the landing is such that the airplane can't be kept within the confines of the runway. The third is the forced landing, where the airplane is landed somewhere other than on an airport or is landed on an airport with some apparent defect. As you might imagine, the latter is the riskiest. Almost 25 percent of the total and 12 percent of the fatal accidents occur as a pilot attempts to land an airplane somewhere other than on an airport, usually because of power problems but also because of inclement weather, or when he attempts an emergency landing on an airport. Overruns account for 4 percent of the accidents and one-third of 1 percent of the fatals. Hard landings are involved in 6 percent of the total and one-half of 1 percent of the fatal accidents.

To put what should be "normal" emergency landings on an airport in context, we have to go to the multiengine statistics. If there is a total or partial power loss in a multiengine airplane, it is reasonable to assume that the pilot will try to go to or return to a runway for the landing. He paid for that option. Twenty-nine percent of the total and 24 percent of the fatal twin accidents follow a complete or partial power loss. The overall twin fatal accident rate is about the same as for singles, so this would suggest that pilots trying to land twins on airports after one engine fails do but half as well as pilots landing singles off-airport after a power failure. This doesn't quite wash when the actual accident records are examined. In a majority of the cases, a twin pilot never gets to the part about having a shot at landing on a runway. Control is lost on takeoff, or en route after a power failure. Cases where the pilot manages the power failure and lands without further ado don't make the record.

So, the risk has proved not to be high when the airplane is being landed normally on an airport, and relatively high when it is being landed somewhere other than on an airport, or when a pilot flying a twin is challenged to get the airplane to any runway after a power loss. Off-airport landings in singles come out better than average when compared with all other accident types, accounting as they do for twice as many total as fatal accidents. But this is as it should be. An off-airport landing in a single should be a low-speed event; most of the other fatal accidents involve higher speed and less chance for survival.

ON-AIRPORT

There are not a lot of serious landing accidents on airports that do not have strong contributing factors. One resulted in destruction of a Super Cub and loss of life; the NTSB narrative offers an example: "The pilot stated to fire personnel that as he approached touchdown, the sun got in his eyes and a crosswind pushed him off the right side of his private airstrip. The aircraft landed hard on the right wheel, veered off the right side of the runway, cartwheeled down the side of a hill and caught fire after coming to rest. The airstrip is on top of a ridge with 30-degree slopes at the edges of the runway. As calculated, the sun was 5 degrees above the horizon and about 21 degrees right of his center vision reference point. Fire department personnel said the winds were about 45 degrees left of the runway bearing at about 17 knots with peak gusts of 30 knots. The factory flight-tested maximum demonstrated crosswind capability of the aircraft is 13 knots. The private airstrip has no wind direction or speed indicators on the facility."

On a larger airport, that would have been a simple ground-loop accident. We do, when using smaller airports, increase risk. A friend of mine was recently cross-country skiing at Sugarbush in Vermont and skied the airport (open in summer only) that is affectionaly referred to as the S.S. *Sugarbush* because of its size. There's a hump in the middle and the length is not generous. He asked if I ever landed there. The answer was "yes, carefully." No crosswind, light weight, is the only way.

SPEED

In discussing approaches, the emphasis is on getting the airplane to the flare point at the correct speed. If that is done, every landing will be about the same. At times people look at the accident history of airplanes like the Tiger or Musketeer and decide they must be hard airplanes to land, because they are involved in a lot of nosewheel collapse incidents. This has nothing to do with the degree of difficulty on landing. It is directly related to the airplane's tolerance for sloppy approaches. Fly the approach too fast, then try to land the airplane out of a fast approach, land it level instead of on the main wheels, and it will be very prone to porpoise—which is what leads to damage. Normal landings are not a problem in either airplane. And it is unlikely that anyone will get hurt in a porpoise accident, so the degree of human risk, other than ego damage, is low.

TECHNIQUE

If the airplane is flown at the correct speed on the approach and the crosswind is managed, what is the technique for a minimum-risk arrival? Simple. Get the airplane in the landing attitude, tail low for a trike or full stall for a tailwheel in a three-point landing, and let it settle gently onto the runway from an inch high. All that is relatively easy except the one-inch business. Even that part isn't as hard as we make it sometimes because of human nature. Go back to shooting landings. They almost always improve as we go along. Concentration is on landing. But if you haven't flown in a couple of weeks, fly a solid IFR trip of three hours, shoot an approach to minimums with a crosswind landing to follow, and it is hard to get into the one-inch mode. Here the first and lowest-risk order of business is to flare at the proper speed, manage the drift, and get the airplane into a landing attitude. On a trike, that means it will touch on the main gear first. Then, if you have finesse left, by all means paint it on. It is true that an airplane can be damaged if dropped in, that is, let settle to the runway rapidly from a number of feet. And if you slow absurdly high, the nose could actually drop on the rapid settle to the runway. But the average drop from a foot or so is not likely to hurt the airplane, even though it might make the pilot blush over the arrival.

An NTSB narrative relates a Learjet hard hit and remarkable recovery: "Crew attempted ILS approach with indefinite ceiling and RVR-O in fog. Copilot at controls. During missed approach, aircraft contacted runway where glideslope intersects terrain with sufficient force to shear all three landing gear. Right engine spooled down during climbout. Crew diverted . . . and effected no-gear landing. Both altimeters bench-checked within tolerances." That had to be one of the hardest semi-successful hits on record followed by some pretty fancy flying.

THE DELICATE PART

Every flight ends in some sort of landing, arrival, or impact, and the record clearly shows that the risk is low when everything is normal and can be quite high when everything is abnormal. Because it is the touchdown and stop that determines the risk, the discussion rightfully belongs under the heading of landings. It isn't over until it is over and the location and nature of the landing is the key to the amount of risk involved.

TWINS

Pilots buy twins because, even after an engine failure, they theoretically can be landed on an airport. Even if it is not the intended destination, an airport will likely have hard surfaces on which to walk, phones, sodas and crackers, perhaps rental cars, and probably someone to fix the ailing powerplant. Contrast that to where you might land a single after the engine fails. Likely mud, cow pies, or a tree to climb down. Nobody immediately at hand to assist, in many cases, and when a battered and muddy pilot bangs on a farmhouse door, the person who answers may or may not be friendly. Certainly it could take more than a moment to make your plight clear.

Historically, as we have seen, twin pilots have not done well at cashing in on the possibilities. One reason for this might be a fixation on the runway part of the reward. Many twins are lost after a power failure because the pilot fails to recognize that there is no way to get the airplane to a runway and loses control of the airplane trying to force the issue. If control is maintained and the airplane is landed in the best available spot, using the remaining power to tweak the off-runway arrival, the risk is small when compared to that found if the airplane crashes out of control.

An accident involving a light twin some years ago got close scrutiny. The aircraft, on an air-taxi flight, departed from a long runway at a major airport. After takeoff, there was an apparent power problem. There was plenty of open space still left for a landing, but the pilot elected to continue. The airspeed decayed below that required for controlled flight and the airplane crashed, with terrible results. The accident caused a lot of rethinking about aborting or continuing in light twins.

One risk factor to consider in choosing between twins and singles is related to the stalling speed of the airplanes and the nature of their construction. Singles have to have a stalling speed (flaps down) of 61 knots or less. If twins meet a specified rate-of-climb requirement at 5,000 feet, they don't have to meet this stalling speed requirement. So any off-airport touch-down in a twin might be at a speed higher than in a single, and the risk in a forced landing increases dramatically with speed. The other factor is that in the single, the heavy part, the engine, is ahead of the cabin, leading the way, so to speak. In the twin the heavy parts are on the wings, dragging the relatively fragile fuselage between them.

Some years ago, when it was clearly recognized that twins were not meeting their safety potential, a number of steps were taken to address this. One was the development of a minimum safe single-engine speed, Vsse. Before, the speed considered a cornerstone was Vmc, minimum control speed. Trouble was, this was on the brink, being the lowest speed at which you could possibly maintain control after the failure of an engine. Having Vsse gives the pilot, by definition, a means of sorting out the possible and the impossible. If it won't do a healthy job of flying and managing the obstructions when flown at Vsse, things would certainly not be any better at a slower speed, nearer to loss of control.

There is no great store of off-airport landings in twins to use in gauging the risk from this. Most pilots simply do not choose this option when confronted with a power problem, and the pilots who make it to a runway are not in the record book; the others are a clear record of what happens when control is lost.

SINGLES

While landing a single-engine airplane on a runway is something that pilots do without great stress and strain, landing one at an impromptu location is something that would get the adrenaline flowing in even the coolest of dudes. It is not something that we do many times, if at all. All the forced-landing practice in the world probably doesn't help us approach the problem with complete aplomb. But after a power failure in a Cessna 210, for example, you have a minute for each 1,000 feet of altitude and what is done immediately after a power failure probably has a lot to do with the quality of the landing that might follow. Most of the time the possible outcomes are pretty good. But occasionally we fly out of airports in congested areas, or over obscured mountains, or on dark nights; at times like these it is probably best not to dwell on the power failing. The times in flying when we accept risk in return for utility have to be flown with a full understanding and acceptance of the risk. It isn't automatic that you will perish if the engine fails at one of these times—flying the airplane under control into whatever is there has proved at times to be survivable—but the risk does take a quantum leap. The pilot who will do best at managing the risk is the one who applies reason and strong thinking while making the most of the energy that is stored with altitude.

PLANNING

Quick, how many feet per minute does your airplane descend, power off, at what speed and in what configuration?

Most of us don't have this number immediately in mind, but it is important. This is the sort of stuff that the FAA writtens ignore in favor of arcane idiocy about figuring out wind drift based on fictitious forecasts. The answer, at least for my airplane, a 210, is about 1,000 feet per minute at 90 knots. That means for each 1,000 feet high, it will glide a mile and a half if there is no wind. I use that a lot. When flying across Lake Michigan at one of the narrower points, it means that at 16,000 feet or above I am always within gliding distance of a shore. It means when I am flying eastbound on J-152 at Flight Level 210 across the Appalachian Mountains I am almost always within gliding distance of a lighted airport. It also means that if the engine were to fail in IFR conditions, I could at least plan a power-off instrument approach to an airport. I have done that in simulators, and you'd be surprised how an ILS approach can work with no power. It is a matter of knowing the descent characteristics of the aircraft, knowing the wind, storing some energy in excess speed, intercepting the glide-slope on short final, and being rewarded with a landing on the runway. It can work in real airplanes, too. My father once shot a power-off ILS, in weather, at Dayton, Ohio, and landed on the runway without incident. Jeppesen kindly gave him an award for setting the world's record speed for extracting the Dayton approach plate from the book.

TOUCHDOWN

The planning part of a forced landing is important. The actual touchdown, though, is where the final grade comes. And one of the most important risk-related items has to do with hardware. The chances are the stop won't be as gentle as it is on a runway and there are a lot of people with highly altered facial features for no reason other than the fact that the airplane they were flying didn't have shoulder harnesses, or they failed to utilize a shoulder harness. In a quick stop with only a belt, the body heads forward and upward at about a 45-degree angle. When the stretch of the belt and body run out, you stop in the middle and your upper section then crashes downward. The way most people and panels are built, this means that your head, about where the eyes are, contacts the upper edge of the instrument panel. I'm not trying to make you barf, but the bloody mess that results has been documented many times, in many ways. People have lost their sight or their lives as a result. Hopefully we will someday develop real five-point shoulder harness systems for at least the front seats. For now, most of us have to settle for the single shoulder strap which, while effective, is still a compromise. A hard hat would also help, but it is unlikely that we can start a big movement in general aviation to wear crash helmets.

SPEED

Regardless of the vehicle chosen, the speed you begin with and the distance over which an unplanned stop is spread have a lot to do with the severity of the stop. In an off-airport landing, the plan should be to touch at the slowest possible forward speed (consistent with maintaining control of the airplane until the stop actually begins) and to spread the stop over the greatest possible distance. It has often been said that if there are trees, go between a couple and let the wings act as big shock absorbers. This was so widely touted that a student was once rather pleased with having been able to successfully do this on a forced landing. However, his instructor was miffed. The student landed in a big, open field and went between the only two trees in the field.

GEAR

In a retractable, should the landing gear be up or down in an off-airport landing? That depends on a lot of things. The pluses of having the gear down include the shock absorption capability of the extended gear as well as the fact that it will, for a while at least, keep the tender belly of the airplane out of the rocks. The negatives of a wing-mounted gear include twisting of the wings and perhaps rupturing a fuel tank. But you might do this hitting a rock with the gear up. Any gear might cause the aircraft to nose over if the nosewheel collapses and the others remain down. Faced with this dilemma, I would weigh carefully the surface on which the landing is to be attempted as well as the size of the area selected. Then the controllability of the airplane after touchdown would have to be considered. In a gear-up landing it will stop in a relatively short distance, but once it is on and sliding, the controls won't have much effect. With the gear down, there would probably be some control, at least as long as the nosewheel remained operable.

What happens after the engine fails on a single is pretty simple, especially if you can't glide to a runway. An incident, perhaps a crash, will follow the failure. The management of the energy in speed and altitude is ours to use in minimizing the seriousness of the event.

GEAR OTHERWISE

Back to more or less normal landings. Most of us would rather fly an airplane with retractable landing gear because these airplanes are faster and, face it, more satisfying to the old ego. But there is one catch. If we don't remember the gear before landing, or if we inadvertently retract it after landing, the ego gets a blow right in the teeth—to say nothing of the pocketbook. There are gear-up landings that are caused by mechanical problems, but the majority are related to the pilot.

The risk in these accidents is low, but they are still worth avoiding. The FAA will go after your license, the airplane might suffer lasting depreciation because of damage history, and the engine will probably have to be refurbished (along with the prop) because of a sudden stoppage.

Most of us develop a system that helps guard against a gear-up landing. Usually, it is when we bypass this system that we get caught.

For a Cessna 210, I follow the practice of always, without exception, extending the landing gear before using any flaps. Making the gear first establishes it as a priority. When it extends, I look at the main gear on my side and have a passenger or another pilot in the right seat check that side. The third check is of the green light on the panel. And I must admit that I have such confidence in my system that I sneak one last look at the grubby black tire when on short final. The rule after touchdown is to leave everything alone until off the runway, where the flaps can be retracted after a double check that it is the right handle; ditto the cowl flaps.

BONANZAS

I fly Bonanzas some and am especially careful with these because on older ones the gear switch is right, flaps left. Newer ones are vice versa. On one flight, I was returning from Washington National late at night in a Bonanza. The race to the airport at Trenton, New Jersey, was with a nocturnal thunderstorm. I beat it easily, parked the Bonanza, asked the line crew to secure it, and went home. The next day one of the folks at the FBO called and chided me for leaving their Bonanza parked out front with the flaps down. "Would you have rather had it left on the runway with the gear up?"

Airplanes are supposed to have squat switches that will not allow the gear to retract on the ground. These switches don't always work though. And once the mistake is made and the cycle started, there's no turning back. With the FAA in a vindictive mood, a pilot who does this had better have the presence of mind to return the gear switch to the down position after the airplane slides to a stop on its belly, in order to claim mechanical failure. The FAA includes gear-up landings under "careless and reckless operation" for enforcement purposes.

PECULIARITIES

Different landing-gear systems have peculiarities that we tend to learn, one way or the other. It can take a long time to experience some of them, as I did in my 210. The tach was well over 4,000 hours when, one day, the gear-down light would not illuminate. The main gear appeared down, so if there was a problem, it was likely with the nose gear. The bulb was checked as okay, the horn was checked, and the emergency system was operated. Still no green light.

On touchdown, the horn quit blowing and the green light illuminated. Turned out that one of the composite "saddles" that the main gear rests in when extended had come loose and would not allow the gear to quite complete the cycle. My landing did the trick. If the main gear on a 210 appears down and you put the weight of the airplane on it, it will stay extended. The nose gear is another matter.

AIRPORTS

Virtually all landings are on an airport, with no problems, thankfully. But different airports bring a different character to some of our arrivals. I based for years at spacious Mercer County Airport in New Jersey. Nice wide and long runways, no bad crosswinds, ILS approach to get down—all the good things. Then I moved to Carroll County Airport in Maryland, a fine county facility but without all the acreage of pavement that Mercer got because of its role in World War II and as state capital. And landings change when you go from a 6,000-foot runway to a 3,200-foot runway. Gone is a sloppiness about speed, or about being a little high on approach. The margins are all there at Carroll County, but they are based on the pilot doing everything correctly. Each landing became a more enjoyable challenge. I have flown a lot with Patrick Bradley and I think he was ready to hand the airplane over to me when we were landing at Carroll. Never before had I bitched at him about less than 5 knots or less than 50 feet. But the challenge at Carroll is to do it just exactly right.

It's interesting, too, that the quality of touchdowns improved at the smaller airport. One reason might be that the runway is narrower and it is, I think, easier to judge height on a narrow runway than on a wide one. But the primary reason is more likely the effort that is put into flying the approach at the correct speed, crossing the threshold at the same altitude every time.

CHAPTER 9

Dark Is the Night

FIRST PART   Patrick E. Bradley

Often I enjoy flying more at night than I do during the day. On an instrument flight, the airspace and the controllers and the pilots usually seem less rushed and harried than during the daytime hubbub. During VFR flights, the clear, calm evening air, with bright stars overhead and shimmering lights below, provides an ideal backdrop for evening travel. Airplanes fly just as well at night as they do during the day. And pilots don't suddenly forget everything they learned about flying as soon as the sun goes down. At first blush, there is nothing about flying at night that should put off any qualified pilot.

There is always the second blush, the more studied evaluation, though, and it bears serious consideration. When push comes to shove, I do view a night flight as something different, something generally riskier than the run of the mill daytime flight. The reason is not so much changes in the airplane or the air traffic system or even the weather. The changes are actually human. I usually don't operate as well at night for a number of physical and physiological reasons, and because of this, night flights may require compensation and additional care.

GETTING YOUR ACT TOGETHER

One of the most challenging facets of night flying grows out of my simple and natural inability to see as much at night as I can during the day. The problem isn't so much a degradation of vision (although I do understand that night vision deteriorates over time) as it is a lack of complete illumination. One example is a flight that I took about a year ago from Massachusetts to Teterboro, New Jersey. I was running late that evening and, although I had planned for the flight to end before night fell, it was pitch black by the time that I arrived at Teterboro.

Although the weather was VFR, there was a high overcast that limited the illumination of the moon and stars. I was basically operating with my flashlight, the overhead red light, and the panel lights. I was flying on an IFR flight plan, so about 50 miles or so from the airport I reached down onto the floor of the airplane to find my book of approach plates. At the time, I was using the NOS plates, and about five different books had gotten scattered on the floor of the cockpit. It was too dark to read the labels on the books without a flashlight, so I just picked them all up to check them. For some reason, the New Jersey book wasn't in the bunch that I grabbed.

Assuming that I had just missed the book, I leaned over to look on the floor. Not seeing anything but en route charts,

I switched on my flashlight to check more closely. There was still no sign of the errant approach plate book. I started to worry that I had left the book on the ground back in Massachusetts, but I couldn't have, because I distinctly remembered seeing the book while I was looking for the one for Massachusetts. Although the weather was good and I probably would just fly a visual approach anyway, it galled me that I couldn't find the book. It also distracted me. More than once during the episode the altitude and heading began to stray while I was leaning over scouring the cockpit's broadloom with my fingers. Finally, I just gave up. As I expected, I received a visual approach and I knew all of the other necessary frequencies already.

After I landed, I made one last-ditch effort to find the book of approach plates. I got out of the airplane and switched on the full-power white beam of my mega-candlepower flashlight. The book was sitting on the floor of the cockpit, but on the left side rather than the right side, where I had concentrated my efforts. I didn't find the book because it happened to be in a location that remained in the shadow of my leg and the side of the seat. It was just hiding.

BE PREPARED

The lesson of this little escapade was not lost on me. The truth is that it is always more difficult to operate in a dimly lit cockpit. Anything from finding approach plates to reading a frequency from a sectional is going to be more difficult. It pays to prepare the cockpit and everything you will need during the flight. It helps a lot to have another person, and it is even better if you've got another pilot who can help with the navigation, but it isn't essential if you are completely organized.

If I'm going to be making a night flight, I will often prepare a good deal more thoroughly than I would for the same flight in the daytime. In addition to studying the route in some detail, I may make notes on the route of flight along with frequencies and changeover points. If you've got this information, you can use the en route chart for confirming the information that you already know at a more leisurely pace. To the extent possible, I also put the maps and charts in order before takeoff, and I double-check to make sure that every chart that I need for the planned flight and any possible deviations are on board. I never want to be caught in poor weather without a chart that I might need.

Finally, I keep lots of lights around. If the flight is going well, I may only use the penlight that I keep on a string around my neck (I haven't lost that yet) and the overhead dome light. For some reason I feel better with lots of lights around, though. Maybe it has something to do with my childhood.

ALL TUCKERED OUT

Another factor that probably increases the risk factor of night flights is fatigue. If a pilot is flying in the evening, there is a pretty fair chance that, unless he is a professional pilot with duty-time limitations and required rest periods, he has been working a full day before heading back. He may not feel tired, in fact he may feel good, but chances are that by the end of the day, fatigue will begin to take its toll. I have found that fatigue will often cause small insidious errors or oversights which, if not caught, could build up into a serious problem.

I recall one night flight in particular where it took two pilots just to keep up with all of the little mistakes that I was making. Collins and I were on our way back from Wichita, Kansas, after a full day of work and flying. It wasn't until the last part of the last leg of the flight that the day really began to catch up to me. The errors began on the final descent, which generally begins somewhere around Harrisburg, Pennsylvania, and proceeded in steps. Again, the weather was fairly good and the air was smooth, but I just couldn't seem to keep the descent rate and the airspeed and the level-offs under control. Most frequently I found myself fixating on a particular instrument or task that I knew I had to perform. Even worse, I would start to daydream (nightdream?) and before you know it, the airspeed would be inching into the yellow or I'd have just missed the assigned altitude.

The problems continued with botched frequency changes and requests to Philadelphia control for repeats on the instruction. Toward the end of the flight, I found that everything I did required two double checks just to avoid foolish errors. Surprisingly, I found that when I really put my mind to it I could do a creditable job, but the effort had to be deliberate and constant, not something that most pilots are accustomed to, even under the most challenging conditions.

Pilots have to make their own decisions regarding their fatigue level and how far they are able to go to maintain the level of safety they demand. The point to keep in mind when it comes to night flying, though, is that fatigue will frequently play some role in the flight. The wisest pilots give the matter serious consideration before setting off. Personally, I am frequently more comfortable getting half a night's sleep and returning at the crack of dawn.

NAVIGATING THROUGH THE DARKNESS

Obviously, if you are flying along airways and are relying primarily on navaids, there isn't going to be a great deal of difference in navigating through the dark rather than through the light of day. VORs have the same idiosyncrasies at night that they have during the day, and pilots are slightly more prone to errors at night. Otherwise, flying the airways will be relatively simple.

What about navigating by pilotage at night? Although I generally fly on an IFR flight plan at night, I've followed roads, too, and there are both similarities and distinct differences. The most notable characteristic of the night terrain is that it is most often defined by lights on the ground. For instance, if you're flying with reference to the interstate, you'll have no difficulty spotting it or any intersecting roads. They're the ones with the red lights on one side and the white lights on the other. If you are flying over deserted forest area, though, it may appear as though you are flying through a sea of black toward the next large city marked by its incandescent halo on the horizon. (I've often thought that the easiest means of navigating on a clear night would be just to set up a course from city to city, but I haven't tried it.) A lake will often appear at night as a black hole with lights outlining its form. If there are no lights around the lake, it could be very difficult to spot until you are quite close to it. Hills also seem to be defined by the lights interspersed at various levels. Again, your eye receives the general outline and your mind must fill in the finer detail. More than one pilot, though, has run into difficulties when his perceived notion of the mountain turned out to be different from reality.

LUMEN OVERLOAD

Ironically, one of the greatest difficulties that I encounter flying VFR at night in congested metropolitan areas is being (figuratively) blinded by the light. One evening I flew to Teterboro Airport just outside of New York City on an IFR flight plan. The procedure was to fly the VOR-B approach, circle to the active runway, and enter the pattern for landing. The procedure is simple, and one wouldn't think that it would require much more at night than the same procedure during the day. I found out differently, though.

The approach part of the procedure went fine, and I flew the localizer and descended on the approach to pattern altitude. A mile or so from the VOR, I looked down for the runway and realized that it was extremely difficult to orient myself. In addition to a web of highly illuminated roads converging around the airport, there was also the incredible candlepower output of the Meadowlands Sports Complex, where the racetrack and the parking lot were fully lit. Just to the east was Manhattan Island, which throws off a bit of light, too. To tell the truth, it seemed as light that evening as it does during the day, but I found the lights confusing. Ultimately, I flew to the VOR on the field and looked for the dimmest lights I could find. They were the runway lights.

IT WAS A DARK AND STORMY NIGHT . . .

Flying through actual instrument conditions at night can be challenging for many of the reasons described earlier. But there are some additional twists that arise only at night. Although actual IFR refers to flight by reference to the airplane's instruments, pilots often learn a lot about the weather just by looking outside of the airplane. For instance, you can get some idea of where a line of thunderstorms is brewing most violently by the darkness of the cloud bases. And you can often determine whether a cloud is packing a wallop by the presence of telltale wisps at the base.

These signs, and the entire tenor of the clouds, become more difficult to distinguish at night. It's not easy to tell whether the cloud is just a menacing black or the black-and-bluish color that indicates how you and the airplane will look if you try to get too close. True, it is much easier to see the direction from which lightning is coming at night, but I've found that the flashes are so dispersed, and light up such a broad area, that this indicator is helpful only as the broadest type of thunderstorm avoidance.

DRIFTING INTO THE MIST

The darkness presents even greater challenges for VFR pilots tangling with marginal weather. The dangers are a result of a number of factors, the most significant being the ease with which you can find yourself in clouds. On a dark night, it can be quite difficult to detect slight variations in visibility.

During the day, you can usually tell when the visibility is dropping. You can see haze become thicker, and you can sense that you just can't see as far now as you could before. Once you've made this assessment, you may decide to proceed and evaluate further as you go along, or you may decide to land or turn around.

My few experiences flying through marginal weather, though, have illustrated how deceptive visibility changes can be on a dark evening. One summer night, flying along on an IFR flight plan, I was cruising at 2,500 feet about 25 nautical miles from my destination. For most of the 25 nautical miles, the ceiling was hovering at about 3,000 feet, so I was dividing my attentions between the cockpit and the outside traffic. Everything was fine until I diverted my attention inside the cockpit for a few moments, perhaps to open a chart or locate an approach chart book. When I looked up, I suddenly got the odd, off-balance sensation that accompanies vertigo. Though I could see the lights of the ground below me, I had flown into a cloud and entirely lost sight of the horizon. I shifted my attention back to the instruments, but I was surprised that I could fly into a lowering ceiling without even knowing that the ceiling had dropped. This particular evening was quite hazy, and that may have had something to do with the unexpectedness of the encounter, but the experience is one that could become a more serious matter for the VFR pilot in a similar position.

SECOND PART   Richard L. Collins

As they say on stage, folks, this is the biggie. Night is where we do the absolutely poorest job of managing risks in flying. No matter what statistic you look at, for whatever phase of flying, the fatal accident rate is always substantially, usually dramatically, higher in darkness than in light. Often when we pore over accident reports we miss that. For years the NTSB didn't include the condition of light in accident reports (they do now) and researchers had to use sunrise-sunset tables to determine whether or not it was dark when the accident occurred. In its regulations on weather minimums the FAA doesn't usually discriminate between daylight and dark. The only night-flying proficiency requirement addresses takeoffs and landings, not where a large number of the serious night accidents occur. They might argue that the requirement is why there aren't a lot of serious night landing accidents, and there might be something to that, but the fact remains that a lot of serious accidents occur in other phases of flight at night and these are not addressed in our training and currency rules.

SCARY?

The day before this was written, I flew an 800-nautical-mile trip. The weather was grungy, with the airplane in cloud most of the way at Flight Level 190. Another pilot was along, and he flew most of the en route phase of the flight. When we started the letdown, though, he passed control of the airplane back. The descent was through almost solid cloud; only below 6,000 feet did we encounter layered conditions. The air ranged from smooth to light chop. The clearances were quick and direct and the final clearance was for a VOR approach to home base, Carroll County Airport in Maryland. There is no weather reporting there, but the reported ceiling at nearby Baltimore suggested it would be a marginal approach as far as ceiling was concerned. The visibility, though, was 5 miles, which was a positive for completion of the approach.

Because Carroll County is home base, I have some extra procedures that I follow there. One is, no circles for a north landing unless the water tank on the north side of the town of Westminster is in full view during the circle, and the circle can be flown without straying over the tank. That ensures that you do not fly over two higher radio towers south of the tank and defines a way you can safely circle for a north landing without flirting with the obstructions that dictate the relatively high minimum descent altitude. As I descended toward the 754-foot minimum, the situation appeared iffy. Then, at minimums, the runway hove into view. A quick little review of the business about having the runway in sight at minimums and being in a position from which a normal landing can be made ran through my mind. I was almost in position for a straight-in to Runway 34 (the wind was out of the north) but had too much airspeed, so it would have to be a circle. The minimums are the same for either approach. So I set out on what is, at best, a scud run, making my tight circle and landing.

No big deal, and what does this have to do with night flying? This approach was shot in the daytime. There is nothing on the approach plate that suggests anything should be different at night. Yet the demands, and the risk, would increase immeasurably on that approach if it were dark. Flying around over the Maryland hill country at night, with obstructions around, circling low and looking at the runway in the distance, trying to adjust airspeed and altitude in the turn, would simply be a first-class way to fly into the terrain at a speed high enough to make survival a doubtful proposition. By day I could see what I needed to see and what I wouldn't be able to see in the dark.

EVEN WITH PRECISION

As we noted earlier, even ILS approaches are fraught with some peril at night. At least pilots seem to botch them more often at night than they do in the daytime. Which has to lead us to an introspective look at why pilots crash more at night than in the daytime.

The first factor has to be the condition of light in the aircraft. Everything is harder to see at night, and we do have to divert some attention from aircraft control to manage the relationship between flashlights or cockpit floodlights and charts. If we need something from the back seat, floor, or right front seat, it is not apparent at a glance. Some auxiliary lighting might be necessary. And where is that flashlight? It had best always be in the same place. I keep mine on the seat, between my legs. The effect of cockpit lighting should not be an overwhelming addition to risk, but it is a factor. To make a night approach without diversions and distractions caused by the light level in the cockpit, we have to have a plan that gets everything set well in advance and leaves our limited vision free to concentrate on the instruments and what little there is to see of the outside world.

The second factor is the time of day. In the wintertime, much of our night flying is done in normal waking hours, but there is still the likelihood that the flight is being conducted after a day of doing something else—working or playing. There just has to be a level of fatigue that would not have been present earlier in the day. Some people can psych themselves up for fatigue flying, some cannot.

On a recent flight, a quite talented pilot had flown three long legs—big headwind that day—and the third one was to conclude in the dark. That he was quite fatigued was shown by minor altitude excursions and one other item that has always been evident in fatigued pilots. When he was supposed to set the bearing selector on 230, he set it on 250, 10 degrees on the wrong side of the prominently marked 240 position. So I was watching the proceedings closely.

The approach was a visual to a major airport and everything progressed okay until it became apparent that, were we to land on that long runway, we had to start down. Even though he had made two perfect daytime approaches, I had to offer advice on application of full flaps and reduction of power. Still, we landed 3,000 feet down the long runway. The pilot had not professed being current at night, but I feel that his misjudgment of height had more to do with his being fatigued from a long day of flying.

HOW DO?

So how do you work around this? Every pilot has to have a procedure for dealing with fatigue, and its development is an individual thing. Personally, I have found that a series of checks and double checks, combined with a running narrative of what I am doing (helpful at all times) keeps the mind active enough to preclude any lapse into fatigue-induced mental numbness.

One of the best examples of this came at the conclusion of a long day, during what I would classify as a difficult approach. Another factor was personal. It was the first time I had flown solo after a bout with the flu. The medicine I had taken was far in the background and I had flown with other pilots and felt okay. But it was a bad bout, and I had let almost four weeks go by since the onset of the flu without flying alone, just to be sure I was back up to speed.

You might say that this would be a time to pick an easy flight. And I didn't think I had picked a hard one. Arrival would be just before dark. The forecast called for ceilings above 1,000 feet with just a chance of a thundershower. The en route forecast suggested I would be on top for the 440-nautical-mile flight from San Antonio to Little Rock. The tailwind would be good, ensuring arrival with a good condition of light.

We do have to be ready for whatever is dished up. First, the flight was not on top at 17,000 feet. Then, when ice started to form at that level, and the turbulence (not in the forecast) became uncomfortable, I descended to 9,000 feet. That meant that the groundspeed decreased. Then a broken line of thundershowers had to be managed, using the radar and Stormscope. Because it was a northeast-southwest line, roughly parallel to where I was going, I tried to find out if the line extended to Little Rock and, if so, was it northwest or southeast of the airport? I sure didn't want to fly through it twice. The controller couldn't help on that. I got the Little Rock weather, and because the surface wind was out of the northwest, I made the decision that the front was past there and that I should get on the west side of the line and head on in.

OOOKAY

Bad decision. As I got closer, the approach controller said that most of the weather was northwest of the airport and the best thing for me to do would be to parallel the line until northwest of the airport and then fly southeast through the lightest area of weather. By this time the Stormscope was popping and a lot of precip was evident on the radar. It was also getting dark. The trip was eventually to take almost an hour longer than planned.

On the southeast heading, I could see that it would be necessary to fly through a lot of precip to get to the airport. The storms were based at about 9,000 feet, which often happens in that part of the country when a shallow cold front slows or stops and the warm and moist overrunning air aloft keeps pumping out of the southwest. I picked a spot with no red (heavy precip) on the radar ahead and asked the controller if I could fly 120 instead of the 100 that he suggested. He said that was fine. There was a lot of wind-shear turbulence but nothing convective at the lower altitudes. It being nearly dark, there was lightning frequently visible. I was number five for the approach, so would have to fly for a while yet.

The easy flight had turned out to be less than that. And while being number five was not what I would have liked, if you launch it you have to take your turn and fly it until you land.

I was trying to put together a picture of the relationship between a strong cell to the southwest and the approach, and when the controller turned me back toward the localizer, I mentioned that it looked to me like I was about to intercept. No, he said, you are 5 miles south of the localizer. Tilt. After a moment of confusion, I realized that I had tuned the localizer frequency but had either not pushed the transfer button, or had not pushed it hard enough. I was still tuned to the VOR. Th relationship I had developed between the weather and the localizer was wrong.

That, I told myself, is a clear warning. I had been concentrating on the weather and had not been talking to myself with a running narrative of what was going on and had not been doing the double checks. Flying in turbulence and avoiding the worst part of the weather had precluded getting other things in the correct order. I went through a quick reorientation, visualized my present position, and started talking to myself about what was happening and what I was doing.

Because of the weather, I suggested to the controller that I turn on the localizer just outside the marker. He concurred. That is not as easy as getting established on a 5-mile final, but it was what needed to happen. By this time I had psyched myself up to a high level of concentration and was driving my mind to comprehend all factors. If I missed the approach, there would be more difficult flying, probably to an alternate because of the stronger cell that was advancing on the approach course and the airport. I was determined to fly the ILS with precision—the only thing that would make me miss would be weather below minimums. And in all modesty I will say that this night ILS after a full day of work and a far more difficult flight than anticipated worked out with some degree of precision. But, had it not been for that moment of confusion when the nav radio was tuned to the VOR instead of the ILS, would I have awaked from a weather-flying (but not navigating) trance? And had it been a non-radar environment, would I have caught the mistake as quickly, or at all? It made me resolve to double up on my double checks at night.

NIGHT AND DAY

That flight started in the daytime and was influenced by the fact that I had worked all day. And the climax came at night, even though it wasn't planned that way. Had I known the level of difficulty that was involved in advance, I might not have made the flight. But once in the situation, the only way down (all stations were worse than forecast and the chance of thunderstorms was coming true almost everywhere) was to sit up straight and perform. I suspect that this happens to us more in the dark than the daytime and that a peak in the level of difficulty of a flight is often what leads pilots to make lethal mistakes at night.

MORE SERIOUS

In one sample of recent accidents, 30 percent of the fatals occurred at night. There is no clear agreement on how much flying is done at night. The FAA has indicated that it is 15 percent. Surveys of active general aviation pilots have always revealed a much lower number—somewhere between 5 and 10 percent. If the number is higher it is probably because of the folks who fly all night carrying cargo, packages, checks, and mail. These pilots know, for the most part, how to manage the unique risks of night flying and have a pretty good safety record. At least they do much better than the rest of us, who fly only occasionally at night. By day we might have thousands of hours of experience. But if we have only flown 200 hours at night, for example, when the sun sets we become 200-hour pilots.

Night accidents tend to be more serious than those in the daytime, which is one reason the percentage of fatals is so much higher. In this sample, over half of the total accidents that occurred at night were fatal. It is quite similar to the picture in weather accidents, where the airplane is flown into the ground in control but at a high speed, or hits out of control. Neither is conducive to survival.

A LIST

To better form a picture of how the risks at night collect on pilots, a review of a list of what might be called typical night accidents sheds light on the subject. These are from NTSB narratives and are shortened to illustrate only the risks unique to night flying.

". . . On his arrival he entered the traffic pattern on a right downwind leg to Runway 35. This pattern was contrary to the published pattern and the lighted segmented circle visual traffic pattern indicator on the airport. He was unable to complete his first attempt to land and made a go-around. After climbing past the departure end of the runway the pilot made a steep left turn of approximately 225 degrees. This turn placed the aircraft on a right downwind to Runway 35, and it descended into high-voltage electrical transmission lines."

It was a dark night with scattered clouds, and you can imagine that the 450-hour pilot would not have descended into obstructions in the daytime, when the visual clues of height on downwind would have been better.

MARGINAL

". . . As the aircraft was descending toward the airport, the pilot reported that he had entered fog at about 4,000 feet MSL. The controller instructed the pilot to climb and maintain VFR, then asked if the pilot would like a localizer approach to the airport. Although he was not certified for instrument flight, the pilot accepted the approach. The airport weather at that time was reported (in part) as 1,500-scattered, visibility 7 miles. Vectors were provided for the approach. As the aircraft was approaching the outer marker, the pilot was instructed to change to tower frequency. He acknowledged but there was no further transmission from the aircraft and radar contact was lost. Subsequently the aircraft crashed approximately 5 miles east of the airport."

It is difficult to see clouds on a dark and hazy night, and where a VFR pilot wouldn't likely have a lot of trouble with the weather conditions that existed in the daytime, this pilot lost control of his airplane and crashed in the darkness.

ILS

"After failing to see the runway on his first ILS approach in weather reported at IFR minimums for landing, the pilot was radar vectored for a second approach. According to controllers, the approach appeared to be normal until the aircraft's radar target disappeared off the scope approximately 2 miles from the runway. Ground rescue found the aircraft impacted on a fog-shrouded ridge in the vicinity of where it disappeared from radar."

The accident records have always contained a lot of examples of pilots crashing on approach after missing one and trying again. Why would the risk increase on a second approach? Trying harder to get down to an altitude from which you can see would be the most logical answer. Couple that with the distractions of night for a really bad combination.

LONG DAY

"The private, non-instrument-rated pilot overflew his home airport by 23 miles upon returning from a night cross-country flight and descended into a hill. Instrument meteorological conditions were reported in the area due to reduced visibility. The pilot had flown ten hours during the last twenty-four hours."

The visibility was two miles in haze which, for VFR navigation at night, is not much.

CHECK LIST

"Witnesses stated that the aircraft started the takeoff roll, became airborne about 1,000 feet down the runway, climbed to an altitude of about 50 feet, rolled to the left, and crashed inverted onto a parallel taxiway at about midfield. . . . Examination of the wreckage revealed that the fuel selector for the right engine was on right main while the selector for the left engine was on the auxiliary tank. The operating manual states they should both be on mains for takeoff."

Would the pilot have caught the position of the left engine fuel selector in the daytime and corrected it before takeoff? There is no way to know the answer to that, but it is probably safe to say that managing an engine failure properly would be easier in the daytime than on a dark night.

OUT OF GAS

". . . As he approached the vicinity of Athens, Georgia, he informed ARTCC that he would like to divert due to low fuel; however, the closest airport was below minimums. The next closest airport was his destination. While being vectored for an ILS approach, the engine lost power due to fuel exhaustion. During a forced landing, the aircraft hit trees, then crashed to the ground . . ."

We always like to say that if you maintain control of the aircraft until contact is made with something, your chances are pretty good. This pilot maintained control and, according to the NTSB, there was minimal compromise of the cabin area. The pilot apparently had on a shoulder harness; evidence indicated that the passenger did not. Yet both apparently hit the instrument panel, according to the report, and both perished. An extenuating circumstance in this case was operation at a relatively high cruise power and rich mixture because the engine was being broken-in after work. But a number one item of managing the risk from engine failure (day or night) remains not running out of fuel, regardless of circumstances.

BROKEN

"Pilot experienced loss of power during cruise flight at 6,000 feet. Aircraft vectored toward Daviess County Airport, 10 miles away. Pilot reported aircraft on fire. Witnesses saw N9307V in a left bank turn, then nose-dive into ground. Post-crash exam of engine revealed number three cylinder departed from crankcase. Further exam revealed the throughbolts/nuts were undertorqued . . . Metallurgical examination of bolts/nuts revealed fatigue failures and 'working' of the number three cylinder for a long period of time."

This Mooney was within gliding distance of an airport when the failure occurred, but the pilot lost control of the airplane after reporting that it was on fire. The failure itself has to be considered as primary, and it is not often that you find the actual mechanical failure of an engine at night to be occurrence number one on the NTSB's list. The FAA requirement that an airframe and engine has to have only an annual inspection might be enough for some, but many pilots who use airplanes at night and IFR at least have 100-hour-type inspections on the engine at the appropriate time. No guarantees, just something that works toward the reduction of risk.

CONFUSED AND DISORIENTED

"The pilot-in-command had flown his aircraft from Springfield, Missouri, to Olathe, Kansas, to have some repair work accomplished and was to return that same day. The pilot never returned to Springfield. The pilot had flown to Salem, Illinois, where witnesses stated that they observed that he was confused and disoriented. The pilot tried to return to Springfield the next day but stopped short at Rolla, Missouri. Again witnesses at Rolla stated that the pilot was confused and disoriented. The pilot was on the prescription drugs Tenormin and Librium. Both of these drugs have warnings that include confusion and disorientation as side effects. Weather at the crash site . . . included low ceilings and fog, and the pilot was not instrument rated. The forecasted weather for the flight to Springfield was VFR."

The NTSB found that physical impairment was the probable cause of this accident, but the weather does illustrate one of the risks of night VFR. Weather is harder to forecast at night, and when areas of fog form away from reporting stations they may or may not be detected on a timely basis.

STUDENT

"The student pilot with no simulated or actual instrument and a total of nine hours night flight time called the Amarillo FSS, which briefed him on weather for a flight from Borger, Texas, to Big Spring, Texas, located 210 nautical miles south. He was briefed on marginal VFR weather en route and instrument meteorological conditions weather with ceiling of 800 feet at destination. He also was advised of a weather frontal system expected to move into the area overnight with widespread IMC by morning. He departed on the night VFR cross-country, but failed to arrive at the destination. The flight was reported missing nine days after takeoff. The wreckage was located 84 nautical miles west of course in flat, very remote range land. The aircraft impacted in a left wing low, 30-degree nose-down attitude."

The attempted flight would have been a very difficult one to fly VFR, even if the pilot were experienced and had an instrument rating.

SO IT GOES

In years of researching aviation safety, the same patterns have always been there in relation to night and your "average" general aviation pilot. Pilots who fly a lot at night tend to get by without an abnormal amount of trouble. They apparently know the risks and keep them at bay. The rest of us tend not to do as well, trying as we do to take the FAA's regulatory word as an indication that there isn't a lot of difference between day and night flying. All of us, though, should be able to study the risks of flying at night, stay current, and eliminate all but the one related to mechanical failure. And, it has been said before but is always worth repeating, this might have something to do with the night record. Most pilots are so concerned with the question of what happens if the engine quits at night that the other risks are not properly managed. Some could, simply, feel bulletproof unless the engine quits. Then an airplane with a perfect engine is flown into something.

CHAPTER **10**

Midair Collisions

FIRST PART   Patrick E. Bradley

One day on a flight that was taking me up the east coast, near Providence, Rhode Island, I received the following warning/notification from ATC:

"Cessna 53 Uniform, be advised we're showing numerous targets in all sectors along your route of flight. Altitude unknown."

And that was it. In terms of grabbing my attention, this warning ranked up there with the "traffic, twelve o'clock, opposite direction, fast moving" warning that pilots sometimes kid about.

My first thought was simply to turn around and flee for safer territory. Numerous targets. Altitude unknown. I felt as though I was flying into a meteor storm, or perhaps crawling through a mine field. What made the experience even more eerie was that I could not sight a single one of these numerous targets. Most likely, the airplanes were down low, taking advantage of the beautiful weather to get in some flying on a Saturday afternoon. And with this in mind, I proceeded on my way with somewhat heightened awareness of what was going on around me. But when it got right down to it, what could I do to ensure my safe passage through this apparently heavily congested portion of the east coast? I could look out the window, but after more than one encounter requiring immediate avoidance, I'm less than certain that this is the answer to a collision-free flight. So often it is just too difficult to spot other airplanes until they are on top of you or already by, unnoticed.

For a time, I held the fatalistic view that there is no good way to avoid a midair collision, so why bother trying? I have also held the view that midair collisions are almost always avoidable if the pilots have been following the appropriate collision avoidance procedures. Now I believe that, to some degree, avoiding a midair collision depends on luck. It just seems unrealistic to think that, given human limitations and equipment limitations and the structure of our air traffic system, all collisions are avoidable. On the other hand, pilots can follow certain procedures and guidelines that will greatly reduce their risk of becoming one of the unfortunate ships that "did not pass in the night." By following certain rules, it becomes possible to reduce the risk of a midair so dramatically that a collision becomes the result of wicked bad luck rather than bad technique.

EYES OPEN, HEADS UP

The number one rule for avoiding other airplanes is, of course, "watch where you're going." I learned this from day one, but there is a difference between knowing the rule and actually following it. This was impressed upon me most emphatically several years ago when I was receiving some commercial instruction at FlightSafety International in Vero Beach, Florida. It was my first lesson, and I was, of course, very much concerned with impressing my instructor. I completed the preflight inspection and the startup, apparently to his satisfaction, and it was time for the takeoff.

The drill was to establish the best angle of climb speed up to a certain altitude and then increase the speed for the best rate of climb up to another altitude. The gear was to be retracted when landing was not possible and, of course, I would need to adjust the manifold pressure and rpm for the climb. There was also a heading for me to follow. The instructor wasn't asking me for anything unusual, but I wanted to get it right, and immediately after liftoff began to work on best angle speed, cleaning up the airplane, and flying the heading.

I was pretty pleased with my performance when I heard, over the din of the engine, the instructor saying something that I hadn't quite caught. "What?" I said.

"Heads up," my instructor said, raising his voice. I still wasn't sure what he meant, which I suppose my expression indicated.

"Keep your eyes outside the airplane," he said in a voice suggesting that his self-control was requiring more effort. "This is a busy traffic pattern," he said, "and that stuff"—he gestured toward the instruments—"isn't going to help avoid a collision." My instructor then proceeded to spend half the lesson showing me how to scan the horizon for other airplanes. Looking back, I think it was one of the most valuable lessons I've ever had. I could see that serious pilots really took this traffic avoidance stuff seriously.

IFR FLIGHT PLAN:
MAGIC SHIELD?

Another misconception that I labored under when I first got interested in flying IFR was that pilots flying on an instrument flight plan are under radar control, and that they no longer have to remain alert for other airplanes. I viewed an instrument flight plan as a magic shield that would protect me from any encroaching airplanes. While I was partially correct—airplanes flying IFR are separated from other IFR airplanes—I was wrong in thinking that IFR aircraft are separated from VFR aircraft as well. It remains critical for a pilot flying on an IFR flight plan to keep a weather eye out for other airplanes that may not be under ATC control.

This situation becomes particularly difficult in low-visibility conditions where you may be inbound for an approach, flying with reference to your instruments. Although you may have decided to make the flight IFR, there may well be VFR aircraft out there coming in from the deteriorating weather or just scud-running to where they're going. If you know there are other VFR aircraft still operating in the pattern, or if you think there may be, then it becomes necessary to shift your attention outside of the airplane as well, which can sometimes present problems. Regardless of the tendency and desire to concentrate on the IFR aspects of the flight, the pilot still has an obligation (to himself, especially) to keep an eye out for airplanes operating VFR. It's like adding another instrument to your scan. Depending on how bad the conditions are, the additional scan probably won't result in more than an inconvenience. It could, though, prove very valuable when you find

yourself neck and neck on downwind with the Bonanza that
was reported to be on final.

TOWER'S NOT-SO-WATCHFUL GAZE

When approaching an airport control area for landing, it
isn't at all unusual to receive vectors or special instructions that
allow the tower controllers to maintain the flow and separation
of airplanes. In fact, sometimes after establishing contact with
the control tower it's easy to fall under the misapprehension
that the tower has assumed responsibility for the separation of
the airplane from other airplanes. Unfortunately, though, this
just isn't true. It becomes important, then, to remember that
even though the tower may be relaying fairly specific instructions regarding the terminal operations of the airplane, the separation burden is still squarely on the shoulders of the pilot.

I recall a recent experience where I called Teterboro Tower
to inform them that I was VFR at the Alpine Tower, one of
the standard reporting points, and that I was inbound for
landing. Teterboro acknowledged my call and told me to proceed to the airport for a straight-in landing on Runway 19. I
was feeling pretty lucky to have scored a straight-in until I
heard the controller giving the same clearance to another airplane. Even worse, the other airplane had reported that he was
just north of the George Washington Bridge at 1,500 feet. I
could not have described my position any better, and I began
craning my neck to spot the other airplane.

Directly after the second airplane reported its position, the
tower advised me that there was other inbound traffic from
my direction and asked me whether I had it in sight. For all

of my looking, I couldn't spot the other airplane, and told the tower so. This continued for the next few minutes with both me and the other airplane reporting nearly the identical position at the same time and neither of us being able to spot the other. It was like an aerial game of chicken, with neither pilot wanting to duck out of the approach, but neither of us wanting to make contact other than visual.

About 4 miles from the airport, neither of us had the other in sight, the tower still didn't see either of us, and I decided that I had had enough. I believed that the other airplane was east of me, to my left, and I called the tower with an offer/request to make a 360-degree turn to the right to assure separation. Directly after my call, though, the other airplane reported a 2-mile final. With this information, I finally was able to spot the other airplane, about a mile and a half in front of me descending to the runway. I announced that I had the other airplane in sight and began to slow the airplane for landing.

Although we were in a controlled environment, neither of us was flying a standard pattern, where one airplane can generally spot the other and both are in sight of the tower. In our case, neither airplane could see the other, and neither of us was in sight of the tower. Looking back on the experience, I think that I should probably have suggested a little earlier and a little more strenuously that I deviate to put more distance between the airplanes.

UNCONTROLLED OR OUT OF CONTROL

I would expect that one of the more dangerous situations for midair collision risk would be entry to the pattern of an uncontrolled airport. Having learned at and flown from an uncontrolled airport for many years, I know that there is nothing inherently dangerous about an uncontrolled airport. The problems begin when pilots behave as though the rules of the road are suspended because there is no tower. If anything, the need for firm rules and strict adherence is even more important at an uncontrolled airport. It is essential that pilots, whether in the pattern or entering the pattern, know what to expect from each other. The only way to ensure this, it seems to me, is by operating from the same instruction manual.

I recall a few years ago taking a biennial flight review at a small uncontrolled airport that I had not flown from before. The flight went quite well until the very end, when, after performing the requisite stalls, steep turns, slow flight, and chandelles, I was to return for a landing. Since I had not flown with this pilot before, I wasn't aware that he was a stickler for pattern procedures. This was particularly difficult, because at the time I was flying regularly from a controlled airport and had grown quite lax in my uncontrolled pattern procedures. What I thought was the end of the flight became the beginning, as we reviewed and I finally demonstrated the basics of good pattern procedure.

PATTERN PRINCIPLES

My transgressions began in entering the pattern, and they continued until I got both wheels on the runway. As I was to be reminded, the standard entry to a traffic pattern is at a 45-degree angle on the downwind leg. There's nothing special about this entry, except that everyone is, or should be, familiar

with it. Pilots in the pattern know where they should be looking for other entries.

Next, I was a bit lax in scanning for other airplanes. It is
important to look for other airplanes not only directly in front
of you, but also on either side. Some pilots, like me, tend to
fly very close patterns. Other pilots prefer a wider pattern
perhaps to give themselves more maneuvering room and time.

Just as important as scanning for other airplanes is announcing and listening, which is one area in which I received
a passing grade straight away. At an uncontrolled airport it is
particularly important to announce your position on downwind, base, and final. Although the unicom can sometimes get
so noisy that it seems not worth fooling with, close listening
and faithful announcing has saved me more than once. It's
also important to advertise your actions while on the ground.
Where there is confusion regarding the active runway, announcing your takeoff may be one of the few ways of alerting
other pilots in the pattern that one of you is wrong.

PREDICTABILITY

Fortunately it is a big sky out there, and the chances of
two airplanes meeting at the same piece of that sky at the same
time are remote for most phases of flight. There are the other
phases of flight, though, and in them the key to separation
becomes predictability. If you stay where you are supposed
to, or where convention dictates that you ought to, chances
are you will see and be seen.

A good example of the value of predictability is the single
VFR corridor throught the heart of the New York TCA. For

a long time I wouldn't go near the corridor, thinking it just too congested and too much of a free-for-all to be safe. More recently, though, I flew up the corridor with another pilot and saw that, even though it is quite congested, it can still be fairly safe.

The corridor runs up the Hudson River, below 1,100 feet. The Hudson is perhaps a half a mile wide at this point, so all of the airplanes passing through are going to be at about the same altitude and the same place. The way that collisions are avoided is by following the rules of the road. Northbound aircraft hug the right side of the river while the southbound airplanes stay on their right, just like cars. In addition, there is a special frequency for use by aircraft in the area to announce their positions and destinations. Because of the TCA, there is no crossing traffic and no descending traffic. As long as everyone follows the rules and keeps his eyes peeled, it's possible to keep the risks within acceptable limits. The critical factor here, and in avoiding collisions anywhere, is "following the rules and keeping a lookout." A failure of either of these factors can, and regularly does, result in disaster.

SECOND PART   Richard L. Collins

The sky was crystal clear and the visibility unlimited as we streaked westbound in a business jet, VFR and level at 16,500 feet. There were two of us up front and one on the jump seat, which afforded him a good view outside. We called ourselves looking for traffic and were all aware that there would probably be some because we were flying near a major metropolitan area. And all three of us became aware of the presence of an airline twinjet at about the same time—eleven o'clock, opposite direction, fast moving, close, descending through our altitude. I was at the controls and instinctively started a turn to the right, but when the airliner was first sighted it was obvious that he would pass to our left, closer than any of us would have preferred. If the relative position of the other aircraft is changing in the windshield, he will go by. If the relative position is fixed, you have a problem begging for a solution. Had we been 300 feet farther south or he 300 feet farther north, you might have read about this in the newspaper rather than here.

So here you have perfect weather conditions, five pilots, and an air traffic control system on which we have spent billions and that is supposed to give IFR airplanes information on other traffic, especially that above 12,500 feet, where altitude-reporting transponders are mandatory. There is even a computer conflict-alert system in place that should have made a call on this. We had been running level for a while, so no maneuvering would have confused the system. We were VFR; fly IFR all the time, you say. Maybe that helps, but one dark night west of Pittsburgh the controller, rather frantically said, "Sixty RC, turn right immediately." The number was wrong but we (Bradley was flying that night) turned right immediately. A moment later an airline captain said, "What was that?" We were IFR at Flight Level 210; through some mixup the airliner was apparently descending through our altitude.

LESSONS

These two incidents illustrate a lot of things. When IFR in VFR conditions, as was the DC-9, you are still supposed to look for other traffic. True, the controller is supposed to call traffic, but if for some reason he doesn't, see and be seen is the only game in town. When you are going to be VFR above 12,500, as we were, it probably pays to try to establish contact with air traffic control even if you are going to be up there for only a few minutes. Had we been speaking with a controller, chances would have been far better for a traffic call and vector. On the IFR incident, we did all we could have done. But it is still a good practice to try to stay aware of the controller's big picture. To isolate ourselves in the system doesn't help us understand what is going on. I like to listen to what the controller says to everyone, to understand his problems and traffic flows. Occasionally controllers make a mistake; who knows, an alert pilot might catch it and help avoid an incident. In either case, VFR/IFR or IFR/IFR, had we connected, upon whom would the blame have been laid? Probably on a combination of factors.

Collisions do have to be put into context. The air carrier–general aviation collisions are rare and random events. Each time one has occurred, the FAA has taken steps to prevent that kind of accident. The Mode C veil proposal (requiring Mode C within 30 miles of an airport with a terminal control area) was a direct result of the collision between a DC-9 and Piper Archer within the Los Angeles TCA. The TCAs themselves came from three collisions in the late sixties. The expansion of the TCAs came as a result of the collision between a Skyhawk and a 727 at San Diego. The requirement for Mode C above 12,500 feet was an attempt to preclude incidents like the one related at the beginning of my part of this chapter. The collision at the Grand Canyon in the late fifties brought positive control above 18,000 feet, among other things. Even the requirement for two-way radio at control towers can be traced to an accident, a collision between a surplus fighter aircraft and an airliner at Washington National in the forties.

With all this regulatory history, it is apparent that the FAA has taken on the task of managing the risk of collision between airline and general aviation aircraft. That does not mean pilots are off the hook. The FAA requirements affect what we have to do. Buy Mode C and learn to navigate precisely around TCA and ARSA airports. Do this, then recognize that the compression of VFR traffic into limited airspace increases the risk of collision with another VFR aircraft while reducing the risk of collision with air carriers.

One remaining inherent risk of conflict is at airports with infrequent airline service, especially regional airline service. The management of risk there is relatively simple. Flying IFR ensures separation to the best of the system's ability. If flying VFR, squawking and talking on the applicable radio frequencies is the procedure. Even at the most remote airfields served by commuters there's a published frequency to use in announcing intentions and positions. As everywhere, keep up an active scan for traffic.

BUSY AREAS

Around busy areas, we have a remaining chore that is left to pilots. Airline aircraft approaching for landing at Newark, New Jersey, for example, are often below 10,000 feet 50 or more flying miles away from the runway of landing and well outside the New York TCA. Under certain traffic-flow conditions, airline aircraft might be as low as 3,000 feet outside the TCA. In other words, they are mixing it up in what is considered good VFR airspace. I well remember a Concorde ride up the Jersey coast, at low altitude, outside the TCA. The autopilot was left to fly the airplane while all four sets of eyes on the flight deck scoured the sky for VFR traffic. As far as see-and-be-seen goes, the slower aircraft is at a marked disadvantage, and this crew recognized that fact. The only way for a collision to occur is for the slow one to begin out front of the faster one. It can even be going in the same direction (as was the Skyhawk at San Diego) and get hit. Because of this, the pilot in the slower airplane might not have a real opportunity to see and thus avoid the faster airplane. In busy areas, it thus becomes a game of strategy, procedural avoidance strategy. Personally, when flying VFR around the New York TCA, I either use the low-level corridor up the Hudson River, or skirt it at a minimum safe altitude to the west and north. By so doing, the risk of collision with faster airplanes is minimized.

Something that is coming soon is the collision avoidance system. Initially the airlines and probably business jets will have this and it will certainly be a valuable new tool. For the first time, pilots will have precise electronic intelligence on other traffic (provided the traffic has an altitude-reporting transponder) and a system that will give collision avoidance commands. Eventually costs will come down and it will become available for more airplanes but, one, it is just another tool, not an end-it-all and, two, while twenty-five years from now we might have far fewer midair collisions, the possibility will still exist as long as we let more than one airplane fly at a time. The worst collision in history occurred on the ground, between two 747s in the Azores, and would not likely have been prevented by the collision avoidance system.

STATS

The annual number of midair collisions has not changed much over the years. They account for just under 2 percent of the total aircraft (two per collision) involved in accidents, or about fifty airplanes a year. But, as you might imagine, they do account for more fatalities. Is it automatic that having a midair is the end? Not really; about half the collisions result in fatal injuries, some years more, some years less. If it were not for that, I wouldn't be writing this book, but we'll get to that in a minute. Searches of the records have not shown an abnormally high involvement by high-wing airplanes. In fact, while there are collisions between airplanes flying cross-country and others, the "typical" midair is between two training airplanes, within 5 miles of an airport. To show, though, that no aircraft is immune, even in areas with low traffic density, there was a midair between a departing ultralight and an arriving Learjet at Auburn, Alabama, fatal to the Learjet first officer and the ultralight pilot.

EN ROUTE

There have always been a few en route midairs every year. And when these are studied with an eye toward minimizing this risk, we don't find a lot of answers. If you either fly IFR or get VFR traffic advisories, some of the traffic might be called some of the time—it is a secondary duty for controllers and many of them are fully occupied with keeping IFR aircraft separated. They are often not able even to offer the service.

Flying random routings instead of airways and avoiding the immediate area of navaids is often a way to go, but in some parts of the country, this isn't easy because of military operating areas, where we can fly but where the risk from high-speed traffic increases dramatically. Still, loran makes this easier and if you have it or a VOR/DME area navigation system, the airway can be paralleled and the military operating areas avoided. The same thing can be done with charts and dead reckoning, which is something that we often forget. When bypassing a major traffic area, remember that inbound fast traffic usually crosses 30 to 40 miles out at 10,000 feet if you want to practice procedural avoidance.

LONESOME

Now we get to the see-and-be-seen part of en route flying. There is some high-visibility hardware to help here. Strobes help, especially when the visibility is a bit reduced. Because of the history of general aviation aircraft being hit from behind, the brightest possible light on the tail is the best deal, and I have always wondered why pilots don't go for this more often. A transponder with Mode C gives the best possible "see" to the controller who might give a fast airplane a 20-degree turn that converts a near incident or accident into a friendly passing in the sky. Then we get to the hardest part, seeing other traffic. The reason it is so difficult is that it is lonesome up there. Once you move away from the busy spots and start flying somewhere, you seldom see other airplanes. That is good, sure, but it tends to lull the senses. Most of us fly through a career with no aerial encounters; many do it without ever having to take evasive action, especially en route. So how is it that you maintain interest in crawling all over the cockpit, minimizing blind spots while looking for traffic? It is taught that the best way is to sectorize your scan, letting the eyes stop in each sector to take it in for a moment before moving on to the next. That is good, and effective, but how many of us are able to do it for the total en route course of a flight, on a methodical basis? As we have evolved into more cockpit complexity, more time is spent running the machine and less looking outside. This is one area where an autopilot can be a real help. Get it and everything else set when operating in VFR conditions, let it fly, and spend more time looking outside.

BIG SKY

We do have to face the fact, though, that when en route most pilots get by as much because of the size of the sky and the relatively small number of airplanes as because of vigilance. Flying from Maryland to Arkansas on a perfectly clear day, the only other airplanes spotted were airplanes at high altitiude, easy to see because of their contrails; aircraft near terminal areas; and one en route IFR aircraft that was called as traffic. Another pilot was flying and not once did we, through our vigilant and methodical scan, find another en route airplane on our own—and this on an absolutely perfect winter flying day. We weren't even able to find all the aircraft called as traffic. You can't see a small airplane much more than 3 miles away, and when looking for one lower with a complex visual background, they can seldom be seen at 3 miles.

It would be foolish to relegate the business about en route collisions to fate and the big-sky theory and just enjoy a newspaper and cup of coffee. While not too many of them occur, they do occur and are an identifiable risk that pilots should try to manage. Hard as it may be to keep interest in scanning alive, it might someday make the difference between daylight and dark.

AROUND THE AIRPORT

Airports are like the small end of a funnel. The traffic is coming from random directions. As it nears the airport it enters the large end of the funnel and eventually all exits the small end and plops onto the active runway. The large end of the funnel might be a number of miles away from the airport in a major terminal area where, because of TCA restrictions on VFR aircraft and procedural handling of IFR aircraft, traffic is bunched together pretty far out. Or, at an idyllic little airport out in the country it might be considered the entry to downwind leg. Or, if the pattern discipline is bad, it could be the final approach.

Even though we emphasize arrivals—and more collisions involve arriving than departing aircraft because the former are converging and the latter are diverging—the departure comes first and has to be considered.

One strong advantage of a VFR departure is that you can search the sky from the safe haven of the ground before launching. With the sophisticated radar systems on high-performance fighters, the crew does a radar search before one of those spectacular takeoffs and climbs. In general aviation airplanes, a slow 360 on the ground before takeoff can reveal traffic. After takeoff, the conflicts with arriving aircraft have to be considered, especially if you are climbing out on downwind leg, where another aircraft might be descending. I like to get a little farther away than the normal pattern before heading off in a direction that would conflict with arriving traffic. In climb we have to be aware that most airplanes flying level will be going faster and that we'll be under the nose of those airplanes, thus hard to see. By the same token, we don't have much rearward visibility. Back in the good old days we did a lot of S-turning to clear the air about to be used. Perhaps this has a modern application.

ARRIVING

It is in arriving that we face the biggest chore. The Falcon that collided with a Piper at Teterboro, New Jersey, was arriving. The DC-9 that collided with an Archer at Cerritos, California, was arriving. The DC-9 that collided with a Baron at Urbana, Ohio, was arriving. The DC-9 that collided with a Cherokee near Indianapolis, Indiana, was arriving. The 727 that collided with a Skyhawk in California was arriving. The DC-8 and Constellation that collided over Staten Island, New York, were both arriving. In most of the others, the second aircraft was either passing through the area or on arrival. At Hendersonville, North Carolina, the 727 was departing and the 310 arriving, an illustration that while arrivals pose the greatest demand for risk management, departures can't be ignored.

CHALLENGES

When I was based at Mercer County Airport in New Jersey, arriving was always a challenge even though it was usually done IFR. Mercer is a satellite airport for Philadelphia, and the procedure they use is to get the satellite traffic low, far out, and underneath the inbound traffic for the primary airport, Philadelphia International. That meant we had to fly past some relatively busy airports at relatively low altitudes, mixing it up with their traffic. The radar coverage is good, starting with Harrisburg approach control 100 miles west of Mercer and proceeding through Reading's area and then into Philly's. But it was always a time of heightened interest and, if flying a high-performance airplane, a time perhaps to slow to less than the legal speed to be better able to spot traffic which included, at various times, sailplanes and balloons in addition to the usual fare. If you stop to visualize the random flows of traffic that feed both the large and small airports in a congested area like Philadelphia, it is easy to see that the VFR airspace is, of necessity, like a supermarket parking lot without lines. It can also be understood why the busy controllers don't have time to call all the traffic.

The time I liked flying in the area least was at night. There probably is less traffic after sunset, but seeing and avoiding the traffic becomes much more difficult. True, if the airplane is above you, the strobes and beacons will make it easy to see, and a quick determination of closure can be made. But if it is below, against a matrix of lights, it will be hard to see and the task of determining whether the aircraft is a threat will be more difficult. Many times I've had traffic called that I could not find, even though it was reported relatively close. Out in the country, where there are fewer lights present on the ground, other aircraft are easier to see.

UNCONTROLLED

When flying in a radar environment from a controlled airport, it is easy to become complacent. Someone else is watching out. But this isn't true: it is a false sense of complacency. A tower operator is really a runway referee. Sure, he'll try to tell you about any traffic conflict that he sees, but he may not see all of them. Nor may a radar controller see, or have time to call, all of the traffic. Don't forget that the Cerritos collision occurred in the LA TCA. The San Diego collision occurred in the traffic pattern of a controlled airport. So did the one at Teterboro, to name the most recent and spectacular.

Still, it is common to feel better at a controlled field than at an uncontrolled. And I experienced this when I moved from New Jersey to Maryland, from Mercer County, where I first started operating in 1958, to Carroll County, a pleasant single-strip general aviation airport. But one thing is key to collision risk management at Carroll County and that is the single strip. At times I fly from Frederick, Maryland, which has two runways and is not controlled. It is where runways cross and there is poor pattern discipline that the collision risk increases.

BACK TO THE PAST

Which takes me back in time to the early fifties. The day was a nice one and the student a sharp one. He was nearly ready to solo, but the crosswind was a bit much for the north-south runway, so we were using the short runway, directly into the northwest wind. The runways didn't actually cross; the short one began about 200 feet after you passed over the long one.

The student was doing well, but the approaches took a little coaching because the runway length was marginal, even for a J-3 Cub. We were well into the session when, on short final, I became aware of an intruder. The airplane was in view, in my peripheral vision, there was a loud noise, and the airplane was gone, followed by another loud noise. And I realized that the Cub was still flying. The first instinct was to add power, to keep flying. This, though, caused a lot of vibration, and the only clear course of action was obvious: land quickly. This I did, and on touchdown I came to realize that the landing gear of the Cub was partly broken. We scraped to a stop on the runway and ran back to a Cessna 120 that lay thorougly crumpled on the other runway. Approaching, I saw the owner of the 120, whom I recognized, standing by the airplane. When within speaking distance, I said, "Who was flying your airplane?" He turned to me with a dazed look on his face and said, "That's the worst landing I ever made in my life." He hadn't shared my brief glimpse of another airplane trying to occupy the same piece of air. The bad fortune was that probably the only two airplanes within 50 miles had collided; the good fortune was that, other than the other pilot having his bell rung quite loudly, we were okay but wiser. To this day, when landing where there is a crossing runway I scour the sky for anyone who might be landing on that other runway.

TRAFFIC PATTERN FREQUENCY

One of the good things that has come to uncontrolled airports since that event has been the traffic pattern frequency, or common traffic advisory frequency (CTAF). I like the former term because it is what my father, Leighton Collins, used when proposing the formalization of the use of unicom frequencies for position announcements in the pattern of uncontrolled airports. Properly used, this can bring as much order to the pattern of an uncontrolled airport as a controlled one. The weakness is in the fact that use of it is not mandatory. And anything like being in radar contact or using the appropriate frequency is only good if we don't let it induce a false sense of security. A no-radio airplane is just as unpleasant in a collision as is one with a radio.

Position announcements can help us find each other in a traffic pattern. A predictable flow of traffic also helps. While it is legal to make a straight-in or left base entry at most uncontrolled airports, this has to be weighed against the risk of other traffic. Flying a full pattern gives the advantage of time in locating and sequencing with other traffic. It also gives more identifiable points for a position report. If the flying is at the proper altitude, the other airplanes are easier to spot. Probably the riskiest thing in a pattern is to be descending and flying quite fast. A lot of training is done at smaller airports, and the average speed of a trainer in the pattern is under 100 knots.

A potential problem, but one that has not caused a lot of trouble over the years, is the mix between VFR aircraft in an uncontrolled pattern and IFR aircraft, when the weather is marginal. I was departing from Auburn, Alabama, one grungy day and right after liftoff spotted a Huey helicopter off to the right, about a half mile away, paralleling my course. I called Columbus, Georgia, approach control and asked them about this traffic. They told me, in no uncertain terms, that Auburn was in uncontrolled airspace, the VFR requirement is 1-mile visibility, and that we just had to look out for ourselves.

FIXATION

As in so many other areas of flying, fixation on one thing can lead to a neglect of the proper scan for other aircraft. In cruise, this is a direct result of seldom seeing other traffic even when you try hard: Nothing out there; the mind goes on to the other elements of flying from here to there. Closer to the airport, the chance of seeing another airplane is better, so there is some motivation. But it is still possible to be completely distracted by another, stronger influence.

The ceiling was 600 feet and the visibility a couple of miles as I worked into a VOR approach to an uncontrolled airport. I had never been to the airport before and was working hard to fly a precise approach. The runway is at right angles to the final approach course; when I saw it I wasn't in a good position to enter a downwind, so I overflew the airport and came all the way back around in a pattern. It was raining, and I wasn't taking in the surrounding scenery but was keenly aware that shooting at a short wet runway in a 210 with the wind calm would require good short-field technique. Everything looked fine and on final a check of speed and approach slope suggested the landing would work well. The landing itself was a thunker, but it was on the money, and I could have stopped in half the runway.

In retrospect, though, I have to get a bad grade for the arrival. I never even gave the first thought to the possibility that there might have been a VFR airplane in the pattern. The VOR approach and then the visual circle and plan for the landing was so totally engrossing that, other than an initial call for an altimeter setting, I didn't make the pattern calls and undoubtedly did a poor job of looking for, or even thinking about, other traffic. That it was a grungy day shouldn't have mattered. The weather was legal for VFR and someone could have been out there shooting landings.

KEEP ALERT, WATCH FOR OTHER TRAFFIC

I always thought the near-collision reporting system to be an inaccurate method of judging collision risk. A near collision is simply a non-event, with the nearness left up to pilots who had a fleeting glimpse of another airplane. How startled a pilot might be is determined by when the other airplane is sighted. In the case of the passing of the airline twinjet related previously, my heart didn't even go pitty-pat because, when the airplane was first sighted, it was obvious that we would pass safely, if closely. The startle factor would have been higher if the airplane had been spotted a second or more later. Startled, I might have considered it a near collision. Otherwise, no. The point is, in managing the collision risk, we have a large enough statistical base of collisions to know that while they can and have happened in almost every phase of flight—high and low altitude, close to and far from the airport, with every conceivable mixture of airplanes—there are places where the risk is higher. A lot of the risk has been addressed by regulations and, as much as we dislike some rules, the system works pretty well. But there are still peaks, especially at uncontrolled airports, in training areas, and in areas where VFR traffic is compressed because of airspace restrictions. But no matter where we fly, the key is in feeling like there might be another one out there, on a possible collision course. Find him and fly safely on.

CHAPTER **11**

Special Weather
Considerations

FIRST PART   Patrick E. Bradley

Flying airplanes presents a wide range of challenges to pilots, but I find the most demanding (and fascinating) to be the weather. Weather is a factor in every single flight that a pilot makes, whether it involves the direction the wind is blowing or the temperature at cruise altitude. But there are a number of special weather considerations that tend to garner a lot of attention, if for no other reason than the degree of risk they pose to pilots and their airplanes and the general lack of knowledge on the part of pilots regarding the finer points of meteorology.

I am a good example of a pilot who has flown through a relatively wide range of weather conditions but who is not well versed in the finer points of meteorology. As a result, I frequently find myself approaching and dealing with weather from an "operational" perspective—on the basis of what I see, what flight service tells me, and what other pilots have reported—rather than from an understanding of how highs, lows, and frontal systems work.

My approach works for the most part, but I frequently

253

encounter new weather variations that leave me with lots of questions about how I should deal with them. At other times, while I may have encountered certain weather conditions before in an airplane equipped with weather avoidance equipment, I may be somewhat unsure of how to deal with the situation in an airplane without such amenities. In either case, the more experience I gain with weather, the more questions I have. I keep threatening to pick up a meteorology book.

THUNDERSTORMS: WHAT'S IN A NAME?

When flying through areas with lots of cumulus clouds, I sometimes wonder when one of these benign-looking but bumpy clouds crosses the line from cumulus to cumulonimbus. In other words, when does a puffball become a thunderbumper? Even more important, when flying along at, say, 5,000 feet, how is a pilot to know when a cumulus cloud is tall enough, and has sufficient convective activity, to make it too dangerous to enter? The question here is one of degree. If there is sufficient moisture and instability in the air, a run-of-the-mill cumulus puff will become sufficiently dangerous to warrant a wide deviation. When does this happen, though? And, even more important for the operationally oriented pilot like myself, how is one to know?

I suppose that the best way of knowing when you are confronting a thunderstorm or a thunderstorm about to be born is with radar or a Stormscope. If the old Stormscope is showing spark patterns, you can be fairly certain you are looking at a well-developed storm. Likewise, if the radar is painting lots of red, then it's reasonably clear that there is also a corresponding level of convective activity. Problems arise, though, when you are droning along without the benefit of avoidance gear. If you're dealing with a full-blown thunderstorm, chances are that you will see either the ominously dark colors or the rain shafts that leave little doubt of the gravity of the situation. In some ways, the bad thunderstorms are the easiest ones to deal with—they make their presence known early and you can begin the deviation correspondingly early.

QUESTIONABLE CASES

There is another class of cloud, though, that may not rise to the level of a thunderstorm and may not have the dark appearance of a thunderstorm, but can still pack enough of a wallop that you won't want to go anywhere near it. The problem that I frequently run into with these clouds is knowing how much of a wallop they are likely to pack and how far away I should stay. The problem, for me, generally arises when flying at a relatively low level near the base of the clouds. On a recent flight, for example, I was flying at around 6,000 feet on an IFR flight plan. I had been making valiant efforts through most of the flight to deviate around the cumulus clouds. They didn't look like they held too much sauce, but to tell the truth, I couldn't see the tops of the clouds, and the turbulence around the perimeter of the clouds counseled caution.

After an hour or so of zigging and zagging, though, I began to tire of the effort, and at one weak point, let my guard down. I came to a bevy of clouds that would have required a deviation of 5 or so miles around and then as many miles back onto course. I knew that I should just fly around, but the clouds looked so fluffy and friendly I decided to take the shortest distance between two points. With the sense of speed and abandon that one feels only when plowing into a cloud, I plunged forward for the yardage. The cloud parted, but within seconds, I knew I had made a mistake. So did my passengers, whom I did not warn. Immediately, the airspeed began to build and I had to lean into the control wheel to keep the airplane from launching upward. I got the throttle back and was able to slow the airplane down to maneuvering speed. The next moment, though, we all saw stars. It was a solid, perfectly timed, and perfectly placed uppercut to the chin, followed by rapid-fire jabs to the midsection. This cloud was not particularly fluffy and friendly and, by the time I escaped, tail between my legs, I gave some serious thought to landing and checking the airplane for popped rivets.

GAUGING THE BUMP FACTOR

Although they can often be quite unreliable, I probably should have at least attempted to obtain tops reports to get some idea of how unstable the air was and how bumpy the clouds would be. I have been told that in general it is unwise to even attempt to fly through a cumulus cloud with tops at over 10,000 feet. The problem, again, is getting a reliable read on how high the tops are if there is a stratus layer above you or if you simply can't tell. I was at about 6,000 feet during this flight and, using this guideline, it would have been a good bet that the clouds were high enough to be rough even if I couldn't tell exactly what the tops were.

Another method of helping to predict the severity of bumps in a developing cumulus cloud is to check the temperature changes at various levels. If the temperature change is greater than 2 degrees centigrade per 1,000 feet, then it is probably unstable air, and the likelihood is that the turbulence is going to be uncomfortable enough that few pilots will want to mess with the cloud.

WHAT YOU CAN'T SEE
CAN GET YOU

Another dilemma that I have stewed over on more than one occasion is the presence of embedded thunderstorms. An embedded thunderstorm is hidden from view by the stratus clouds generated in connection with the associated weather pattern. Thus, you could be cruising along in the clouds and run the risk of encountering a full-fledged thunderstorm. I don't think the risk is so much that I won't know that I'm encountering a thunderstorm—certainly there will be sufficient turbulence and precipitation to remove all doubt of this—but that I really won't know when or where to turn to evade the thunderstorm before I actually enter it.

Pilots confronted with the embedded thunderstorm scenario don't have many choices and, unlike most other weather encounters or potential weather encounters, there aren't many choices if you do end up encountering storms. I recall, during one flight, running into thunderstorms in the midst of the thickest and calmest murky precipitation. At first, I could sense the danger from the increase in the turbulence. After that, I began to encounter very heavy rainshowers. I was debating

whether to attempt to get vectors from ATC around the
weather or to descend lower beneath the ceiling when the
approach controller just gave me a vector "to avoid the thunderstorm" directly in my path.

Although I gratefully accepted the controller's assistance,
it is never desirable to be in the position of having to rely
on ATC for weather avoidance. Often the controller cannot
or just will not provide the information with the reliability
that I like before shoving off on a flight into questionable
weather. The only other alternative, flying beneath the
clouds, often is not particularly desirable. In some situations,
the ceiling will just be too low to fly beneath and remain
on your IFR flight plan. The other alternative is to climb
above the stratus layer and fly between the thunderstorms.
Again, this could be limited by ATC and the airplane's capabilities. Where all else fails, the best approach is probably
to land and cool your heels while the thunderstorm moves
on to trouble someone else.

ICICLE TIME

With the exception of thunderstorms, the phenomenon
that I find most difficult to deal with is airframe ice. All pilots
learn early on in their careers that, in certain conditions,
water droplets which are supercooled to temperatures below
freezing will form on the airframe of the airplane and will
reduce the airplane's lift and efficiency. The real difficulty
with ice, however, is the problem pilots have in predicting
where icing may occur and in deciding what to do once it
does occur.

Although my experiences with significant ice (the type that requires action) have been relatively few, I have spent a fair amount of time worrying that I would encounter it. The problem is that, on the east coast at least, it seems as though there are few weather reports or forecasts that do not make some mention of various possibilities and probabilities of icing in visible moisture. The difficulty is that anytime you fly in a cloud when the temperatures are at or below freezing, it is possible for ice to form on the airframe. The accumulation could be gradual and steady, or it could be sudden and dramatic. Whether you will encounter gradual, dramatic, or any ice accumulation at all, though, is apparently difficult to predict with any certainty, even if there is access to accurate weather information. And therein lies the difficulty for pilots.

RULES OF THE ROAD

In situations where there are reported icing conditions for your selected route and altitude, there is little for the pilot to decide. A pilot on an IFR flight plan will have to find another route or altitude unless he has approved deicing gear.

Most frequently flight service seems to forecast the "chance" of icing. And in such a situation, that wouldn't seem to preclude the pilot's going up for a look. The burden, then, is on the pilot to evaluate the conditions and to make the final decision. Usually, where there is no report of actual icing, moderate or worse, and where there isn't any other information indicating that you're going to pick up a load, I usually feel obliged to take a look. But because the prospect of picking up substantial ice is so ominous, I always try to have a plan for dealing with ice before the possibility becomes reality.

FINDING THE FRIENDLIER ALTITUDE

I was always taught that the first step to take upon learning that you are accumulating ice is to find a different altitude. Because airplanes don't climb well when iced up, the prevailing wisdom is to climb higher while the airplane is able to. By doing this, there is the possibility of climbing to a colder altitude, less amenable to icing. Since I get spooked at the first sign of ice, I almost always immediately request a higher altitude. Also, when the request for the higher altitude is preceeded by the mention of ice, there are few controllers who won't bend over backwards to assist you.

The ideal situation is to climb above the icing conditions, and, even better, out of the cloud altogether. Where I am unable to climb out of cloud, though, and where the ice continues to accumulate, I usually don't waste any time asking for a lower altitude. The hope is that the temperature will be sufficiently high to prevent the accumulation of ice or that I can descend beneath the clouds.

What happens where there is icing at all levels and the ceiling is too low to permit cruise under the clouds? This is the stuff of nightmares for pilots, but, nonetheless, it's a contingency for which we must plan. I suppose that the only choice is to head for the nearest airport and execute an approach and landing with all due dispatch.

NEW AERODYNAMICS

Even if it is possible to make it to an airport, landing an airplane carrying ice can be a new and different experience— no matter how many times you have had the misfortune of attempting it. In addition to adding weight and drag, ice changes the aerodynamic qualities of the wing. Because of this, I was always instructed not to forget two things: first, don't even think about using flaps for the landing; second, maintain power and airspeed until the runway is made. The reason for these warnings is that the effect of lowering the flaps will be completely unknown where the airplane is carrying ice. Even one notch of flaps could result in an untested airflow over the horizontal tail and a loss of pitch control. The reason for holding power is that you really don't know what the airplane's stall speed will be with the addition of the ice, except that it will most likely be a good deal higher. The obvious approach, then, is to play it safe and to leave as wide a margin as possible for surprises.

SECOND PART Richard L. Collins

One look at the title of this chapter suggests that it is going to be about low ceilings, thunderstorms, ice, and high surface winds. And those things will be addressed, but long ago I did some research into weather and my flying and found one factor that was more important than all those time-honored and very real elements. It has to do with your location. When at home and headed out, I found that I had some cancellations due to weather every year. But when out and headed home, I found few, if any, cancellations. That is a little scary, so I went back through my logs to see if I was tackling weather that I should have been culling. It wasn't really so, but the exercise did suggest at least that when headed for the hearth at home, perhaps I put more effort into dealing with whatever is there. Other folks might do the reverse. Whatever, when considering the types of weather that have proved unhealthy for pilots and passengers, it is best to weigh the reason that the "start" decision is made, and, along the way, to think about why the "continue" decision is made. A sign of a good pilot is the ability to scratch a flight regardless of the reward that would come from continuing that flight.

LOW CEILINGS

Low ceilings when VFR are rather cut-and-dried items. The risk is extremely high when we are scud-running, because the ground is close and the slightest miscalculation can put the airplane in contact with pretty solid stuff. Most "Continued VFR" accidents, as they have come to be called, are fatal because of the speed involved. Anyone who presses on VFR in marginal weather is running an almost extreme risk and should be aware of that fact. It doesn't help to have an instrument rating or a lot of scud-running experience. It is just a flat dangerous operation that leads to a relatively high percentage of the accidents every year. Either the airplane is flown into terrain, or it enters clouds and the pilot loses control.

The IFR deal is a better one, but still involves some increased risk. And the risk is really the same as when VFR. As long as we follow the approach procedure, everything is fine. It's when we get to the part about maneuvering for landing that the trouble starts. In truth, like it or not, the last part of an instrument approach involves scud-running and the associated risks. The best way to manage the risk is to separate desire from reality and to fly the approach as an exercise in keeping the airplane out of the weeds, not one of completing the approach. One factor is very important here: fuel. In approach accidents, fuel is often a factor. If the supply is low, the pressure to complete the approach is strong. Any pilot who has flown much IFR has been in a situation where all the forecasts have gone to pot, and where the mind is just not overflowing with thoughts about what to do next if this approach is missed. That is indeed a risky time in life and one that should have been avoided with a fuel stop a while back.

THUNDER

Thunderstorms, probably more than anything else, strike fear into the hearts of pilots. And, indeed, there is probably no worse place to be in an airplane than in the midst of a thunderstorm. Avoidance of them is deeply rooted in several things, none of which is magic. Suspicion is one, caution is another. What you see counts for a lot. Finally, we add the electronic devices that can help—airborne weather radar, ground radar, and a Stormscope or other detector of electrical discharges. The electronics were listed last on purpose. A lot of pilots view them as magic, and as giving yes or no answers to the question about going straight ahead, zigging, zagging, or cutting and running. They do not do this. They give additional information for a pilot to use in making a plan. I'll hasten to add that the information they give is very valuable.

A lot of folks feel that the risk from a storm is in the turbulence being so bad that it breaks the airplane. That isn't always true. A 30-foot-per-second vertical gust is the requirement for strength in most light airplanes. It was later increased for newer certifications, but the criteria for the gust was changed to soften the onset, with the result that there is probably little difference in actual strength. Also, some designs have been tested to destruction and have often proved to be much stronger than the certification requirements. Even at the requirement, a Normal Category airplane bends at 3.8 g and breaks at 5.7 g. That is a lot of load, and if the builder went, say, 30 percent further, then it would be at 7.4 before breaking. Also, the gust consideration is at the top of the green on airspeed and hopefully most of us fly them slower than that when turbulence is in the offing.

Before you go away thinking that the airplane is tough enough for anything, put 30 feet per second into context. It is less than 20 knots. How many thunderstorms have you seen where the first gust exceeded 20 knots? The first gust is an indication of the up-and-down activity within the storm and, in truth, in thunderstorm research flying, vertical gusts far in excess of 30 feet per second have been measured. They come as quick pops, too, which is hardest on the structure of the airplane.

Still, most thunderstorm accidents don't involve a turbulence-induced overload of the structure. There are some, and there have been some involving airliners, but if there is a "typical" thunderstorm accident, it would be one in which the pilot lost control of the airplane in turbulence and the actual failure of the airframe was a result of exceeding the design limits and the pilot overloading the airframe with control inputs.

POSSIBLE?

Which brings us to the real question. If you do everything incorrectly and wind up inside a thunderstorm in a light airplane, is it possible to control the airplane and survive? Certainly you wouldn't want to just give up and start listening for the angels to sing through your noise-attenuating headset. If ever there was a time for a pilot to try and calm himself and be smooth with the airplane, this would be it. The airplane is being tossed and twisted, and loaded to near its limits. The pilot can add to that load with jerky control movements, or he can at least leave it be with smooth flying. Altitude and precise airspeed control is not really possible; the key is in avoiding a loss of lateral—roll—control. If ever there is a time to concentrate on the attitude indicator, this is it. If you are trimmed for maneuvering speed—the proper procedure—the airplane will try to take care of pitch excursions. It will pitch nose up or down in response to gusts, but the old nose will go back in the right direction once the gust is by. But the airplane lacks this stability in roll; there it must be controlled, and it is in roll control that we insulate ourselves from a loss of longitudinal control. If the vertical speed is showing a mad dash for orbit or the ground, the airplane is not out of control if the wings are level. It is just riding with the currents of the storm. There is an altitude below which you must not go if the ground is to be avoided, but in cruising flight it is unlikely that the storm will dash you to the ground. In mountainous terrain, it might put you below ridge levels or otherwise cause the airplane to be in a difficult position in relation to terrain, and this would have to be considered.

STRUCTURE OF THE STORM

It helps to understand the structure of a storm. This lets us visualize what will happen to the airplane as it passes through. This is totally basic, but it serves the purpose: The storm is surrounded by air that isn't involved in a lot of vertical motion. But it is sucking air inward and upward. This occurs mostly around the outside of the storm so it is what we hit first. The updraft is entered quickly. The turbulence probably starts a moment before it is reached because of the interaction between the vertical currents and the surrounding benign air. Look at rapids in a river for a visualization of this. The fast-moving water rolls and tumbles, but there are calm pools around the edges. Entering the updraft, the airplane will climb and the airspeed will increase until the updraft is fully entered. Theoretically, the nose would pitch up but what actually happens is probably more related to the twisting air.

The next stage will be to fly from the updraft into the downdraft. This might be where the maximum level of turbulence will be found. If the air around the storm is benign and the updraft 25 feet per second, the turbulence will be related to the change in velocity over the distance it takes to enter the updraft fully. Go from the 25-feet-per-second up air into the downdraft, which is maybe 20 feet per second, for example, and there is a total change of 45 feet per second over a relatively short distance. That is a lot, and will cause rolling and tumbling as the opposing vertical flows rub against each other. It is not difficult to visualize how a light airplane might be contained within an eddy and be, at least momentarily, difficult to control.

MOTIVE

If you think that I am trying to paint a bleak picture, you are right. If you fly any airplane into a storm, the risk is high. The smaller and lighter the airplane, the higher the risk. Big airplanes are no stronger, but they are bigger, they have higher wing loading, and they are less susceptible to a loss of control because of their greater momentum. I rode through an active storm on the flight deck of a 727 once, and while the ride was rough and the captain wasn't exactly riding along with his feet on the dash and a cup of coffee in hand, the complete control of the aircraft was never in question. It rolled and pitched a little, and some of the passengers in the back barfed, probably because the flight engineer accidentally nudged the temperature control up past 90 degrees, but it was no big deal. In a light airplane, though, it would have been a truly bad spot, one where survival would have been in doubt.

TURN AROUND?

A lot has been written about what to do once you are within a thunderstorm, and most of it suggests that the best way out is always straight ahead. Turning around would increase the chances of a loss of control. Maybe this is true, but when flying from west to east, from the back of a storm to the front, the onset might be relatively mild, whereas the turbulence on the front side of the storm would be much worse. In truth, the remedy is much like using orange juice to avoid pregnancy. Before or after? No, instead of.

HOW?

Having been through all of that, how, pray tell, do we stay out of thunderstorms? Fly long enough, and you'll inevitably be headed into an area where embedded storms are advertised, or toward a line of storms.

The first key is a thorough understanding of what sort of weather system is spawning the storms. This has to be updated by the minute, because storm systems can actually pulse. What was fairly benign an hour ago might turn exceptionally mean a bit later. The Southern Airways DC-9 crew that lost both engines in a severe storm had been flying the area all day with no major problem up until the time in the afternoon when they penetrated that exceptionally mean cell. It is often said that the best time to negotiate an active area is mid to late morning. Certainly I have seen that to be true, but it is by no means automatic.

The strongest storms are usually in squall lines that form ahead of cold fronts. These are supported by a strong southwesterly flow aloft that brings cold air down around the tip of a low pressure trough aloft and then heads back northeastward over warm and moist air beneath. The area of highest wind aloft is called a "jet core," and there is a rotation in the core that causes lifting to the east (all this is in the Northern Hemisphere) and aids and abets in the formation of really mean stuff. Avoidance of squall-line storms is relatively simple because they are generally quite visible. Flying through small gaps in a line is extremely risky business. The best procedure is a long detour—there will be a surface low-pressure system; the farther away from it you get, the more likely there will be large breaks in the line. Or you can just land and wait. It is not uncommon to get surface wind gusts of 50 or more knots out of squall-line storms. That is a lot more than the 30-feet-per-second design criteria of our airplanes. Having radar and/or a Stormscope is not such a great advantage when dealing with a squall line. Human vision does a pretty good job, and anything that would suggest to you that you might find a way through a squall line is not doing you a big favor.

On long trips there is usually a way around. For example, flying from Colorado Springs to Auburn, Alabama, one stormy day, I went by way of Waco, Texas, because of a squall line. It probably added an hour to my flight time. But had I been going to Oklahoma City that day, the only sensible action would have been to wait until the line passed there and then go on in. I would add that this squall line was a definite exception to the thought that midmorning is best. Before noon, tornados were reported out of this one.

EMBEDDED

It is when embedded thunderstorms are forecast that we come up with the most questions. I once knew an experienced pilot who scoffed at the thought that there could even be such a thing as embedded thunderstorms. Nothing with that much energy, he mused, could hide within other clouds. But this pilot was from the northeast and spent most of his time flying in the northeast. Those of us who have prowled the sky farther south know very well that there are embedded thunderstorms and that they can dish it out, especially to relatively light airplanes.

When you hear one of the classic "I flew through a thunderstorm" stories, it is usually about an embedded convective event. And the reason the pilot is able to tell the story is related to one of the characteristics of certain types of thunderstorms. In a warm frontal condition, or where a front has become stationary, there is stable air from the surface up a ways—how far up depends on the nature of the condition. It may be a few thousand feet, or as much as 10,000 feet—you can't count on it because nobody really measures it or makes an attempt at forecasting it. In such a condition, any convective activity that forms will be based at the level where the air becomes unstable. The inflow into the storm will be at or above the level where the air becomes unstable, and the cooler air below will mitigate the effects of the downdraft from the storm. There will be plenty of wind-shear turbulence below the base of the storm because of the southerly flow above the slope of the front and the northerly or easterly flow beneath it, which might lead a pilot to believe he has successfully flown through a thunderstorm. But if you watch the instruments in the jarring bumps, you'll see that they reflect shear, not convective turbulence. There are only sharp jabs, not major upward and downward excursions. True, there might be lightning and thunder, and a pilot flying higher, above the base of the storms, would get the full thunderstorm treatment. But lower it might be manageable and this is where some pilots have formed the quite erroneous opinion that thunderstorms are really not so bad.

STAYING OUT

The question that we always reach is how best to stay out of thunderstorms, using whatever equipment we have. The most basic is human vision, and this works well a lot of the time. If it looks bad, don't fly through it. To this day, after flying for 10,000 hours barefoot and for 6,000 with a radar, Stormscope, or both, I still put more faith in what I see than in anything else. At times what I see might be a radar depiction before takeoff that tells me that there is a squall line out there. At other times, it might be the texture and color of the clouds ahead. And every time that I have used the electronic devices to go through a place that didn't look good, it didn't feel all that good either. There are a lot of wild and bumpy clouds out there that emit neither electrical discharges nor rain. One really nasty day, flying near Dayton, Ohio, a front was occluding in the area, a cold front was overtaking a warm front, and all the pilots with radar were commenting that cells were popping up all over and that the turbulence was "moderate plus." There was not one single dot on the Stormscope, though. There was rain, and there was enough shear turbulence to convince any pilot he was trespassing, but there were no cells as such. The point is that with radar and a Stormscope or other detector of electrical discharges, you can't always steer clear of the bad spots and get a smooth ride.

EXAMPLE

Even vision will leave you lacking at times. Flying my Cherokee Six between Tulsa and Fort Smith, Arkansas, a number of years ago, I eyeballed a nasty storm and made the decision to go what appeared a comfortable distance north of the dark, heavy rain area. When I flew under a cloud shield that extended north of the storm, the old Six went wild. A suitcase in the rear baggage area was actually tossed all the way to the front. I quickly told the controller that I had to make a 90-degree turn to the left and descend, the thought being that I was too close to the clouds both horizontally and vertically. This was approved, and then the controller asked for a description of the turbulence. I told him it was "severe," the only time I have ever used that term in a pilot report. He told an airline jet following behind that severe turbulence had been reported. The pilot asked what kind of airplane the report came from. The controller told him. The airline pilot said he would stay on course. A few moments later his mike keyed, horns blaring in the background, and the airline pilot asked what the Cherokee had done to get out of the turbulence. He did the same.

TRAFFIC RADAR

At times, in some areas, air traffic controllers will pass along information about what they see on their radarscopes. This has to be treated properly for it to be anything other than hazardous. They do see rain, and heavy rain is identified, but they do not have the specialized information that is available with weather radar. One key to interpreting radar data is the gradient between no rain, light rain, moderate rain, and heavy rain. This can identify a thunderstorm, and the gradient is not all that clear on traffic radar. Whenever you hear a controller say that he'll vector you through the lightest area, he is trying to be helpful but is perhaps not doing you much of a favor. The better way would be a vector around a whole area of weather, or a trip to the closest suitable airport for a soda pop and a further check on conditions.

AIRBORNE WEATHER RADAR AND STORMSCOPES

This is good stuff, but not magic. And it must be used in conjunction with a knowledge of the general weather synopsis, what the sky looks like, and a high degree of caution. Buying it can help you manage risks, but it neither removes risk nor makes it possible to fly through thunderstorms. Weather radar seminars are available on videotape, as well as in person, from Archie Trammell of *B/CA* magazine and this is without doubt the best way to learn the fine points of radar use. The Stormscope is also a valuable device, with the same caveats as apply to radar.

A good example of how everything has to work together came one stormy March day in the Chicago area. A lot of storms had moved through; once they passed I got an accumulation of ice off the airplane and headed out. Initially, the Stormscope was worth its weight in gold. Before departure, I used it to calculate a heading that would take us south of the activity. After takeoff, the controller suggested a path over South Bend, but the Stormscope didn't back this up. It wanted the airplane on a heading of 120 degrees for a while. Because of the nature of the condition—stable cold air low and unstable warm air higher—the decision was to stay as low as possible, which came to be 4,000 feet. In a bit we could see heavy precip on the radar, and we were soon beneath an overcast with a line of dark-bottom clouds ahead, based at about 5,000 feet. Most of the precip was north of our path. I was giving it a generous berth, using the radar. As we passed under the dark clouds, there was definite churning in the air but nothing more than light to moderate turbulence. But you could look up at the bases of the clouds and tell something was about to pop. And it did. About thirty minutes later, a sigmet was issued for a line of thunderstorms from north of South Bend all the way down to St. Louis. Apparently precip had started falling all along the line shortly after we passed.

Several lessons there, where I used the Stormscope, radar, and human vision to get the best possible ride. One is that the electronics can help a lot. What you see is still important. The controller's radar won't always give the best path, and when you break away from his advice, you are on your own. And convective weather can change rapidly. Had I given a pilot report that a reasonable passage was available at 4,000 feet, the way would have been closed before the information reached other pilots.

FROSTY STUFF

Ice is next on the list, and while it is often thought of in the same context as thunderstorms, it is entirely different. Ice comes on more slowly, and once you are in ice, the opportunity exists to get safely out without great risk. If the airplane is flown from where there is no ice to where there is ice, then the air where it didn't exist is close by, still there, waiting for your return. The saddest thing about the icing accidents that we see in general aviation—they claim about the same number of airplanes (six to ten) as thunderstorms each year—is that, in every case, the pilot had a lot of chances to get out.

The ice problem that exists in general aviation is at least partly the fault of the FAA. They write the written test, and the ground school programs are all geared to helping applicants pass that written test. And they concentrate on arcane interpretations of the regulations as well as flying lore that, honestly, is rooted in World War II. In one of the dumbest actions ever, the FAA proposed in 1989 to define "known icing" as any time the temperature is less than plus 5 centigrade and there is visible moisture. Don't go to whoever thought that up for a highball—the ice cubes might be water. The other contributor to the icing problem is the forecasts issued by the National Weather Service. In a constant attempt to cover their buns, they forecast ice all winter. "Icing in clouds and in precipitation" is a standard. As an illustration of the lack of understanding, there can actually be ice in only one kind of precipitation—freezing rain. Snow might make a white line down the leading edge, but because it is already frozen, it doesn't create classic airframe ice. The kind of ice they mean is that found in clouds. And don't take this to belittle ice. It is a very serious problem. It's just that as pilots we get zero help in managing the risk from the regulations and the forecasts.

INVERSIONS

The best friend we have in winter, as related to ice, is the temperature inversion—where the temperature increases with altitude. These are very common and they are not well forecast.

In fact, the National Weather Service will often show an inversion (and warm air aloft) on the winds-aloft forecasts (which include temperature-aloft forecasts), but will forecast icing on the area forecast. One winter I made a lot of trips on days that a friend and neighbor deemed unflyable because of forecast ice. As with thunderstorms, you have to consider the synopsis to judge the potential for ice. The real icebox is north of a developing low-pressure system. Your airplane can turn into a popsicle in record time there, and the lifting and mixing of warm and cold air can overwhelm any inversion you might have counted on.

Strong, warm overrunning air is where we get the best inversions. The temperature might be near freezing on the surface, but if the wind aloft is strong and out of the southwest, there might be warmer air above. At times, it can be significantly warmer—enough that when you climb into it the airplane, including the instrument faces, will break out in a sweat. This would more likely happen when the low-pressure system is to the west and there is a warm front to the south.

There are a lot of tales about ice. One is that ice clouds are never more than a few thousand feet thick. Watch out for these. If you are in silky-smooth air, meaning stratus clouds, it is probably true that there will be an altitude within a few thousand feet that is more friendly. But if you are getting ice in bumpy clouds, cumulus types, then the likelihood of finding better conditions within a few thousand feet is less of a possibility. Turbulence and ice together call for an immediate retreat.

SHOW ME THE WAY
TO GO HOME

The nature of ice is what makes it something that we can deal with easily. It isn't there and then it is there. When it appears, we need an instant plan to get out of it, even if the airplane is equipped with deicing equipment. The simple fact is that no airplane should really be flown in continuous icing conditions. When it appears, go up, go down, or go back.

One other thing has to be considered. Pilot reports on icing are totally unreliable. Why? Because of the effect of airspeed. When we fly faster, the temperature rises on the structure of the aircraft because of surface friction. The ultimate example is Concorde, whose Gallic nose reaches 127 degrees centigrade at Mach 2. No ice there. Closer to home, if a DC-9 reports no ice on a climb, twirl your Jeppesen whiz wheel and see that if he is abiding by the 250-knot speed limit below 10,000 feet, he has a temperature rise of just under 10 degrees. By the same token, if you are climbing at 110 knots, your temperature rise is but two degrees. Thus, if the temperature were, say, minus 3 centigrade, you would get ice on your Bonanza where the DC-9 pilot reported no ice. This tells us that ice is quite a personal matter that has to be handled on a case-by-case basis. And the risk from it is minimized by fleeing at its first sign.

One final ice item. You have probably heard that some airplanes carry ice better than others. This is true. If the wing is big and fat at the leading edge, the airplane will probably fly with a lot of ice. But that doesn't mean it should be done. If an airplane isn't approved for flight in icing, that means it has not been tested in icing. There is no assurance even that the engine will continue to run. And if ice forms on the prop and sheds unevenly, you have big trouble in little airplane.

WIND

Strong winds pose an operational consideration, and it is up to each one of us to set some limits for normal operations. The more conservative, the less the risk. The higher the limit, the more utility you get out of the airplane. Nobody in his right mind would suggest a limit to another pilot; this is truly something you have to decide for yourself, with the guidance of a more experienced person if you are a new pilot.

Wind comes in different levels. A lot of pilots consider wind under 20 knots not to be an operational consideration unless it is 90 degrees to the runway. Upwind obstructions that would make wind variable in both direction and velocity would make it more of a consideration. When the wind strengthens to from 20 to 40 knots on the highest gust, it is very much an operational consideration. There will likely be low-level wind shear, the turbulence will be quite uncomfortable at lower altitudes, and even taxiing becomes risky, especially in airplanes with lower stalling speeds. Over 40 knots, wind might well become the master of the airplane.

The risk from high winds is substantially more than the typical wind accident where the airplane tips over on the ground. Landing accidents become more serious. Wind shear on an approach can cause a short landing, or, at the other extreme, if we pile too much speed on to compensate for the gusts, an overshoot becomes a real possibility, especially with a crosswind on a relatively short runway.

Surface wind forecasts are not accurate at times, but usually they are in the ballpark. If you decide, for example, to cull flying when the forecast calls for gusts over 30 knots, there might be a surprise a year, but not more frequently.

One item of wind technique does vary with airplanes, but the simple facts relating to it are just that, simple facts. An airplane's behavior in wind depends in part on the relationship between the wind speed and the stalling speed of the airplane. On most airplanes, extending flaps lowers the stalling speed. When the airplane is flown slower, the controls are less effective. In honor of these simple facts, on my 210 I use 30 degrees of flaps for normal landings, and cut 10 degrees for each 10 knots of crosswind. Or, if the wind is down the runway, I cut 10 degrees for each 10 knots of velocity over 20. On the 210, the reference speed on approach goes up 5 knots for each 10 degrees of flaps not used. That simple little rule-of-thumb makes my landings easier. Some pilots, especially ex-military ones, will argue with this, saying that if you have flaps, use them all. I think they bust more props than the rest of us, though.

As in so many other areas of aviation, special weather considerations have a lot to do with the individual. And as long as we don't harbor the mistaken opinion that we can fly through hell for love and understand the various phenomena, the balance between risk and utility can be managed.

CHAPTER **12**

Messing Around

FIRST PART Patrick E. Bradley

There is no rule that says all the people who become interested in flying must use airplanes as a tool, or that they
must eventually become instrument rated, or that they use
aircraft for transportation. On the contrary, many of the most
devoted aviation enthusiasts fly just for the fun of it. And who
can blame them? But weekend pilots, as they are sometimes
known, have developed a bad reputation in some quarters.
The thinking is that because you fly for pleasure, you are
somehow less safe or less capable than your business/pleasure
or strictly business pilot counterpart. For some reason, the
pilot who blusters onto an approach control frequency, unable
to quite manage even a request for traffic advisories, is labeled
a weekend pilot, and thus tars a large segment of the aviation
community.

The critical factor that all pleasure or recreational pilots
must keep in mind is that the standard of airmanship applicable
to them is the same as that applicable to the business/personal
pilot who flies frequently in a wide range of conditions. The
only difference is that the pleasure pilot has greater control of
the conditions in which he flies, and therefore need not be

proficient in some aspects of flying. Even so, the pleasure pilot is still susceptible to many of the risks that confront pilots that fly more often or for longer distances. Because of this, even the pilot who does nothing more than take his airplane out to look at the scenery or to shoot touch and goes has an obligation to himself to maintain the standards.

KEEP A CRITICAL EYE

Since I am not a professional pilot, and since I certainly don't fly every day, I find it extremely important to evaluate my performance on a flight-by-flight basis. During the en route phase of the flight, did I let the altitude wander? Did I miss calls from approach or center? Did I transition from the cruise to approach phase of flight smoothly? Each phase of a flight has special demands, and it is extremely important to compare your performance to that of the ideal on every single flight.

Even if a pilot is flying just for pleasure, he ought to consider how well he maintained altitudes and speeds and particular flight configurations. He ought to consider how good a job he did navigating or landing or operating in the pattern. Each of these things is critical to remaining a safe pilot after the rigors of training have ended.

NEVER STOP TRAINING

Another ground rule that I try to follow is to fly with an instructor at least two or three times a year. The flight doesn't have to be anything fancy or formal. Just tell the instructor that you want to go up to practice stalls or landings or maneuvers. I've never met an instructor who was not delighted to fly with me on a one-shot basis, and very often he can pick up small flaws in technique, a bad habit or quirk, before it becomes something worse. An instructor can reinstill in you the respect for the standards that was the basis of your prior training.

Unfortunately, many pilots perceive flying with an instructor as an admission that they are less than perfect pilots. The attitude is, "I've got my license and I had a BFR last year. Why should I spend the money for an instructor when I've already gotten all the instruction I need?" Again, people forget, and skills do get rusty without our even perceiving the changes. Better to find out in the controlled environment of a lesson than during an emergency that could have been avoided in the first place. Furthermore, professional pilots are exposed to a rigorous and ongoing program of recurrent training. Why should we view similar practices on our own part as a blow to the piloting ego?

VFR PILOT / INSTRUMENT RATING

Pilots sometimes tell me that, although they've got an instrument rating, they keep it in reserve—in case of an emergency in which they get caught in instrument conditions or have to climb through instrument conditions to VFR conditions. Often they don't spend much time practicing the full panoply of instrument procedures because they don't really ever plan to get fully involved in the instrument environment.

Although I don't see any problem with getting an instrument rating even when you don't plan to use it, it seems to

me that the temptations would be pretty strong to get yourself
into the IFR system even though you were less than fully
prepared for the task. For example, about eight or nine years
ago, on one of my Cessna 150 trips to Florida, I encountered
just this situation. As usual, I was weathered in at an airport
because of low ceilings and rotten weather up north. I was
hanging around the airport where I saw a pilot squinting over
some en route charts with a flight computer and a look of
complete unease.

At one point, the pilot asked me whether I had come from
the north. I answered that I had tried to fly north earlier, but
that I had to return because of deteriorating weather. The pilot
then went on to quiz me about the conditions, whether there
was much turbulence and where the tops were and where the
ceiling was. He seemed quite nervous, and not at all anxious
to get his airplane wet. As it turned out, the pilot was instrument rated, but it had been some time since he had flown in
instrument conditions. I didn't ask whether he was current.
In any event, the pilot was hoping that he would be able to
climb on top and fly to his destination. I told him I wasn't
sure, but I didn't think that the tops were all that high. My
question was what he was going to do when he got to his
destination. They were IFR, weren't they? The pilot conceded
that this was the case, and this was what worried him: the
chance that he would have to fly an approach.

I'm not sure whether the pilot decided to launch IFR or
not, but I didn't envy him his predicament. It has always
seemed to me that there is no good way to be half an instrument pilot because, as this pilot found out, whenever you enter
the IFR system, there is the possibility that you will find yourself shooting an approach to minimums. If you're not ready
for that, then I still think that you ought to reconsider the

flight entirely. It just seems to me that it would be more difficult to limit a flight to a particular level of instrument conditions than it would be to practice up for full-fledged actual conditions.

FUNNY BUSINESS

Some people tend to associate pleasure flying with fooling around in an airplane, and I think this is erroneous. Fooling around tends to connote irresponsible flying, while there is nothing irresponsible about pleasure flying. But it is true that lots of pilots fly irresponsibly just for the fun of fooling around, and it frequently gets them into trouble.

The problems arise when ill-equipped pilots attempt aerobatic or semi-aerobatic maneuvers to show off or just thrill themselves; buzzing is a perfect example. The danger is that the pilot will forget the power lines or the radio tower just down the street from the house he was buzzing and end up crashing. Even if he doesn't hit something, a common scenario is to pull the airplane up into a zoom or a steep climbing turn after the buzz job. The zoom is followed by a stall, which is followed by a low-level spin into the ground. The risks are obvious, and I am sure that too many pilots lose their lives this way each year.

Even if the pilot manages not to hit anything, and succeeds in returning and landing in one piece, there is always the possibility that one of the pedestrians being buzzed will take the airplane's tail number and give it to the police. The police will probably give the the registration number to the FAA, which takes an extremely dim view of these things. If it's only the first time the offender has been caught, he probably will only receive a suspension and a fine. If he is a repeat offender, then it's a pretty good bet that the FAA will look for a revocation, as well they should.

On the other hand, the pilot may be letting himself in for even worse. My brother told me the story of a buzz job that he witnessed one day at the beach. Apparently, a pilot made several low passes at about 75 feet or lower. Besides endangering himself, the pilot succeeded in clearing a good-sized stretch of beach of petrified sunbathers, who thought that the fellow was crashing. When they realized that they had just been buzzed, most of the witnesses were furious, and some, like my brother, went across the street to express this sentiment to the pilot. You see, the stretch of beach was located across the street from a small grass strip at which the pilot, obviously no rocket scientist, landed after completing the buzz job. When my brother got to the airport, he saw that he was not the first to arrive. The pilot was spread-eagled with his palms on the side of his airplane; one policeman was frisking him while the other held off the angry sunbathers. Within a few moments, the pilot was seated in the back of the black-and-white for a trip downtown. This was actually fortunate for the pilot, because if the police had not gotten there first, he probably would have been dragged to the beach and fed to the sharks.

SECOND PART   Richard L. Collins

There is no question that airplanes are fine recreational devices that can honestly be fun to play with. But when you look at the fact that the fatal accident rate in personal flying is far higher than in any other form of flying, you have to wonder whether or not airplanes, while fine toys, are also hazardous toys.

This depends entirely on the individual. Aerobatic flying, for example, is a fine sport. And when it is done within the confines of the rules (or waivers of the rules for the really expert), there is no unusual risk. A properly trained pilot out doing approved maneuvers (meaning the airplane has been thoroughly tested in those maneuvers) and following all the rules is simply not doing something that is daring. Those of us who have tried to keep airplanes upright as a career might think this is letting it all hang out in the name of fun, but it can all be within very safe envelopes if done in an aerobatic airplane by a pilot who knows what he is doing.

On the other hand, playing with airplanes that are not toys can be lethal. Two new business jets have been destroyed in low-level aerobatics on demonstrations, examples of what happens when you try maneuvers that are outside the envelope of an airplane. It is all fireballs, black smoke, and grief. There is no truer fool in aviation than the person who aerobats in an unapproved airplane, without the requisite parachutes, and at low altitude or in congested airspace. Call me a stick-in-the-mud if you will; if I were to list the names of friends who have perished toying with airplanes at low altitude, the length of the list would probably change your mind.

BUZZ JOBS

Different than low-altitude aerobatics, in a way, is the time-honored buzz job. This is usually just low flying done because it is difficult to show your aeronautical prowess to nonflying peers unless you take the airplane to them, at low altitude. The fact that this tends to alienate the public is one thing. The fact that it is dangerous is another. The latter is what we have to consider when thinking about risk management.

Why is buzzing hazardous? We are flying close to things, we are consumed with the idea of showing off, and there is little or no margin for error. For example, one of the best thrills of a well-executed buzz job is the pull-up that follows the high-speed low pass. In many of the accidents that occur in this phase of flight, the pilot stalls the airplane at the apogee of the zoom, and spins in. In fact, if you get an airplane in enough of a nose-up attitude with a rapid enough decay in airspeed, the airplane is in a position where a stall can not be averted well before the stall actually occurs.

It was once said that in buzzing, pilots make one critical mistake. That is in the repeat. Perhaps it is like shooting a second and third instrument approach when the weather is below minimums. Trying too hard to make it work, or to make the buzz job better, leads to shaving what are already minimum margins. Probably few pilots have ever been caught as a result of a first pass. That one surprises people and few, if any, would get an N-number or even the color of the airplane. Do it again and again, and they will catch you every time. That is, they will catch you if the law of gravity doesn't intervene.

Please don't take this as a recommendation to go out and do one-pass buzzing. This is so harmful to the public relations effort in aviation that it can only be viewed as being totally bad, as well as dangerous. But if ever you get carried away, just remember that the risk is extremely high to begin with, and multiplies after a successful first pass.

RIDING AROUND

Most pilots choose neither low-altitude aerobatics nor buzzing as an outlet. The more common thing is to fly somewhere for the legendary $100 hamburger, taking along some non-flying friends on an idyllic day. A marvelous way to spend time, sightseeing as you go along, and giving folks a look at a slice of life that they don't often see. And there is nothing risky about this. It can be, and probably is, as safe as flying along with your briefcase, in search of the almighty dollar.

Whether the personal flight is for the purpose of taking friends to a nearby airport, or to a far away place for a little rest and relaxation, there is only one requirement when it comes to managing risk. And that is a proper attitude about flying. Some say that we should always take a professional approach, but to me that word is a bit severe. It suggests that you have to have an airline transport pilot certificate for all operations. I would just rather think that pilots flying for personal reasons can do so at minimum risk as long as they are proficient, as long as they know the risks, and as long as they take the prudent steps that can minimize those risks.

One of the keys is managing external factors. We will delve more into that in the next chapter, but for now just consider the time pressures that you put on yourself. Physicians who fly are a good example of this. The airplane is to them an escape, a way to get away from a very high pressure environment. Maybe they use it to go to faraway places on weekends. But when they start home, there is a very real pressure to get back. People are depending on them. In such conditions, it is perhaps difficult for some to make decisions that are based totally on aeronautical considerations.

THE PILOT
AND AIRPLANE

When we fly purely for personal reasons, a lot of the standards by which we fly are reduced. The third-class medical is less demanding, the pilot-proficiency items are different, and the airplane has only to have an annual inspection, as opposed to 100-hour inspections for airplanes that are flown for hire. This need not have a bearing on the risks of flying, but that is true only if we use the greater freedom carefully. This is especially true in regard to the airplane, and the pilot's proficiency level. Maybe a nice simple airplane like a Taylorcraft does just fine with but an annual (or biennial, when and if the new primary-aircraft category comes into being) visit to the shop, but a turbocharged and sophisticated single or light twin probably needs a lot more than the minimum. Usually, but not always, when we do find accidents that are directly related to something on the airplane breaking, the flight is for personal reasons. That is logical—if maintenance is a write-off, we are much more likely to get it done than if it is something that comes directly from the old pocket. Logical, but too bad. The fact is that airplanes are expensive to maintain, even if they are used only for fun, and if the maintenance money is not spent, then the risk increases. Many pilots address this by doing some of their own maintenance, but that has to be done within the applicable rules.

RUSTY

The more frequent cause of problems in recreational flying is the rusty pilot. It is always sad to hear or read of a pilot crashing a homebuilt airplane on its first flight, but it takes little imagination to see why this happens. The pilot has been engrossed, usually over a long period of time, in building the airplane. Not a lot of flying has been done, none in that particular airplane. On a first flight, an airplane might be out of rig or need some other adjustment to ensure proper handling qualities. It is really the same task faced by a professional test pilot.

For most pilots, though, the rusty skills are taken to a familiar airplane, or at least one that used to be familiar. In some areas, following the FARs helps, but in some other areas we need to go well past the FARs. For example, the rule says that we must have made at least three takeoffs and landings in the category and class (airplane, single-engine land, for example) in the past ninety days before carrying passengers. That might be fine for Skyhawks and Archers, but in more sophisticated airplanes we might need more. For example, do three takeoffs and landings in a Seneca make you okay to fly a King Air? Or does instrument currency (six hours and six approaches in the past six months) in a Warrior make you okay in an Aerostar? Those are things that we have to address on a personal level. Certainly it is a bad feeling to take off, especially IFR, in an airplane with which you are not completely familiar. Even a different set of avionics can lead to enough confusion to endanger a flight.

HOW MUCH?

A big question faced by infrequent fliers is, how much is enough? That probably depends on the type of recreational flying done. For example, a pilot who goes and shoots three landings every week on twenty-minute flights might well stay current on landings and pattern work on less than twenty hours a year. If it is a tower-controlled airport, currency on radio procedures might well be maintained. That would be far different than the pilot who elects to make one twenty-hour trip a year, a long cross-country that might take place in three days and involve but five landings. The simple fact is that a small number of hours flown solely for the purpose of maintaining proficiency and practicing skills is worth more than a larger number of hours spent droning along.

This is especially important for the instrument-rated pilot. In recent times the fatal accident record in instrument flying has seemed to worsen. More pilots have instrument ratings than ever, and a lot of these pilots use those ratings for personal flying. But we do have to recognize that instrument flying requires a high level of precision and is not something to do with doubts in your mind. It has been said that flying is unforgiving. Instrument flying is totally unforgiving. Lose control of an airplane in cruising flight at, say, 10,000 feet, and you can hit the ground in thirty seconds or less. Which is where we do have to make an honest division on flying. The recreational pilot who wants only to enjoy the pure joy of flight, on nice days, has one set of needs where the pilot who wants to use the airplane for personal or recreational travel, IFR, has another set of needs. The requirements for the latter are far more like those for the professional pilot.

OUT MANEUVERING

Going out and doing airwork falls under "messing around" except when part of a training program. And where we see little trouble with this in training, it is likely more of a problem when done as a lark. Any of the ground-reference maneuvers, most of which involve turning flight at relatively low altitudes with attention diverted outside the cockpit, increase the risk of being involved in a stall/spin accident. We might have been crackerjack at these when getting a commercial certificate, but those skills rust, too.

Stalls fall into the same category, especially as airplanes get heavier. Light airplanes are nice to stall, and indeed some heavy ones do well. The trijet Falcon 900 is one of the nicest airplanes to stall that I have ever flown. It is fully controllable in roll while in the stall. But all airplanes are not like this, and any airplane that is not licensed to spin has to be suspect in anything other than approaches to stalls, with recovery begun at the onset of the stall. The reason for this is that while singles not approved for spins do have to be spun in certification, it is only one turn, and then they have an additional turn for recovery. This is done by a professional test pilot with a spin chute mounted on the aft of the aircraft to use in case the airplane should enter an unrecoverable spin mode. So if you go out flying around in a new retractable, for example, start doing full stalls, and the airplane spins, congratulations. You just became a test pilot and have one turn to figure it out. No spin chute, either. It is a risk that need not be taken. For full-stall practice, the world has plenty of Skyhawks and Cherokees. At this writing, the Warrior and Cadet were not approved for spins but those airplanes have docile stall characteristics and are likely to be approved, as was the Cherokee.

THE TOTAL

Perhaps the best caution against messing around relates to the "envelope," the diagram that plots allowable speeds and g loads for our airplanes. In military flying they push airplanes right to the edges of the envelope. Our training does not really teach us to do that, and one of the ways to make up for a lack of the familiarity with the outer edges of the envelope is to plan to stay well within it. Then, if things do not go as planned, there is some left to use in a recovery. And, while low flying can be fun, the ground is hard and the obstructions unforgiving. Just flying is fun in itself, one of the most enjoyable things that we can do, and it doesn't need a lot of embellishment.

CHAPTER 13

Human Factors

FIRST PART   Patrick E. Bradley

There is no doubt in my mind that some of the most important variables affecting the safety of a flight are human factors, the things that affect the way we perform or react in a given situation. For instance, will a pilot perform better if he is well-rested than if he hasn't slept in the last twenty-four hours or his sleep cycle has been disrupted? Obviously. What about the pilot whose mind is on major business negotiations that he is about to undertake? Would this also affect his ability to perform? This is a less clear case, and it is probably very much dependent upon the person, but if the person is preoccupied or anxious, then it is likely that his flying will be affected—and not for the better.

The problem I have always had in considering human factors is that physical or psychological variables affect the way that a pilot behaves on every flight. It is impossible to create the perfect, well-rested, no-stress, healthy flying environment in the real world, and because of that, there are probably not many flights in which a pilot will be operating at peak capacity. The question, then, is to what degree any given factor will affect any given flight. Are there some flights that ought to be scrubbed due to adverse human conditions, the same way we would for adverse weather conditions? I've always found this a tough call, and I think that we pilots are probably less adept at evaluating our own mental and physical conditions than we are at evaluating weather factors or the condition of our airplane.

THE Z-Z-Z FACTOR

Who hasn't experienced the wonderful feeling of waking up in the morning after a long, relaxed, uninterrupted, and completely peaceful sleep. Few things color my world so dramatically—at least until I've got to get on the New York City subway to go to work. In any case, there is little doubt that a good night's sleep leaves us more alert and better able to face the rigors, both physical and mental, of the upcoming day. Unfortunately, we don't always have the good fortune of experiencing the type of ideal sleep promised in the Sominex commercials. In fact if we did, there probably wouldn't be any Sominex commercials. So how should a bad night's sleep, or no night's sleep, or irregular sleep at irregular times affect a flight? Should we scrub flights unless we've gotten a good six hours, four hours?

Not many pilots I know would or could scrub a flight on grounds of lack of sleep, although the FAA does impose certain duty and rest requirements on pilots that fly in certain commercial contexts. As I mentioned in chapter 1, I once attempted to get some insight into this question by attempting flights in various stages of fatigue. What stands out most in my mind was my ability to function adequately in a wide variety of flight conditions on very little sleep. What I found most worrisome, though, was the unpredictability of the times when an error —perhaps minor and perhaps severe—would show up and gum up the works.

BEWARE THE MUNDANE

Surprisingly, I found that lack of sleep did not disable me in even the most demanding of situations. In fact, when the heat was really on, I found that the increase in adrenaline would do wonders to bring me back to an acceptable level of performance. I had the most trouble, I think, during the less demanding times. Staying alert (or even awake) during a long leg could be absolute torture, and the potential for missing a dogleg on an airway or a navaid change or a frequency was very real. I found that I would have to work to stay awake and to double-check nearly everything that I did. Although I was able to manage, I was much less efficient than I would be with normal sleep.

The other interesting effect of lack of sleep that I noticed was the unpredictability of the effects. Instead of becoming progressively more tired during the course of the flight, I found that fatigue would hit me in waves. For a while I would be managing quite well, when suddenly I would get the feeling that I just couldn't go on unless I got some shut-eye, maybe just a few winks, just a short nap. When the need for sleep hits, there is precious little you can do to overcome the intense desire to shut down operations for a brief siesta. This, I think, must be one of the greatest dangers of flying under the effects of no sleep.

INJURIES

Another physical consideration that pilots must sometime confront is when to take themselves out of the game due to injuries. I've faced this question twice in the last year or so, though each case presented different considerations and different results.

My first injury was a broken knee. Agile fellow that I am, I tripped over one of the tiedown cables at a local airport. As a result of the injury, I found my right leg wrapped for six weeks in a device aptly named a leg immobilizer. Although the unit prevented me from bending my knee, my ankle was free and I could walk—almost like a human. Initially, I thought that I was going to have to lay off flying for my leg's period of entombment. The problem was operating the rudders of the airplane. I just wasn't sure whether it would be possible without bending my right knee. After a week or two, though, I began to become more comfortable with the apparatus, and began to reconsider the restriction on my flying.

Eventually, I decided to try flying. First, I sat in the left seat to see how restricted I would be in my use of the rudder pedals. Though I had to move the seat of the Cessna 210 back fairly far, a combination of wriggling, twisting, and turning permitted me to control the rudder about as well as I do normally. In the air, I found that the same procedure worked well, even during a crosswind landing. In all, I was just sorry that I hadn't tried to fly the airplane earlier. Still, I flew only with another pilot until the leg was well.

BRUISED

My second injury was a bit different, though. It came on a crisp fall day in Lebanon, New Hampshire, where I had flown to visit family. During the course of the visit, I went on a bicycle ride that I succeeded in marring with a nasty bicycle spill. It's easy to visualize the scenario: I went flying without an airplane and landed on my head. Although I was wearing a helmet, my lip still required several stitches, and then there was a fair amount of miscellaneous road rash. Though none of my injuries was particularly serious, I was confronted with the question of whether I should fly back to New York that day as I had planned. Besides my own desire to get back in time for work, there were others who were not particularly anxious to take a vacation day. Putting off the flight would have meant a significant inconvenience all around.

The countervailing view was raised by the doctor who sewed me up. Although I appeared fine except for my cuts and bruises, it is not uncommon for head injuries to manifest themselves hours after the actual trauma. There was some risk that I would suffer dizziness or fainting. "Would you like to faint up in the airplane?" the doctor asked (I hope rhetorically). Although I felt fine, I decided that I had better not push my luck. I decided to scrub the flight and returned early the next morning, almost on time for work.

I did not experience any dizziness or fainting spells for the rest of the day, and looking back, I doubt that I'd have had any problem making the return flight at the planned time. This is 20/20 hindsight, though, which isn't particularly helpful at the time the decision has to be made. If there is a chance that you could be incapacitated, or become unable to complete the flight, it is foolhardy to begin the flight without at least having another pilot on board to take over the reins. Anything less is simply accepting too high a risk.

AFFAIRS OF THE HEAD

Psychological as well as physical considerations frequently affect flights, and they can be major factors in the degree of risk that a pilot will assume in embarking on a flight. Because of this, it is probably as important for us to take a moment to consider our mental preparedness for a flight as our physical preparedness. For instance, there may be business concerns that so preoccupy a pilot, that it would be impossible for him to devote the necessary attention to flying the airplane. Perhaps in such situations it would be better to arrange for another pilot either to fly one or both of the legs or simply to be there. Personally, I often find flying an airplane a welcome distraction, but this might not be true under some other circumstances. The important thing is to evaluate your own ability to devote the necessary concentration to the flight and to make other arrangements if you are at all doubtful.

PUSHING THE ENVELOPE

Another consideration that can make or break a flight for me is my ability to make timetables that I didn't have the luxury of setting in the first place. As I mentioned earlier, I believe that one of the most disruptive influences on a flight is rushing. I don't dally when preparing for a flight, but, on the other hand, I find that when I am forced to rush to get off or to get down, I inevitably begin to forget things—sometimes important things. Because of this I consider timetables very thoroughly when I'm making the initial decision regarding whether I will make a particular flight. Where the schedule is entirely unforgiving, and where I can't leave early enough to allow the necessary time to prepare for and make a flight, I may simply scratch the flight. Of course this is more of a problem for longer flights, but it is always one of my initial considerations in determining whether a flight is an appropriate one for me to make, long or short.

Even where there is not a set timetable that I must make or break, I tend to be wary of spur-of-the-moment flights. I don't mean to say that I don't make flights on short notice, because I do, and I consider such flexibility a valuable quality of general aviation. At the same time, a spur-of-the-moment flight may become a rushed flight under some circumstances, and when it does, an alarm should go off. Are you cutting corners to accommodate others or even yourself? Is this compromising the safety of the flight? Sometimes a few introspective moments prior to takeoff will end up saving time in the long run. It can also go far in reducing risks.

WHEN THE UNEXPECTED OCCURS

Just about every pilot considers how he will react in the event of an emergency. I've thought about it lots of times, primarily with some dim hope that I may be able to prepare myself better if I do experience a serious emergency, one where the clarity of my thinking and the steps that I take could determine the outcome of the incident. I tend to think that pilots are better able to deal with such situations if they practice them. For example, I believe that a pilot will be able to deal more effectively with an engine failure if he has run through the procedure in his head so many times that the response, to the extent possible, becomes automatic. It becomes another maneuver to execute the best you can and, with luck, you will succeed.

I also think practicing responses to emergency situations instills in one the confidence necessary to deal with the emergency. When the fateful moment comes, I think that the most important instrument in the airplane remains the pilot's mind. If he has the confidence to address the situation calmly, if he avoids the temptation to surrender to panic, I feel strongly that there are few inflight emergencies short of an explosion with which a pilot can't deal effectively. Again, the secret in such a situation is keeping your head and remembering that, short of a structural failure, you still have control; even in the event of a structural failure, you might still have some control of the airplane. And as long as you can remain master, you can escape the worst situations. I think that the rational and workmanlike approach to an emergency will stand a pilot in better stead than the hope that he will be able to pull off some sort of virtuoso performance that will save the day.

SECOND PART   Richard L. Collins

A lot of study goes into the relationship between the pilot and the airplane, and this is all to the good. It would be foolish to think that we can cover it all with machines and rules, even if pilots tried to follow all the rules. Some studies have identified undesirable traits in pilots, but they are not going to be rehashed in total here for one reason: to expand the discussion. The fact is that pilots with all kinds of personalities fly airplanes, and try as we might to achieve some level of standardization through training and regulation, it simply does not happen. Each pilot takes a personality to the cockpit. Most are able to overcome what might be perceived as a weakness with a burst of brilliance and exceptional flying skill, but for some the time comes when they are overwhelmed by events. For some pilots there is a personality change during a flying career. This can go both ways. One pilot might become more conservative with age, the next might become less conservative. A pilot might get more cautious as he ages because he doesn't want to make a mark on an otherwise good career of flying. That is probably coupled with a recognition of slowing down a little with age. The pilot who becomes more daring with time might well be looking at the calendar. Each day older, one less day to lose.

THE RISK EQUATION

Perhaps it is appropriate that this is chapter 13. Some might choose to skip that number and go on to the next. But somehow the number well illustrates one of the truths about flying. We start with the basic low level of risk that is found flying on a calm and clear day off a large airport in flat country, in an airplane with which we are very familiar and which is in excellent mechanical condition, and when we feel in perfect physical and mental shape. Then we, as individuals, according to our proclivities, add to that basic low level of risk. That is what most of the preceding chapters have been about. How we do this, and the risks we take, are directly related to our personalities and the way we look at risks. Walk under a ladder on Friday the thirteenth? Maybe not, but that is superstitition. Go scud-running on a marginal day? That is a lot more than superstition—that is quite a real risk. The decisions to take risks occur both on the ground and in flight. The process might be easier on the ground but the fact is that risks change as a flight unfolds and the challenge is there until the airplane is parked and secured.

EXAMPLE

I'll share with you flights that were made a few days before this was written. It was an exceptionally active early March, with crazy weather. All the thought processes are fresh in my mind; we'll look at what they mean.

The first run was from Carroll County Airport in Maryland down to Vero Beach, Florida, to visit the Piper factory. The weather was not good to the south. A low had been off the Florida coast for several days and was still there, whipping up wind and rain. The forecasts for arrival were not bad, mostly low VFR. No day for beach walking but okay for flying. It appeared from the information on my complete CompuServe briefing that the flight would be on top much of the time at 12,000 feet. In total, it appeared a fairly easy IFR flight. I had recently added a 30-gallon O&N Aircraft baggage compartment tank to my P210, so it was both reasonable and legal to file to Vero Beach with Orlando International as an alternate. According to the computer flight plan it would be five hours and three minutes en route, six plus forty-five on the fuel.

ALONG THE WAY

There was cloud cover starting in northern Virginia, and the air was quite choppy at 12,000 feet. The airplane was in cloud and soon ice began to form. A descent to 8,000 feet fixed that as it was warmer there. The wind was not as forecast at that level; the temperature was higher than forecast and the air was turbulent. I was between layers; the lower layer appeared to top at about 5,000 and the surface wind was out of the north. All this suggested that if I descended into the lower layer, I might get some of the benefit of the north wind. I went to 4,000, where the groundspeed increased to 185 knots. What I thought would be an easy flight was requiring more thought than anticipated.

After an hour or so in the clouds, I got tired of that and thought I'd go back on top to have lunch, some coffee, and to take a visual rest. I enjoy flying instruments, even doing it all day, but if you can take a break, why not?

The wind was better on top by this time so I thought I would just stay there until close to the destination.

I dropped off for a weather check, and when they gave me the Vero weather it came with a kicker. Lower than forecast, and the VOR was out of service.

"When will it be back on the air?"

"Don't know, it burned up in a grass fire."

I looked back through the briefing papers and, sure enough, it was there. I had read all the way through, but that notam on the VOR just hadn't registered. With no VOR, that meant no approach to Vero Beach. The closest airport is Fort Pierce, but the approach there is off the Vero Beach station as well.

So a new plan was required. Melbourne, Florida, 27 nautical miles north of Vero Beach, has an ILS and was reporting 800 overcast and 5 miles. Shoot the approach there and get a Special VFR down to Vero? That didn't remain a consideration for long—for some reason I thought of the sick cartoon that was on airport bulletin boards years ago. Two buzzards, smiling, one saying to the other, "Oh look, here comes our hot lunch on a Special VFR."

THE REAL PLAN

The real plan then became to shoot the approach at Melbourne and rent a car.

The low off the coast was obviously strengthening and not moving away as forecast. When I flew by Daytona they had read their new ATIS and had gone down to 400 overcast and 4. I tuned ahead to the Melbourne ATIS, they now had 500 broken, 1,000 overcast and 4 with the wind from 320 at 20 with gusts to 30. They were using a back-course approach to Runway 27. Hmmm. Back course, that means a lot of overwater maneuvering, which is a risk I would rather not take but is something that you often have to accept in coastal areas. I looked up the circling minimums for the ILS; they were higher. I checked weather at Orlando and, instead of the forecast low VFR, they had 400 overcast and 3. Also, moderate turbulence was being reported on approaches below 3,000 feet.

THE REAL REAL PLAN

This was starting to take a toll on the thinking procedures. As often happens when the old brain has been whirring excessively, a mild headache developed. When Melbourne's ATIS changed and the reported ceiling became 400 feet, I came to another decision time. The MDA was 433 feet. I still had plenty of fuel, but shooting the approach and missing would use some of that and with weather worse than forecast, what might happen next? I was coming close to the end of a five-hour flight, so I was not what you would call well-rested. Would I start that approach, with a reported ceiling below the MDA, with a determination to make it work? Once down in the low-level wind-shear turbulence, in clouds, would there be a heightened desire to get down? The final question asked whether it wouldn't be better to go for a surer thing, an ILS to Runway 36 at Orlando. It would involve a couple of more hours of driving on the roundtrip to Vero, as opposed to Melbourne, but appeared to be something that I could define, so I went for that option. There was moderate turbulence on the approach, which probably would have been worse at Melbourne because the surface wind there was substantially stronger than at Orlando.

ANOTHER OPINION

The next day I described these events to another pilot. He said he'd have gone for the approach at Melbourne, that it was always good practice to get down in the bumpy clouds and get a workout, and that he always tried the approach regardless of the reported weather. Whether he would have actually done that is totally open to question. What we say we might do from a desk chair and what we might do in a bouncing airplane are two different matters. But both thought processes are worth considering, because when we examine the psychological factors that play on our flying, we do have to dissect every decision. At times one personality trait might drive us to an incorrect decision, from which we get a chance to fly out and then make a good decision. At other times, the way we feel—tired, for example—might cause a different personality trait to take over. A tired puppy is usually looking for the easiest way out, and often the easiest way involves less risk. Had I this flight to fly over, I think that I would have done it about the same way. But the question that has to be asked is whether I would have done it the same way ten years ago. Or would I have done it the same way if it had been at the end of a one-hour flight instead of at the end of a five-hour flight? In retrospect, the approach at Melbourne had many of the ingredients of the accident reports that we read on a continuous basis.

NO JEKYLL AND HYDE

This is not to suggest that pilots undergo wild personality swings. But most pilots do have a little in them that can be associated with personality traits sometimes identified as harmful. "Macho" is one of the identified traits. That is a poor word to use in relation to this subject because it relates more to ethnic pride; those who tend to put it in a negative context simply don't take the dictionary at face value. But in their favor, most of us know what they mean when they say it: Here is a pilot who feels like he can fly through anything because he is the greatest. Had I shot the back course at Melbourne after the end of a five-hour flight, would that have been macho? Had I flown it at the end of a one hour flight, would it have been macho? Maybe we need a balancing category. Maybe had I shot the approach it would have been macho; by going to Orlando I became an instant "wimp."

UTILITY

Much is said about setting limits and then adhering to them. One of my limits that helped me make the preceding decision is not starting a nonprecision approach if the ceiling is reported below the MDA, or a precision approach if the visibility is below minimums. Both of those are based on a lot of accident reports that tell of pilots shooting approaches in below-minimum conditions. If you do it by the book, it should not be a high-risk maneuver, but it has proved to be so. I wouldn't try to identify the personality trait that drives pilots into the ground, but we can look at it in another area: departing in less than ideal conditions, when you are comfortable in the warmth of the FBO's office and elect to go out and challenge the elements.

MARCH IN CHICAGO

Whenever you go flying in March you shouldn't be surprised if the wind blows, or if the weather gets screwed up far beyond the wildest expectations of the forecaster. It happened to be on a St. Patrick's Day that I wound up headed from Maryland to DuPage Airport near Chicago to make a business call. Along for the ride was my FBO, Jack Poage, who wanted to go look at a Pitts to buy and fly on the air-show circuit. That Jack is an experienced lad we'll leave to your imagination: His certificate number is 60,000 lower than that of Rudy Peace, the man who taught me to fly. Jack is probably of a different discipline in flying than I am, but somehow the air can't tell the difference when we get to it: He is a good guy to go flying with and respects my desire to stay upright as much as I respect his to do otherwise. The trip home was the one used as an example of the use of radar, the Stormscope, and vision in storm avoidance.

The forecast was good, with the worst called for in the whole period for Chicago to be low VFR or high IFR with light rain and, later, light snow. There was a stationary front across the area and a low was expected to form around Cincinnati in the afternoon and move northeastward.

The trip out was fine, but with one sign I made note of. The wind aloft was stronger and more southerly than forecast. That generally means weather worse than forecast. The Stormscope seconded the motion by showing a lot of electrical activity west of Chicago. Thunder was not in the forecast, and even the morning's TV weather maps had shown thunderstorm activity to the south but not in the Chicago area. The wind above 2,000 feet agl was strong southerly and the surface wind was easterly, so there was wind-shear turbulence on the approach. But no surprises at all.

We landed at 11:00 in the morning. By noon, there was strong thunder and heavy rain. Now we had something different. Because the surface temperature was varying between 31 and 32 degrees Fahrenheit, the rain was freezing. When I got back to my airplane at 2:30 in the afternoon, it was fes-

tooned with ice. There was a rough coating atop all the surfaces. The thunderstorms were through the area, and it
appeared that we could fly southeast for a while, then east,
and miss the activity. But first the ice had to be dealt with,
both the ice on the airplane and the potential ice in the clouds.
The thinking exercise was made more interesting by the fact
that there were four crews there trying to leave. One, the crew
of a Beech 18, had just landed. They said that there was an
inversion, warmer temperatures aloft, and that they had a
smooth ride up from Indianapolis with nothing other than
rain. But their airplane iced over while the cargo was being
loaded, so they were in the same boat as those who had been
there for a while. The other airplanes, in addition to my P210,
were a Baron and a 310.

The FBO, Planemaster Services, was the best I have ever
seen at handling pilots with ice on their eyebrows and wings.
Whether you wanted glycol, or your airplane in a warm hangar,
the line crew was right with it. At first I thought glycol, then
I changed my mind. Put it in the warm hangar and thaw it;
I would wait until the rain abated and then make a decision.
All the while airplanes were landing. Each reported some icing
on the last part of the approach.

It is in a situation like this that the macho tendency can
be the most dangerous. Lots of peer pressure, other airplanes
flying, why not have a go at it? My flying partner, Jack, was
laconic about the whole thing: "I don't have to be home until
midnight." When I asked what he had going at midnight, he
said, "I need to go to bed by then."

The first airplane to leave was a 310. Pilot and three. The
airplane had been left out, deiced with glycol. When the passengers showed up they felt sure they wouldn't be leaving.
The pilot assured them it would be okay. The only bad grade

he got from a distance was for leaving the chocks under the nosewheel. I suggested to one of the line crew that he could make a friend for life by going out and pulling the chocks as if that were the way it was always done. A few minutes later, before the 310 took off, there was some discussion about the condition of the airplane and one of the line crew said something to the effect that the deicing of the 310 had been ineffective. But it left without apparent incident.

NEXT

If you don't have proper respect for the folks flying freight around in old airplanes, consider that the Beech 18 crew was the most pragmatic of the group. The captain was not young; I got the feeling that he and the Beech had done all this before and had a good understanding of who does what to whom. He wasn't about to take off with ice on its wings. But he was the first to notice a slight temperature rise. The wind had shifted from the east, off Lake Michigan, to the north. That would usually indicate a decrease in temperature, but the surface to the north was warmer than the lake to the east.

Decision time. It was only a bit more than an hour into the thinking process. The surface temperature was 34, it was raining rather enthusiastically, and the wind was blowing. The airplane was in a warm hangar and was melted down. The line crew said we could load inside; they would pull us out and send us on the way. I looked at Jack and said I thought we should go for it, but if he had expressed doubt I would have deferred. "Let's go," he said. We did, there was no ice to mention on climb, and at 4,000 feet the temperature was plus 10 degrees centigrade. The trip through the line of developing activity was okay, as related, and in total it was a low-risk flight.

The question remains whether or not the decision was affected by other things. Right after they pulled us out of the hangar, while we were waiting for the clearance, a Bellanca Viking landed. I remember thinking that this was good. If he made it okay, things were fine. That is like following someone through an area of storms. If the airplane ahead makes it, you can, too. But what do you do if the controller suddenly loses radio and radar contact with that airplane ahead? Watching what the other guy is doing is okay but should never be considered a mandate. He might have made it just by the skin of his teeth.

A lot of thought was put into the decision to launch that day, and the favorable signs overwhelmed the negatives after the surface temperature went up two degrees. Had it not gone up, the decision would have had to be a no. Anything else would not have been macho, it would have been dumb. The whole exercise took only a bit over an hour, including deicing the airplane, becoming familiar with a weather synopsis pretty far from forecast, and getting a clearance out of a major metropolitan area. It was not an easy hour, but the type in which you had best understand yourself. At other times, the decision to do something is made over a longer period of time.

FACTORYVILLE

The pretty airport at Factoryville, Pennsylvania, Seamans Airport, poses interesting questions to anyone flying other than a basic airplane. And some of the questions are not obvious before you go there. The runway is 4/22, 1,988 feet long and a whopping 28 feet wide, with a precipitous drop-off at the northeast end, and along both sides of the runway for the last 300 or 400 feet at the northeast end. This is not obvious from the approach plates and airport diagrams that I consulted before going there for the first time. After looking at the charts, though, you do give a lot of advance thought to flying to such an airport.

I had word that, in a crosswind, landing there was real sport. The diagrams were clear on that, showing trees to the west side of the runway, close. I was taking my 210 there to get the baggage compartment tank installed, and with word of the crosswind problem and study of the airport diagram, I started putting limitations on wind for an arrival. Not more than 10 knots crosswind was the final decision. The VOR approach for the airport shows a 471-foot agl minimum descent altitude, which looked reasonable as long as everything else was good. The 1-mile visibility minimum looked sparse —more than that would be appreciated.

Anytime you put as much thought into an arrival as was put into this one, you know full well that there has to be some doubt lurking back in the corners of your mind. Nobody but you will make the final decision; is there some driving force that will make the decision an impossible one?

ARRIVAL

The day to go came, and the weather forecast for Wilkes-Barre, nearby, showed well above IFR minimums—good visibility and a 1,000-foot ceiling with a 10-knot wind out of the southwest. That would be virtually right down the runway.

The flight there was routine, but some things were not as forecast for the arrival. The visibility was a couple of miles with light rain, and the ceiling at Wilkes-Barre was 600 feet. The elevation there is about 240 feet lower than Factoryville, so if ceilings are in fact above sea level over a wide area, which is not always the case, the approach into Factoryville would be close, if not impossible. The case could have been made not to attempt the approach, but I had a telephone report on the weather at Factoryville: "Looks good." There was no wind shear and no turbulence. I was shooting the approach after a short flight. The VOR was shot. At the MDA I was clear of clouds, and the airport was sighted from a comfortable and legal altitude for circling. Concentration on the approach was good, so much on the runway that even after landing to the southwest I was oblivious to the precipitous drop-off at the approach end of the runway I used. I was more into the sight picture of the runway and having the airspeed bang-on than I was into the surroundings. As I came over the threshold of the runway, I was aware of some unusual visual sensations, but by that time the primary task was power back and land. In retrospect, had I been aware of all the characteristics of the airport I would probably have waited for a better day. Certainly I didn't qualify as a wimp.

SECOND ARRIVAL

After leaving the airplane at Factoryville for a couple of days, what had to follow? Right, a return trip. And the return was with full knowledge, so there were no excuses. Mark Twombly was taking me back in the Warrior we had at the time, and we agreed that, in the post-cold-front conditions that existed, we would not go unless and until the wind forecast was under 10 knots, or right down the runway. That condition was met as we launched to go back to Factoryville.

The weather was much better this day, though we did have to shoot the approach to get beneath the clouds. But the wind was stronger than forecast as Wilkes-Barre, at about 15 knots, out of the northwest instead of the north as forecast. So what do you do after putting all that thought into limits? We continued. The velocity was within the crosswind capability of the airplane, so why give up early? I did resolve that if Mark decided it looked chancy on the first approach and elected to go around, we would go away. The landing would be to the northeast, which meant any overrun would be into the precipitous drop. Mark had the approach exactly correct and we reached the end of the runway before the effect of the wind through the trees was felt. Was it a macho arrival? I didn't think so. Too much thought was put into alternatives, and I was fully ready for Mark to leave me off at Wilkes-Barre to find ground transportation.

LEAVING

The story of this little airport's relationship to the thinking process doesn't end there. We both had to depart. The wind freshened while we were there, and shifted to at least a 90-degree crosswind on the runway, blowing through the trees. Both airplanes, the Warrior and 210, were quite light on fuel, so there was no real question about takeoff performance. Either airplane should fly in less than half the runway length.

But what about the crosswind and the width of the runway? There always seems to be a question.

We debated the best direction for a takeoff, and, after close study of the swinging wind sock, decided that it was six one way and a half a dozen the other. The locals cinched the deal. They said that with the amount of wind, about 20 knots, it would be much better to take off southwest. Go back to the carefully laid plan that was based on the wind being out of the north. Would a southwest takeoff be dumb, considering the things that had changed? The decision was made that it was okay, and it was, though when I flew out from behind the trees, with a lot of extra airspeed that was added instead of altitude, the airplane went through some weird gyrations. Was the decision to leave macho? Not totally so, but there might be some question about it.

PINCH THYSELF

How you feel has a lot to do with all this. While the FAA would like to sit back smugly and think that its medical certification system guarantees a sky full of superpeople, that simply is not true. There are people out there every day, a lot of them, who have colds, residual bad feeling from an illness or a party, or who are pissed off at the world or someone in particular. These are internal deals. We live in our own world and seldom have outside help on making the decision on whether or not to fly. Whether it is the challenge of a back-course approach to minimums, ice, or a marginal airport, it is up to us to merge this with an assessment of current ability. And ability does ebb and flow with personal feelings. Even the FAA's bottle-to-throttle rule doesn't apply to some events. Hangovers come in all shapes and sizes and while the letter of the law might be met, there are days when you shouldn't go flying with yourself.

SNEEZE

I ran into a case one winter where rules about ailments didn't work. It is no fun to go flying with a cold. In my case, I can't fly or do much of anything else after taking antihistamines and always put twenty-four hours between one and flying—forty-eight hours if more than one dose. And I always try to give flu or a bad cold ten days.

I had met all the criteria after a flu-like episode, but as I was driving to the airport I kept wondering if I really felt like flying six hours that day. I must have psyched myself up for the trip because I kept driving. At the airport, I opened the hangar, loaded everything into the airplane, and did a thorough preflight. Then I attached the towbar, for use in pulling the airplane out of the hangar.

I have always had a personal attachment to airplanes, especially to ones I have flown a lot. The 210 had 4,850 hours on the tach at the time, all flown by me, so we were pretty good buddies. And when I straightened up, grabbed the prop, and looked the airplane in the eyes, it seemed to say that it didn't want to go flying with me. I dropped the towbar, unloaded the airplane, closed the hangar, and went home. The airplane was right. The macho person who drove to the airport turned into a wimp who consulted a physician about an ailment for the first time in twenty years.

PECULIAR TO THE AIRPLANE?

Is there anything peculiar to an airplane that rates special consideration in our dealings with ourselves? Absolutely. Once we take off, the management of risk is ours alone until the airplane is parked, and in flying more time and effort is involved than in any other activity. If you are driving a car and want to stop, it is a relatively simple process. The only thing that comes close to an airplane is a sailboat or any boat that you take a distance from shore. There's a line about the air, like the sea, being unforgiving, and it is very true.

The personality trait that can result in high risk is one of resignation. If a pilot develops a hopeless or helpless feeling in an airplane, the risk becomes very high. This shouldn't be confused with the terribly lonesome feeling that sometimes comes at a difficult time in an airplane. The lonesome feeling—"nobody but me can get me out of this"—is probably positive because it reinforces the truth. But if the airplane is, for example, in the bowels of a thunderstorm and the pilot loses control of the thought process because of a feeling that it is an impossible situation, then all is lost. Any pilot who hasn't flirted with this thought hasn't flown a lot. Whether facing a turbulent and strong crosswind on a runway, a bad and bumpy cloud, a horrendous mechanical failure, or an incredible wind shear, the thought has to pass through the mind. If you won't acknowledge it has been there, how many times have you wiped your sweating palm on your shirt?

VALUABLE VIBE

The sweaty palm or bad taste in your mouth serves well, too. It is a message that a trespass is being committed, that you are in a position you don't particularly like or enjoy. It is time to take stock. What are the alternatives? If there is no better alternative, haven't you been able to handle this before? Overconfidence is a bad thing, but to manage risk properly we have to have confidence in our ability to do so. Where this is harmful to the risk-management process is when it leads to impulsive actions—"I can do anything, so full speed ahead without thinking it through." And I think most of us with sweaty palms first think about the quickest way out. That isn't always the best way, though, and the value of the phenomenon comes only if it prompts a burst of thinking about why it is happening and how to make things better. I remember in my beginning flying days, crosswinds would always raise doubt about landings. Then one day the light came on. I realized that I had finally learned how to land with a crosswind and could tell when the condition was too much for my ability or for the airplane.

IN-FLIGHT ANXIETY

Another form of doubt has to be dealt with by some. I've had letters from pilots who, for no obvious reason, have had what might be described as anxiety attacks in airplanes. Usually the symptoms are those of hyperventilation, where rapid breathing causes light-headedness. That's great to diagnose it as such, but until the pilot determines what caused the rapid breathing, a question remains. At times, an odor in the airplane might cause the pilot to suspect carbon monoxide. This has been a factor in some accidents but is relatively rare. A mild form of hypoxia might also be a cause. Some of us can do okay at 12,500 feet without oxygen or pressurization, but you should probably subtract an inch, or some portion thereof, for each hour you have lived, each cigarette you have smoked, and each drink you have taken. You can probably add some back for the other.

A valuable thing to do is to go through the altitude chamber. It is available at military bases and the local FAA Flight Standards District Office can supply details. This will teach you how you relate to altitude and might well change the way you operate. I can, for example, function okay for five or more minutes at 18,000 feet. I'd estimate that I might last as long as fifteen or twenty minutes before serious impairment. But at 25,000 feet, it's a matter of just over a minute. What that has done is limit the altitude at which I will fly solo, or with another person if we are both using the same oxygen supply. Above 21,000 feet, the chances of catching an oxygen-flow problem and descending before becoming unconscious would not be good. In a pressurized airplane, notice of a failure is dramatic, but unless there's a quick-don mask at hand you'd be in trouble if above 21,000 feet. The FAA says that 25,000 feet is okay even with no oxygen in a pressurized airplane, but a lot of things that are legal involve risk that shouldn't be taken.

PILOT ERROR

Big numbers are bandied about in relation to the percentage of accidents that are "pilot error." While the number usually given is about 85 percent, you could easily reach 100 percent, because if the pilot had made the decision not to attempt the flight, the accident would not have happened. On the other hand, risk management would be better served if "pilot error" were trashed as an accident cause. What is really meant is that the relationship between the pilot and the airplane became impossible. No mechanical problem existed, and no error was made by air traffic control, for example. Midair collisions are almost always pilot error because one or both pilots failed to see and avoid the other aircraft. The lessons for risk management are in why the relationship between the pilot and the airplane soured. Often this is because of one of the bad traits, but more often than not we find that the trait was instilled in the pilot, as far as flying goes, by some action or lack thereof in the training process. That isn't to say that training is magic. Pilots have completed the finest training in the world and made a humongous mess on their first flight after training. If there is a lack here, it would be in sending a pilot away without the feeling that airplanes can be hazardous to your health. When you are at 200 feet above the ground on an ILS approach, airspeed 110 knots, there are three possibilities. One is a successful landing if you can see the runway. Another is a missed approach. The third is a collision with the ground that probably won't be survivable. The best two out of three might be acceptable odds in sports, but in flying the third is a bad option. We have to fly always with that understanding.

AND SO

You can tell by how much of the book is on the left and how much is on the right that we are nearing the end of this exploration of risk in flying. There will always be risk here, too, as in any other activity. I have taken a few I wish I had not taken and would not take again. And there are some I probably take on a routine basis that other people cull. That is well and good, because it is really up to each of us to understand, evaluate, and then manage risks. For example, I have always and will probably always accept the risk of a low-visibility takeoff. With passengers, I modify the risk and always explain it fully. Same goes for night flying. I just don't want anyone in my airplane who doesn't understand that flying involves more risk than some other things—if for no other reason than that a third dimension is added. And while I have used this in previous writings, in closing I offer a quote from the aviator of all time, Charles Lindbergh. He forever changed the face of aviation; had he not succeeded, a lot of us who are flying today would probably be bank tellers. From *The Last Hero: Charles A. Lindbergh* by Walter S. Ross (Harper & Row): "Why should man want to fly at all? . . . What justifies the risk of life? . . . I believe the risks I take are justified by the sheer love of the life I lead." He took the risks, managed them, and lived out a natural life. It can be done.

Index

Northwest MD-80, Detroit
    accident, 71
Nose baggage compartment, 39
Nose gear, 202
Nosewheel:
    collapse, 192, 199
    steering, 116
NTSB, 11, 35, 65, 68, 84, 89,
    113, 114, 115, 119, 143,
    165, 168, 213, 225

OBS knob, 156
Obstacle clearance, 130, 131
Oil, 26, 27, 38, 44
    cap, 38
    lines, 21
Overruns, 189
Oxygen, 320

Panic, 120
Parachutes, 286
Passengers, 31
Pattern, traffic. *See* Traffic
    pattern
Perfect Flight, The (Collins),
    123
Performance charts, 2
Pilot, 294–322
    anxiety, 319–320
    currency of skills, 10, 11,
        213, 216, 291
    emergency situation
        response, 108–109,
        300–301
    error, 320–321
    familiarity with plane, 70–71
    fatigue, 10, 151–153, 163–

164, 207–208, 215–216,
    223, 294–296
flying while ill or injured,
    225–226, 297–299, 317
focus of attention outside
    plane, 230, 243–244, 251
loss of control due to
    disorientation, 110
personality, 302, 303, 307,
    318
ratings, 94
"rusty," 290
self-evaluation, 9–11
stress, 23–24, 288
student, 226
weekend, 280–293
Piper airplanes, 27, 245, 303
Piper Archer, 186, 238, 245,
    290
Piper Arrow, 27, 185
Piper Navajo, 42
Piper Seneca, 170–171, 290
Piper Warrior, 88, 169, 290,
    292
Piston-powered airplanes, 37,
    166
Pitching, 265, 266
Pitot heat, 41
Pitot tube, 35–36
Pitstops, 5
Planemaster Services, 310
Position, announcing, 134, 249
Power levels, 183
Power-off:
    approach, 117–119,
        150–151
    landing, 184–186